Max Reinhardt: A Life in Publishing

Max Reinhardt, 1982 (photocredit: Caroline Forbes)

Max Reinhardt: A Life in Publishing

Judith Adamson

First published 2009 by
PALGRAVE MACMILLAN

Palgrave Macmillan in the UK is an imprint of Macmillan Publishers Limited, registered in England, company number 785998, of Houndmills, Basingstoke, Hampshire RG21 6XS.

Palgrave Macmillan in the US is a division of St Martin's Press LLC, 175 Fifth Avenue, New York, NY 10010.

Palgrave Macmillan is the global academic imprint of the above companies and has companies and representatives throughout the world.

Palgrave® and Macmillan® are registered trademarks in the United States, the United Kingdom, Europe and other countries.

ISBN-13: 978–0–230–54542–7   hardback
ISBN-10: 0–230–54542–4   hardback

This book is printed on paper suitable for recycling and made from fully managed and sustained forest sources. Logging, pulping and manufacturing processes are expected to conform to the environmental regulations of the country of origin.

A catalogue record for this book is available from the British Library.

A catalog record for this book is available from the Library of Congress.

10 9 8 7 6 5 4 3 2 1
18 17 16 15 14 13 12 11 10 09

Printed and bound in Great Britain by
CPI Antony Rowe, Chippenham and Eastbourne

*For Max's grandchildren
Marina, James and Holly Reinhardt*

Contents

List of Illustrations

Acknowledgments and Sources

To write this book I used the thousands of letters and business papers in Max Reinhardt's private archive. I am grateful above all to his widow, Joan Reinhardt, and to Judy Taylor, his literary executrix, for giving me access to these papers and allowing me to quote from them liberally, for patiently answering my many questions and kindly reading my manuscript. The late Belinda McGill was invaluable in helping me sort through Max's papers and in providing wise and often practical assistance. To a lesser extent I used papers in The Bodley Head Archive at the University of Reading Library. Michael Bott and Verity Andrews deserve special thanks for their generous assistance there.

I am also deeply indebted to Sue Bradley, whose interviews with Belinda McGill, Max Reinhardt and Judy Taylor for *National Life Stories' Book Trade Lives* I have relied on heavily, and to Carmen Callil, who allowed me to quote from Bradley's interview with her for *Book Trade Lives* (tapes which are otherwise closed until 2026), and who made time in her busy schedule to talk with me. These tapes are in the British Library Sound Archive. Graham C. Greene was also extremely kind in helping me and in allowing me to quote from our conversation.

I have relied as well on tapes I made of talks Max and I had between 1994 and 1998; some of the material from these talks is in his privately published *Memories*, a copy of which can be found in the British Library. Max's daughter, Veronica, kindly shared memories of her father and upbringing. Andrew Gammon, the husband of Max's late daughter, Alexandra, added many lively stories about his father-in-law. Francis Greene generously allowed me to quote extensively from Graham Greene's letters to Max.

This book could not have been written without the help and trust of many other people. I would like to thank especially: Jack Ashley, Richard Attenborough, Eric de Bellaigue, Jill Black, Euan Cameron, the late Margaret Clark, Cecily Coales, Mary Connell, Louise Dennys, Diana Fowles, John Goodwin, Gordon Graham, Jeremy Lewis, Wyndham Lloyd-Davis, Peter Mayer, David Machin, Vincent McDonnell, the late James Michie, Peggy Miller, the late Richard Rougier, Holly Rumbold, Barbara Slater, Guido Waldman and Gavin Wraith.

I would also like to thank the estates of Alistair Cooke, J.B. Priestley, Francis Meynell, Anthony Quayle, and the Ralph and Meriel Richardson Foundation for allowing me to quote from letters to Max.

I am grateful to the staff of the following libraries and institutions: the British Library Sound Archive (Mary Stewart), the Garrick Club (Marcus Risdell), Georgetown University Library, Special Collections Research Centre (Nicholas Scheetz), the London School of Economics (Simeon Underwood), the Harry Ransome Research Centre, University of Texas at Austin, and the Random House Archive (Jo Watt).

Finally I want to thank Alan Adamson and Nicholas Adamson for their constant encouragement, and Barbara Steinman for her critical comments and friendship.

In my notes readers will find reference to whatever newspapers, books and journals I have used, the provenance of letters I have quoted, and the call numbers for the *Life Stories* tapes in the British Library Sound Archive.

This book was written with financial assistance from the Social Sciences and Humanities Research Council of Canada.

Prologue

One afternoon in late 1941 a handsome and cosmopolitan young RAF Aircraftsman 2 on leave from Northern Ireland went down to the squash courts below his London flat in Kensington Close looking for a game. His name was Max Reinhardt. There he found the actor Ralph Richardson, now a Lieutenant Commander on leave, waiting for a player to come along. Equally matched at squash and both having a quiet war they decided to play again next time they were in London. This chance meeting led to a lifelong friendship and to the establishment in 1947 of a small publishing firm called Max Reinhardt Ltd. It specialized in books about the theatre, which was not surprising; Max had been fascinated by the theatre since, as a young boy visiting Vienna with his mother and grandparents in the early twenties, he had seen the theatre Max Reinhardt's name on tram advertisements. Even when he became a prestigious London publisher with a list of famous writers that included Graham Greene, William Trevor, Georgette Heyer and Alexander Solzhenitsyn, he would occasionally say after meeting someone, 'they must have expected the other Max Reinhardt'.

When as a child he returned home from Vienna to Constantinople he sent a fan letter to his doppelgänger and was rewarded with a reply, but not with a picture. The great man said he did not sign pictures. So the young Max began to buy movie magazines with his pocket money in the hope of finding a picture of the other Max. He was taken to the cinema by his nanny and wrote to the stars he saw on the screen. His first love was Charlie Chaplin, whose autobiography he would commission and publish in the 1960s. The year before his death in 2002 he told *National Life Stories' Book Trade Lives* interviewer Sue Bradley that while he had never believed the stories he read about actors in his youth, the glossy magazines had shown him another possibility outside Turkey where, by the time he was in high school, he felt 'a foreigner, more and more stranded'.[1]

His collection of movie magazines was so important to him that when he left Istanbul in 1932 to study at the Ecôle des Hautes Etudes Commerciales he took it with him to Paris. The other Max Reinhardt had a film in town and our Max had his name printed on visiting cards, which gave him a certain advantage dating chorus girls. Max lost his film books and pictures when he left Paris for London just before the Second World War, but when he met Ralph Richardson in 1941 something of the possibility the magazines had shown him began, as a movie might.

Because Max had graduated from the English High School in Istanbul he never thought of himself as an immigrant in Britain, even when he had been declared an enemy alien and interned for several months on the Isle of Man the year before he and Ralph Richardson met. But he had an immigrant's keenness to know what he needed to know. As though his new actor friend had said, 'Why not play your part like this', he allowed Ralph to direct him in the role of English gentleman.

At Ralph's suggestion John Morgan and Company tailored his well-cut double-breasted suits, Trufitt and Hill cut his hair, George Cleverley made his shoes, the Savile became his club. The year Max Reinhardt Ltd was set up Max married Margaret Leighton, Ralph's protégée and, according to his biographer Gary O'Connor, Ralph's love. The following year the theatrical connections of both Ralph Richardson and Anthony Quayle made it possible for Max to publish the correspondence of George Bernard Shaw and Ellen Terry. Ralph Richardson sat first on the board of Max Reinhardt Ltd, then on that of The Bodley Head when Ansbacher's, the merchant bankers to whom he recommended Max as managing director, bought the firm with Max from Sir Stanley Unwin in 1957. By then Max had become a director of The Nonesuch Press, too. He asked Graham Greene to help him revamp The Bodley Head list and he made it one of the world's top publishers.

Perhaps because he loved the feel of books more than he liked to read them, his were consistently among the most elegant in bookshops. And perhaps because the magazines and pictures he bought as a child had helped him to become the man he was, he championed children's books when few in publishing took them seriously, creating with Judy Taylor and her team the finest children's list in Britain.

In the decades between wartime paper rationing and the takeover of independent imprints by international conglomerates, Max built a small and highly respected publishing empire on gentlemen's agreements, protecting his editors and staff as long as he could from the market forces that changed the trade forever. He called his authors his friends and for several decades he had fun publishing their work. He could not have taken more pride in their books had he written them himself. Caring for his authors became his life. He was a brilliant enabler, a backstage man who so thoroughly enjoyed his part that he took on a similar role at the Royal Academy of Dramatic Art in 1965, prompting the council with financial advice for thirty years as the academy became the world's leading theatre school.

'Ralphie' and 'Maxie', as they were to one other, played squash every Sunday they could for the rest of their lives. Not a particularly sociable man, when acting abroad Ralph often stayed in his dressing room after a show to write to Max. He asked for books and news and finally for assurance: 23 September 1976 – 'I stagger about the world and am uncertain that anything of our world exists but I think of you and hope that you are SOLID and HAPPY. I have no news…All affection to you and love to you ever.' Soon after Ralph died in 1983 Max made a business mistake that would cost him his beloved Bodley Head four years later when the firm was sold to Random House in New York without his knowledge. After sadly recommending to his old friend's widow that she sell Ralph's shares for the £9613.40 they were worth, he quickly turned defeat into a notable victory against the conglomerates by launching Reinhardt Books. He wanted to call the new company Max Reinhardt Books, but the way The Bodley Head had been sold made that legally impossible, so he could not share the other Max's name on his last imprint. No matter – in championing independent publishing he had become a kind of British hero in his own name and under it he continued to publish Graham Greene, Alistair Cooke and his other favourite writers for another decade.

1

From Istanbul to London on the Orient Express

Max Peter Reinhardt was born on the Grande Rue de Pera in Constantinople on 30 November 1915, a few weeks short of the evacuation of British and Dominion troops from the Gallipoli peninsula. He told Euan Cameron, head of publicity at The Bodley Head for many years and one of his obituarists, that as a young child he had glimpsed decapitated heads impaled on spikes as he was wheeled through the streets by his nanny.[1] But Max more usually recalled the First World War with a less traumatic story set in the city's main railway station built in the late 1880s to receive the luxurious Orient Express in which he would cross Europe many times. In 1918 Max's father, Ernest Reinhardt, was the Austrian captain in charge of the station. He had grown up in Trieste, trained as an architect in Vienna and Prague, and been sent by his firm to Turkey before the war. On duty one day he spotted two of his wife's brothers, both ordinary privates in Italian uniform, arriving as prisoners. He marched them out of the station, then took them home to lunch. 'That was the kind of humane thing that could happen then,' his son was later to say. 'That was the way things were done.'[2]

Max's mother, Frieda Darr, was born in Constantinople into a large family of secularized Jews who had come from the Ukraine, lived for some time near Trieste on the Italian side of the border, then migrated to Constantinople. The Darrs owned Comptoir d'Anatolie, a shipping, insurance and trading agency which represented British firms and well into the Second World War dealt with the Germans too; it certainly faced no financial problems in the First World War when free maritime passage of the Dardanelles was blocked by German mines and submarine nets.

An early photograph shows Max standing on a table between his parents, his arm on his father's shoulder. He looks a sturdy toddler, serious, even stubborn. In another picture, taken when he was four or five, he seems quite pleased with himself alone in the street on his tricycle, proudly watched from a low window by his favourite uncle, Richard. At maybe ten he appears entirely independent on his bicycle, his hand on his mother's shoulder briefly to balance himself for a quick picture. He was a handsome child, an only and much loved child.

According to Max's *Memories*, his grandfather Haim Darr had eight brothers and sisters, all of whom had children. He said Haim Darr and his wife Dina Klimak added three to the tribe – Emil, Frieda, who was Haim's favourite, and Richard, who became Max's close friend and mentor, and was called Oncle Richard by everyone in Max's second, British life. But Max remembered his family's history propitiously. By another account Haim had 13 children; four are listed in the burial records of Yüksekkaldirim Synagogue in Istanbul. Another Darr is buried in the plot closest to Haim. Perhaps she was an earlier wife, which might make Max's story correct, except that Emil is listed in the synagogue wedding records as the son not of Haim but of Nathan, who was either an older son of Haim, or one of the uncles Max thought were Haim's siblings. But these early records are often inaccurate and even now very difficult to verify. Max certainly knew Mary Wraith, the daughter of one of Haim's sons, Josef, who emigrated to Birmingham and sold goods made there in the Middle East. According to Mary's son, Gavin Wraith, as a child Mary had met her Uncle Maurice, who had moved from Istanbul to Finland where he was eventually awarded the White Rose. When Max moved to London in 1938 Mary Wraith was enormously helpful to him and in turn Max was kind to Gavin. But in later years Max called Mary a distant rather than first cousin. What happened to Haim's other progeny, and to theirs, one of whom may have been born in a French concentration camp?[3] Max never talked about these relatives even when asked. But one day on holiday a few years before he died he said out of the blue to his son-in-law, Andrew Gammon: 'The holocaust was a terrible thing' – nothing more.[4]

The Darrs spoke French to one another, which was the language of international Constantinople, and as a child Max was read to in French – Jules Verne, the Comtesse de Ségur, Alexandre Dumas. But he learned Greek first, from his Greek nannies. There were three or four of them before he began school just after the British and French occupied the city at the end of the war and the Greeks occupied Smyrna. His father spoke to him in German and insisted that his first school be German, which would accent Max's English for life. Otherwise Ernest Reinhardt remained a distant figure remembered as a strict father, a shy man who enjoyed Wagner and walking alone. At four Max fell from a wall and injured both arms badly enough to leave a scar on each below the elbow. Ernest said he could not play the piano, which he wanted to and which his mother played well, or the violin. In high school Max came to love jazz and asked if he could play the sax but his father said it would be bad for his lungs. Max knew nothing about his father's siblings or their children. Ernest was entirely overshadowed by the extroverted and wealthier Darrs, who had no interest in architecture and whose taste in music was decidedly jazz.

Ernest had a small office on the north side of the Galata Bridge, which linked Galata and Pera above it, spiralling among the cypresses, with Constantinople proper where the Darrs' firm was. As a child Max was taken down to the harbour only when visitors came from abroad. The waters were thick with battleships, the quays of Galata piled with munitions for the Greek army fighting in Anatolia. He loved the bridge, the Bosphorous and the Sea of Marmara on one side and the Golden Horn on the other with tiny rivers flowing into it. When he worked in the office of the Darrs' firm for a while in the thirties he crossed it several times a day. The magnificence of the churches and mosques, the Yeni Cami seeming to rise from the south side of the bridge itself, the wharfs and landings on the Galata side where he and his father docked when they came to the city together from their summer quarters on the Bosphorous, the clutter of taxis and people, the boats and ferries spewing smoke, the surrounding old wooden houses with their jutting upper stories, the cemeteries with their forests of derelict tombstones fenced in stately wrought-iron, the packs of dogs, the maze of market streets with their commerce of stalls and small shops – these memories lived in Max's 'buried' life along with his ancestors and the famous Reinhardt name on the Viennese advertisements. If asked to share them he would allow that his childhood sounded rather glamorous but block discussion of it with details of how problematic things became for his European community after Atatürk defeated the Greek army in 1922.

When the Treaty of Lausanne replaced the Treaty of Sèvres (imposed in 1920 as part of the Peace of Paris), more than a million Greeks whose ancestors had lived in Asia Minor for centuries were expelled to the Greek mainland and replaced by about half as many Turks who had been living in Greece. The Allied troops left Constantinople and an infantry division of the Turkish army moved in. Turkey would thereafter be for the Turks and resentment of the foreign ownership of business continued to grow. The foreign post offices and consular courts which had served the European community were closed. All shops and offices were forced to shut on Fridays and Muslim holidays, although in his determination to modernize Turkey Atatürk decreed that religion and state be otherwise separate. In 1924 women were unveiled, religious schools barred and religious courts replaced with a legal system based on that of Switzerland; in 1925 the fez was banned.

British merchants exploited the fez law scandalously. The Darrs' friend Sir Telford Waugh, Evelyn Waugh's uncle who was British Consul in Constantinople but on holiday at the time, reported: 'a hat manufacturer in London ... had had an inquiry from Constantinople for an order of 30,000 hats and he could not understand it. Nor could I, until on my return I found that the fez had completely disappeared; so had several old hats of mine, given away to Turks who came begging for them.' Even years later Max sometimes saw porters in the street 'bent double under their loads wearing elegant hats with veils'.[5]

Surnames too were adjusted. In 1968 when Graham Greene was writing *Travels With My Aunt* and looking for a name for Colonel Hakim, Max sent him a long explanation about the change Atatürk had demanded. 'Before, one's surname was connected with one's father's Christian name. Then overnight Atatürk decreed that all the Turks should get themselves proper surnames, and there was pandemonium ... I haven't a clue what my old Turkish friends' surnames are now.'[6]

As Max grew up his Greek nannies were replaced by Greek-speaking maids from the Italian Dodecanese islands. But when internal passports were reintroduced in 1925 they became almost as difficult to employ as a man's hat was to find, and fairly soon so were the Turkish-speaking Greeks and Armenians the Darrs' business depended on. Since it was forbidden to hire foreigners in the costal trades, shipping began to avoid Constantinople (now Istanbul) for Piraeus. Insurance companies were driven out. Bribery became the easiest and, according to Max, in many cases the only way to do business.

Was Max's father more sympathetic than the Darrs to the changes Atatürk and his nationalist government were making toward modernization? He did maintain friendships with the Turkish nationalists he had met in the First World War and by the mid-twenties he was staying for months at a time in Ankara, where the narrow streets were being converted into broad boulevards on which large ferro-concrete structures were erected. The post office and several other public buildings were to Ernest's design. All serious negotiations were conducted in the new capital, a long 300 miles from Istanbul and the magnificent embassies where much of the international community's social life was centred. Sir Telford said the major function of the new British Ambassador, Sir George Clerk, who arrived in Turkey in November 1926, was to defend the right of nationals to stay and work in the new country. American Ambassador Grew rented space in Ankara and said there was nothing to do there but play bridge.

His father away, Max was moved to the English school system run by the British Council, first to the High School for Girls, which also took in young boys and was across the street from his family's flat in the Grande Rue, the most fashionable street in Istanbul, lined as it was with crowded restaurants and shops full of the latest Parisian art, clothes and jewellery. But a year later after telling his teacher that a girl in the gym had dirty knickers, he found himself quickly transferred to the English High School for Boys where Sir Telford chaired the board of governors.

The girl's school taught Max English, which his mother could not then speak. The boy's school taught him an independence which his father could not understand. The boys were given considerable responsibility in running the school and Max was made a prefect for two years and then head boy. He was good at French, English, Turkish (which Atatürk had switched from the Arabic to the Latin alphabet at the end of 1928 and which Max had previously spoken only in the street) and especially good at arithmetic. He also showed himself to be a mature, tactful and compassionate leader.

As prefect he was responsible for discipline in and out of class. Late one afternoon he discovered an older Greek boy who had matriculated from another school and come for a year to learn English, sexually playing with a young English boarder. The Greek boy, who was a popular football player, said he would kill Max if he was reported. Max had been brought up with the 'pretty strict moral attitudes'[7] of his parents. He sent the younger boy to his room and when asked by the embarrassed headmaster what he thought ought to be done said courageously that only the older boy should be punished. His reward was the friendship of the shy headmaster, C.H.R. Peach, with whom he was able to discuss his problems as he could not with his father. The headmaster continued to take a protective interest in Max's future and gave him a strong, if idealized, sense of English freedom and gentility. Max said that 'at the English School ... we were conscious that we had great benefits and privileges and, I thought, good schooling'.[8]

Summer holidays lasted for four months and Max readily acknowledged their charm. He spent them sometimes in his grandparents' large two-storeyed wooden house on Bunyük Ada, the biggest of the Princes' Islands in the Sea of Marmara. The house was surrounded by gardens of magnolia, lilac, honeysuckle and jasmine and its many bedrooms were kept full with visiting family. More often Max went with his mother to

Therapia on the Bosphorus, another favourite resort of his affluent community and its ambassadors. There they rented a house on the water next to the Summer Palace, a club owned by the originally Yugoslavian Medovitch family, who also owned the famous Tokatliyan Hotel in the city, where Trotsky stayed in 1929 before he moved to Bunyük Ada for the next four-and-a-half years.

The air in Therapia was filled with the scent of pine trees under which myrtle and arbutus grew. Max played tennis on the Summer Palace courts, once making it to the semi-finals of the Turkish national championships. Thereafter he and a Swiss school friend, Raymond Zinguilli, whose family were wealthy jewellers, were in demand as partners for doubles with the British and American ambassadors, a uniformed servant arriving by boat to announce that their excellencies would like to play on a given afternoon. Max water-skied on a board behind the boat of an Italian surgeon who drove from the city every weekend in his Lancia to stay at the Summer Palace. He fished. He bicycled everywhere, daily to his Uncle Emil's house at Yeniköy twenty minutes away, where Ambassador Clerk's summer residence was. Max and his friends swam across the Bosphorus to touch the Asian shore less than a mile away and felt themselves very international. In the evenings there were supper parties and when the moon rose over the Asian hills to cast its silver light across the water to the European shore he danced happily to the foxtrot and tango. The summer he was 15 he fell in love with Christine Medovitch, as did all his friends. He was also fond of Ambassador Grew's daughter, who was older and with whom he played mixed doubles. But none of the boys had a girlfriend. The community was too strict with its daughters for that.

When he passed the London Matriculation Examination with honours in June 1932 Max was encouraged by his father, headmaster Peach and Sir Telford Waugh to go to an English university. But Oncle Richard had other plans and since he was paying the bill Max had little choice. He was to go to Paris, where Richard had opened a branch of the family's firm, to study at the Ecôles des Hautes Etudes Commerciales. Richard was a handsome and enormously charming man, who had been severely deafened by gunfire in the war. He treated Max as the son he never had. Wanting to be in Paris herself since so many of the old Istanbul families had moved there, Frieda sided with Richard. And Max's best friend Stathy (Eustace) Eugenidi was going to Paris too. Stathy's banker grandfather had been part of the first game of bridge played in Constantinople in August 1873 and although Max's father disapproved of bridge, along with gambling of any sort, Richard and Frieda hooked Max on the game early. In his last winter at the English High School he lied about his age to join the Club de Constantinople with Stathy and by the end of the summer of 1932 the two young men were used to bidding three no trump with the best players in Istanbul and were looking forward to taking on Paris together.

* * *

Richard and his Russian wife, Anya, had a flat on the Rue Labie, off the avenues des Ternes and de la Grande Armée. Anya was a White Russian who, along with well over a hundred thousand others, had fled the revolution for Constantinople in the early twenties. The refugees had worked as waitresses in hotels, opened restaurants with Russian names, driven cabs, sold newspapers or shoelaces and, according to Philip Mansel, did whatever they could to keep themselves alive. 'Since they needed money to buy visas for western Europe they were ready for anything' and in the years of the Allied occupation they gave Pera especially a reputation for extravagance and degeneracy.[9] Max said Anya had 'started as a manicurist to the family and made a good marriage'. In fact, she made two, the first to one of those old uncles lost in Max's reconstructed family and when he died, to Richard. Anya was colourful and Max was very fond of her.

Richard got him a small flat of his own across the hall in their block, with a view of the courtyard and the Rue Labie. Max filled it with books he bought at Brentano's – Somerset Maugham, Bertrand Russell and P.G. Wodehouse were among his favourite authors. He went to parties at W.H. Smith's shop nearby. On an afternoon there were cakes and tea and sometimes there was an author to sign books. Max walked the tree-lined boulevards and sat in cafés reading English newspapers. Sunday mornings he rode in the Bois de Boulogne with Richard and Anya, lunched at Prunier's on oysters, lobster and dry white wine, then sat outside over coffee on the Avenue Victor Hugo. In the evening Anya took them to the nightclubs her Russian friends had opened. There was always a band. They danced to Viennese waltzes and Russian tunes and drank a little too much vodka and threw their glasses into the fireplace.

Max's sitting room doubled as a bedroom for his mother when she visited. She had been 'a little spoiled by her father' Max said, 'and Richard spoiled her too'.[10] Frieda did not ride horseback so when she was with Max they drove into the country on Sundays in Richard's black Chevrolet to lunch at famous restaurants in Fontainebleau or Rambouillet chosen from a guide book. Max took driving lessons and the car became his. Oncle Richard was very generous.

Max and Stathy found their first year in the preparatory section for foreigners at HEC easy. They attracted a group of friends that included Jacques Palaci, who had attended the same German school as Max in Istanbul and was becoming a doctor, and two HEC students, an Austrian named Fritz Gross and a Belgian, Georges Artus. They played bridge and tennis together and skated on an indoor rink. They ate in restaurants recommended in Oncle Richard's guide book. They saw Mistinguette dance, Maurice Chevalier sing, and the famous Max Reinhardt's 1935 musical film of *A Midsummer Night's Dream*. They had visiting cards made up – 'With the compliments of Max Reinhardt' – and used them to meet chorus girls they took dancing at their favourite night clubs in Montmartre. Was it here that Max added the 't' to his name? Or is it an error on the burial list at Yüksekkaldirim Synagogue that his father is recorded as Ernst Reinhard? 'We were so happy to be in Paris', Max remembered. 'I was so happy to be out of Turkey. It was like a dream. We just amused ourselves at first and embraced it.'[11]

The second year in the regular programme at HEC was tough and Max and his friends took amphetamines to cram for exams. He was saved from failure by the complex grading system in which each subject had a coefficient with a required number of points to pass. As extra points could be transferred from one subject to another, Max's proficiency in English and German compensated for his losses in chimie industrielle and other subjects of no interest to him. One of his examiners asked how had he been admitted – what school had he attended? When Max said he had been at the English High School in Istanbul the reply was, 'Ah, les anglais! Ils ne savent rien.'[12] Max smiled and slipped across the Channel whenever he could. He missed the sensibility of his English schooling.

At the end of the 1934 session he was awarded his diploma, without honours, and was sent back to Istanbul to work. He was nineteen. His parents had moved to a block of flats near Taksim Square in Ayapaşa, overlooking the Bosphorus. Every morning Max queued with his Uncle Emil for a communal taxi which took them down to the family business across the Galata Bridge. In the narrow street outside their building *hamals* (porters) waited for something to carry – a local parcel or message, canary seed or tragacanth to be taken to a ship, British cotton goods or metal to be brought from a ship for sale in Turkey. Max once saw a *hamal* transport a small Ford on his back. The basement housed the goods for export. The ground floor was let as a shop. Above were the offices – accountants and clerks on the first floor, partners and cor-respondents who guaranteed the amounts of wheat, barley and other commodities bought from merchants in Anatolia and sold directly to firms on the Baltic Exchange on the second, typists and other staff on the third. Max sat on the second floor behind a counter, the safe behind him, giving out cash when it was requested and keeping a record of where it went. He was good at maths and he quickly became a very good accountant. He wrote the English and French correspondence for the sec-retaries to type and was responsible for having the work redone if errors were made. And he sent coded telegrams accepting or rejecting offers for goods. The code was not complicated, nor much of a secret since it was in a book every international business in the city had a copy of, but it kept the Turkish clerks in the post office from understanding the bids. At least that was Max's theory and its use certainly illustrated the Darrs' distrust of the Turks.[13]

However watchful his uncles had become outside the office, within there was an atmosphere of trust in which young Max learned a patri-archal graciousness that would make him a pleasure to work for years later at The Bodley Head. As an only child he was used to the com-pany of adults, to taking direction from older men and to holding his own among them. Although Max said his father never provided quite enough money, the Darrs were generous with gifts and he was accustomed to privilege. Certainly he had never wanted for money and had been surrounded by servants all his life. He had been taught to take care of both. The English High School had instilled in him the wider responsibility of communal discipline and of keeping your word. His family and community had shown him the value of trust. They called people with whom they did business their friends, as Max would all his life. The Darrs had high expectations for him and Max liked going to the office despite the day-to-day difficulties the business faced. But especially after Paris he felt increasingly restricted in Istanbul, and uneasy.

His father spoke very good Turkish and had many Turkish friends, mostly army people, some of whose children had been educated with Max. He was a popular architect and was building houses all over the country. Max remembered particularly liking an imposing block of flats in Taksim near where they then lived. There was certainly no question of Ernest leaving Turkey, although Stathy Eugenidi, who met him only twice, had the impression of a man with a fine brain who was con-strained by his employers.[14] In 1934 when the professions were restricted to Turkish nationals Ernest may even have become a Turkish citizen.

But Max's life was confined to the European community in Istanbul and Therapia. His mother was vivacious and highly sociable. She enjoyed parties and dancing the night away. When Atatürk and his hard-drinking entourage began to frequent the same clubs and hotels as the Europeans – the Tokatliyan, and later the Park Hotel opposite their flat – her social life became as guarded as the Darrs' business life began to seem insecure. In the evenings Max played bridge at the club, but the movies were his greatest escape from what was becoming an 'increasingly dreary life'. The films he saw 'encouraged [him] that there was a different kind of life possible. If you are unhappy with one part of your life', he said, 'you tend to read about [or watch] other people's lives.'[15] Since the cinemas were rather smelly he bought himself a small projector and began to see movies at home as well. Screened life was so much more attractive than his own.

Then one day in late 1935 the office was occupied by the police. For the next six days the business was entirely shut down. Not even a telegram or letter was allowed to be sent while the Turkish lawyer the family had long employed as a middle-man to protect their interests negotiated a bribe. After it was paid the police vanished. Max's uncles were not surprised by the occupation; the same thing had happened to other foreign businesses and the firm's money was secure in Switzerland. What it did was stiffen Max's decision to leave. He spent the last two weeks of November 1935 with the Eugenidis in Greece, then he went back to France. He knew Oncle Richard wanted him to take over the Paris firm, but he was determined to play another role in London.

* * *

The Spanish Civil War broke out in mid-July 1936. For many the situation seemed clear – an elected government had been attacked by a fascist junta and young volunteers from Britain and North America were soon on their way through Paris to join the Republicans. Max professed little interest in politics, except in the abstract. His ambition was to learn what he could from Oncle Richard and to start his own British branch of the firm. Still, from November 1936 when Germany and Italy agreed to act together, he felt increasingly insecure. Since his family was not religious, he had never been especially aware of himself as a Jew. But he was unsettled when many of his HEC acquaintances showed fascist sympathies and Hitler's racial laws made him 'very uneasy and very anti-German'.[16] After the bombing of Guernica in April 1937 and the fall of Léon Blum's Popular Front government in June, Max used every excuse to visit London. He contacted his cousin, Mary Wraith. He made himself known to people Stathy's influential family had told him to see. He contacted the businesses in London his own family represented.

When Hitler's tanks rolled into Austria in March 1938 the immediate question was what would happen to Czechoslovakia. France was treaty bound to defend her; Britain was not and had no desire to fight. Max headed to the Darrs' London bank, the foreign branch of the Westminster in Lothbury Street, to ask the manager how he could set up a London office for his family. He was put in touch with the accountancy firm of Spicer and Pegler, and there quickly found that British business practices were 'much more down to earth than the French methods, which were a lot of talk and little action'. The firm was in a building at 19 Fenchurch Street. Max said Richard Pegler was surprised to see so young a man turn up. 'He must have been expecting someone like the other Max Reinhardt.'[17] Pegler was impressed enough to discuss Max's plan with the senior partner, Ernest Evan Spicer, who a few days later told Max they could provide him with a small office and a secretary whenever he was ready to come.

Oncle Richard thought him too young to start on his own but he was soon to acknowledge how wise Max was. There was no avoiding the rapidity of Hitler's advance. In Paris young men were being mobilized. A few of Max's friends had joined the army; others had left for their own countries. In early September Max's old headmaster, Mr Peach, sent a letter recommending him for British nationality to the Commercial Consul at the British Embassy in Turkey. In late September there was Munich, and peace for another year. But with an Italian passport and an Austrian name that was obviously Jewish (however spelled) Max was increasingly at risk in Paris. At the end of October Hitler sent 15,000 Jews in box cars to Poland and a few days later orchestrated *Kristallnacht*. Max said people began to ask why he was in France. The French police wanted to know why he was not in uniform. His mother was advised to return to Turkey and Richard said they must all leave Paris although it would be unsafe for Max to be in Istanbul as non-nationals of his age were being sent to work camps.

Abandoning everything, Richard and Max quietly closed the Paris branch of the firm and Richard took Anya with him via Italy to Istanbul. Being interviewed sixty years later in England when he was still horrified at the suggestion he was an immigrant, Max said: 'when I fled – [then firmly] I didn't flee – I mean – my mother and I followed' to Turkey.[18] In the process he lost his papers, his books, his photographs, his lists of actors and films; Oncle Richard lost much more. But Max had established his foothold in London and he was young and determined. He bribed Turkish officials for two entry visas and one to exit, deposited his mother at home in Istanbul and returned to England with his Italian passport in hand and a carbon copy of Mr Peach's letter. It read as though written in an earlier century. Max was proclaimed 'exceptionally manly and honourable, correct in his conduct and most pleasant in his address. His work was always excellent. He was a good sportsman in the correct sense of the word, could take a beating without fuss and showed all the characteristics which we aim at forming. Of all the boys that have passed through my hands I know of only one other of whom I could testify so well. I feel more than justified in supporting his application as I believe him to be a person who would be ready to shoulder the responsibilities of a British subject.'[19] It was January 1939. Barcelona had just fallen to Franco's troops.

2

Enemy Alien, Student, Spy

Looking back Max realized how difficult it must have been for the family to let him go, but as he slipped into his new identity he felt no particular worry. Mary Wraith was in Ladbroke Grove, friends from HEC were elsewhere in London and Stathy was in Cambridge. He rented a bedsit in Bayswater and got on with setting up Fimex Limited, an acronym for Finance Import Marine Export – which was what he had been groomed to do. His Spicer and Pegler acquaintances put him in touch with British companies and the Darrs were soon the agents in Turkey for the steel plate conglomerate Richard Thomas & Baldwin and the Dewhurst cotton concern. He joined the grand Baltic Exchange – he later said because 'the food was better there than anywhere else in the City'[1] – and transferred his family's business account from the Lothbury branch of the Wesminster Bank to the St Mary Axe branch opposite the exchange, then to Mincing Lane, following the assistant manager, Stanley Whitbread, who would help him almost to the end of his publishing years. When Whitbread became the manager at Lombard Street, Max's account went with him.

At 19 Fenchurch Street the Spicer and Pegler partners gathered each morning for coffee and gossip in the boardroom near Max's office and he made a point of getting to know them. Leonard Coe, a former tax inspector, told him never to plan his life in order to save tax but to do what he wanted and leave it to him or another tax expert to figure out the least amount of tax he had to pay. Max continued to follow this advice, and he continued to be of interest to the partners. Here was an amiable and trustworthy young man who knew his way around; when Max moved his family's account to Lombard Street, Spicer and Pegler's account followed.

Flush with Oncle Richard's money, Max found a serviced flat for himself in a nearly completed block in Wright's Lane. Kensington Close was like a club and Max was very clubbable; the building had squash courts, a swimming pool, bar and restaurant. He was soon comfortably installed, his shelves filled with books from Norman Denny's shop next to his office in the City; collecting English books lent him status and an intended permanency. His evenings were filled with bridge and the new friends he made playing the game. 'As in business you have to have an understanding with your partner', he said about bridge. 'It absorbs you.'[2] So did the plays and movies he saw. Rex Harrison, Sybil Thorndike, Emlyn Williams and John Gielgud were on the stage, Ralph Richardson, Merle Oberon and Laurence Olivier on the screen.

On 15 March 1939 Hitler took Prague. At 23 Max already knew the advantage of turning his back on difficult situations, but he could not avoid the war. A huge piece of sailcloth was strung across the centre span of Waterloo Bridge: 'National Service – have you offered yours'? Other advertisements began to appear enticing men into the volunteer services. On 26 April it was announced that 20 and 21 year olds would be called up for three months' training. Soon conscription included 22 to 25 year olds. At Kensington Close military officers and civil servants moved in as Max's friends disappeared into the forces.

By June slit trenches had been dug in Kensington Gardens. Barrage balloons floated above. Posters showed you how to recognize mustard gas and decontaminate yourself after an attack. Hotels and restaurants sandbagged their windows. Registrars were ordered to report the marriages of aliens to British subjects. Papers ran stories of Jewish persecution in Europe, of concentration camps; it was believed 10,000 Polish Jews had already entered Britain; by August Jewish refugees were arriving penniless from Czechoslovakia. On 21 August Germany and the Soviet Union signed their non-aggression pact and the next day Britain and Poland signed one of mutual assistance. Lights on the trains changed to dim blue. In London some underground stations were closed, kerbs painted white, basements converted to shelters. When the German army crossed into Poland on Friday 1 September the British Navy, Army and Airforce were mobilized and all men between 18 and 41 were warned that they could be called up.

Next day the sun shone but as the prime minister dispatched his ultimatum to Germany James Agate reported tremendous lightning across London. 'It was more like stage lightning than the real thing ... One moment complete darkness; the next a sheet of vivid green showing Westminster cut out in cardboard like the scenery in a toy theatre. The flashes lasted so long that you could count the buildings.'[3] War was announced on Sunday morning at 11.15 and a few minutes later the first air-raid warning sounded. Kensington Close residents went to the basement since the newness of the building made it a perfect shelter. Max remained alone in his flat.

On Monday Max went to the office as usual. The place was empty. Clerical staff had been evacuated to the country and he spent the day answering everybody's telephone. By mid-week office life had returned more or less to normal but Max got in touch with Sir Telford Waugh, now retired and living in a small hotel in Wimbledon, and Brigadier Mance, the public relations officer of the Ottoman Bank and a family friend. What should he do? He had not been naturalized. Both men advised that he wait and see what would happen.

Not much did happen until early April 1940 when Hitler's armoured columns marched into Denmark and his warships entered Oslo Fjord. Holland fell on 10 May, Belgium soon after. At the beginning of June more than 300,000 British, French and Belgian troops had to be evacuated to England from the Dunkirk beaches. In the next few days some of Max's French HEC friends who had been attached to the British forces as translators came to him desperate for shelter and money. On 10 June Italy entered the war and two days later Max too was in trouble. The porter at Kensington Close knocked on his door at seven in the morning to say that a policeman was waiting for him downstairs. The station sergeant was named Tennant and before the war he had worked for a rubber broker with whom Max had done business. He was very polite but Max's network of connections was useless. Max was sent to Kempton Park Racecourse where he and many others who had been rounded up slept rough for two nights. On 14 June Paris fell to the Germans without a battle and Max was moved to a disused cotton mill in the midlands.

The conditions were appalling and no one seemed interested in differentiating fascists from Italians who were so anti-fascist that they refused to speak Italian or, like Max and some Greek restaurateurs from the Dodecanese Islands he befriended, could not speak it at all. There was a tremendous public outcry about the arrests. Max was quick to protest to the commanding officer that his small group were not fascists and they were lucky to be separated from the main group; 613 other enemy aliens were shipped to an internment camp in Canada on the *Arondora Star* which a German submarine sank on 2 July, drowning 470 Italians, hundreds of whom had been in England far longer than Max. His group ended up on the Isle of Man where thousands more Italian passport holders had been taken from all over Britain. The boarding houses and hotels on the front were commandeered to house them and were surrounded by barbed wire. Max was quartered in a pleasant enough building, and he did not mind the routine. What he hated was being treated like a foreigner. He formed a protective gang with the Dodecanese Greeks and never took the daily walk he was allowed outside the barbed wire because he refused on principle to be accompanied by an armed escort. Instead he talked with the officers inside the camp about his English education. 'They were decent chaps', he said, 'who had been sent to the camp for a rest.'[4]

The internees had been made to give over their money on arrival. Max said it had been banked in the name of one of the officers and getting any back to buy cigarettes, sweets and other available things was difficult. So he suggested a different system and was allowed to set up a separate account for each person which could be drawn on once a week. It was not an arduous job and doing it gained him a certain authority and better treatment. Soon Professor Della Vida, a tropical disease specialist in Max's camp, became leader of their group and Mario Milano, the head waiter from the Savoy, reorganized their kitchen. Car designer Sampietro took charge of helping people petition the Home Office for release. Max wrote to friends for clothes and books, and to Sir Telford Waugh for help. By return post Sir Telford assured him everything was being done to gain his release and that his family knew he was safe, if interned. So Max settled into a not entirely unpleasant routine of bridge, banking, reading and concerts given by fellow internees. Then one day in late September he was told to pack, was escorted with a few others to the mainland and released. He sat beside Sampietro on the train to London and talked about the manufacture of cars. 'We looked like perfect Englishmen',[5] Max remembered. That night he got his first taste of the Battle of Britain. He remained alone in his flat preferring the danger of bombs to the confinement of even the basement at Kensington Close.

* * *

Some months later Max received a letter telling him to report to room 055A at the War Office which he later learned was used for interrogating spies. There he met a gentleman in civvies who introduced himself as Mr Stewart. The War Office, Mr Stewart said, wanted to offer Max a chance to do something for Britain. Would he become a British agent? He would be flown to Turkey to become 'Number Two to Number One'. He would travel on his Italian passport but have in his pocket Turkish, Austrian and British ones for emergencies. Would Max think about it at the weekend and return on Monday with his answer?

Max went straight to the Kensington Library. Although he later claimed he did not at first understand what it meant to be 'Number Two to Number One' he knew enough to borrow all the books he could about spies and Sir Telford Waugh's *Turkey Yesterday, Today and Tomorrow*. In it he discovered that during the First World War Sir Telford had been head of the Levant Service, a Foreign Office branch of Intelligence. Although Max had been told not to talk to anyone he saw Sir Telford who advised him to 'turn the job down. What they want is your family connections.'[6] If Turkey were invaded Max might be saved by the Austrian passport, but where would he end up then? If he used the British papers his family and friends would certainly be at greater risk for having helped him. So Max declined the offer. Mr Stewart said he was making a mistake but that he would give him a reference for related war work. In July 1941 Max used it to join the RAF. It had become difficult for an enemy alien even to walk in the streets at night, and he wanted desperately to look British. The recruiting office pronounced him unfit to pilot an aeroplane because of the childhood injury to his arms, which Max thought strange since it had never affected his tennis or his squash. What Mr Stewart's name got him instead was a desk job at RAFNI in Belfast as Aircraftsman 2, the lowest rank possible.

For several months at the beginning of 1939 the IRA had set off bombs in England. Hammersmith Bridge had been damaged, as had Madame Tussauds, innumerable letter boxes and finally King's Cross Station, where one person had died and several had been hurt. Ireland was neutral in the war but full of spies, so the Belfast base was not without importance. Nonetheless, Max found his desk job in the operations room boring, and despite the friendliness of the men he lived with in the Dunlambert Hotel, he kept to himself to hide his foreignness. He was very lonely. He read Bertrand Russell's *History of Western Philosophy* with such exigency that he philosophized in his dreams. For practical support he fell back on family business connections. The manager of linen manufacturer William Stewart & Sons lived in Belfast and Max spent many days off with him, having a bath at his house, on occasion crossing into Ireland for the races and a decent meal.

On leave he returned to London where one dull afternoon he found a Lieutenant Commander Ralph Richardson patiently waiting at the Kensington Close squash courts for someone to give him a game. Ralph had joined the RNVR in 1940 and been stationed at Eastleigh where he and Louis Albert (Boy) Hart, a solicitor who would head Ansbacher's bank after the war and play an important role in Max's publishing life, had guarded secret documents – and painted together in their off-duty hours. By 1941 Ralph had been promoted and sent to Lee-on-the-Solent to allot aircraft to stations as they came off the production line.[7] As the war had changed the custom of having to book squash games in advance he and Max took to the court. They found themselves equally matched and liking one another immediately agreed to play again when next they were in London.

Their meeting left Max feeling even more strongly that he should have accepted Mr Stewart's offer. At least being 'Number Two to Number One' would have had a certain glamour; he might even have been able to convince Turkish firms still dealing with Germany to stop. He felt marginal. He missed his family. News was scant except by cable, which was how he learned at the end of 1941 that his father had died. Max wrote Stathy that 'he had been very ill but I was not told of anything until he died; it was a terrible shock'. Ernest's heart had failed during prostate surgery performed by friends who were Turkish army surgeons. 'Their skills were out of date', Max insisted. 'The operation lasted too long.'[8]

The RAF offered to fly him home for a week but Max declined the gesture. Would people in his billet discover his nationality? Would he get back? He was angry with the Turkish surgeons, with the father he was fond of but had never known well, with the confinement of war, with himself for not having become a British subject, for not having taken Mr Stewart's job. Already diminished by his status, he retreated further into himself. He 'did not want to face a grave, and to find everyone crying and mourning'. As he had shut himself up in his flat during the Battle of Britain, Max confronted his father's death alone. 'Going home', he said, 'would serve no purpose.'[9]

Soon after, he heard that his new friend, Ralph Richardson, had nearly been killed going to visit his wife in Wivelsfield on his Harley-Davidson. (She had suffered for more than a decade with the lingering effects of encephalitis lethargica and she died a few months after the accident.) Ralph's bike had gone into a spin and he had landed on his head forty feet away, been unconscious for several days and in hospital for several weeks.

Every so often news of Max's other friends broke through his Belfast isolation. Fritz (now Freddy) Gross had become a British subject and was a lieutenant in the army on his way to becoming a captain in the Intelligence Corps. Georges Artus had been imprisoned in Belgium then released. Jacques Palaci had fled the Turkish army to become a doctor with the American forces. Stathy was in Detroit. He had badly broken his leg in a skiing accident and in April 1942 had the first of two operations in New York to remove necrotic fragments of unhealed bone.

Max was probably the only holder of an Italian passport in the Royal Air Force and he said they really did not know what to do with him. There was no possibility of advancement. His commanding officer recommended him several times for Air Force Intelligence but no commission came and Max stubbornly decided when it was first refused that if the Air Force would not make him an officer because he was an enemy alien he would not seek promotion to Aircraftsman First Class. The quick solution was to get invalided out of service in July 1942. 'The disability in my arms proved too great a handicap', he later told Stathy without irony.[10]

He returned to Kensington Close. Because Fimex was a British company it had not been affected by wartime legislation concerning enemy property, but there was little work; most of the companies the Darrs traded for in Turkey were now dealing directly with the British government. When the Foreign Office informed Max that someone had reported that one of the family's firms was trading with the enemy he acted quickly, cabling his uncle to go immediately to the consulate in Istanbul or the entire Comptoir d'Anatolie would be blacklisted. Was Mr Stewart watching out for Max as Max thought at the time? Or was Mr Stewart keeping an eye on Max for his own purposes? Years later Max concluded that the report had come from an American commercial attaché who disappeared after the war, a man he suspected was a double agent.

Disheartened and without enough work, Max looked again to the Darrs' contacts for direction. Before the war Tube Investments had done its business in Turkey through his family and they suggested Max might fill in time at the London School of Economics. The company would soon be hiring people in the Middle East and they would get permission from the Foreign Office for him to travel there with one of their directors.

He registered as an external student at the University of London, then applied in March 1943 for admission to become an internal student working toward a BSc in Economics at LSE, which had been evacuated to Cambridge. He was admitted at the end of April to the summer session and wrote to Stathy on 20 July from 31 Chesterton Road:

You may be surprised by my address. Didn't you live in Chesterton Road? The Backs are as lovely as ever and on the whole you still find that at Cambridge there is less war atmosphere than in most other places. The students are much younger. All those who are here do some kind of national service, and the strain of war if not evident is always latent. The library of the Union Society was badly bombed but has opened again and debates at the Union are still lively. Fitzbilly's

manage to have good cakes still from time to time and there are as
many bicycles as before, if not more. Punting on the river is still a
popular thing though I prefer canoeing (I can't punt, that explains
it). The Red Lion in Grantchester and the Orchard are still serving
teas and are very busy on Saturdays and Sundays; the boat races still
take place. Tennis and cricket are still being played at Fenners and the
Arts theatre has a good repertory company. Many of the professors
are away on Government work and many new ones have come. I've
met quite a number of Turkish students from Istanbul.

He enclosed a list of the books he was reading: Fisher's *History of Europe*,
Carr's *Conditions of Peace*, Nicolson's *Peacemaking 1919* and *Curzon*, Hob-
house's *Morals in Evolution* (which he thought outstanding), Tolstoy's
War and Peace, Russell's *Power*, Dickinson's *A Modern Symposium* and *The
Greek View of Life*.

By mid-January 1944 Stathy's leg had still not healed and he had
spent months of confinement in Detroit and New York. Max agreed that
'mental agony [is] more unbearable than physical pain ... We are all suffering from it at present. We are surrounded most of the time by tragedy.
There is nothing we can do to mitigate it hence feelings of helplessness,
uncertainty, frustration and depression which are often difficult to bear.'
He told Stathy he had found the reading of history 'a great solace. It
enables you to see things in a truer perspective; it makes you take a more
lenient view of people and events; it shows you that the basic problems
that face us are the ones that have always faced human beings; and if
it makes you feel impatient with the pettiness and wickedness you see
everywhere, it also enables you to see the beauty of man's achievements.
Above all, it makes you tolerant, the supreme virtue.'[11] Bridge was Max's
other remedy and he and Stathy shared their successes through the mail.

* * *

Ralph Richardson had been released from the RNVR to run the Old
Vic with Laurence Olivier and John Burrell so Max often came from
Cambridge to play squash on Sunday afternoons. Ralph remarried on
26 January 1944, and their post-game suppers included his new wife,
Meriel (Mu) Forbes and Max's girlfriend, Molly Usherwood. Although
in March Max told LSE that he was in Cambridge most of the time
'except a day or two in London' the reverse was probably more truthful
for he was soon warned that 'a simple essay and a number of promises
and general statements about your Intermediate work cannot form the

basis for a satisfactory report'. An internal account read: 'Works very well when interested, but not inclined to self-discipline and systematic work when interest is lacking. Fortunately interests are wide and he may do well.'[12]

In June Ralph began rehearsals for *Peer Gynt*, which opened 31 August at the New Theatre in St Martin's Lane. He had chosen for the company two new actresses from the Birmingham Rep, Joyce Redman and Margaret Leighton. He wondered if Max could find a flat for Leighton who was only 22. She moved into Kensington Close as the first V1s hit London. 'Margaret was very, very slim,' Max said, 'very elegant, really a beautiful woman.'[13]

At LSE Professor Manning said Max was 'an admirable man' who 'knows what he wants and how to set about acquiring it', but he thought him 'bored with the Intermediate subjects' and had him enrolled instead in October 1944 for an MSc in economics under himself and Harold Laski. Max's thesis topic was a dry 'Comparative Study of the Control of Foreign Affairs by the French Parliament and the American Congress and the Lessons that Can be Drawn from this Control'. But the spirited Bertrand Russell, who had just returned to Cambridge from America, drew his attention. By mid-November Max was so unsuccessfully juggling Russell's lectures with setting up a Palestinian branch of Fimex to trade with the Near and Middle East after the war that Laski concluded he had 'not yet really settled down to any field of study'. Nothing in Max's letters to Stathy shows any concern about what was happening to Europe's Jews. What interested Max was what the world would look like after the war and how he could fit into it as a British subject. 'A new spirit is needed', he wrote.

> Let us call it Europeanism. The best way to foster it is to organize the functional services in Europe on a European basis so far as it is possible ... a European medical relief system, a European railway system (what Hitler has achieved in some respects), a European postal system, a European air service (this would make frontiers look silly, don't you think) ... I predict a period of leadership for Great Britain after this war: moral leadership and leadership in the field of new ideas, mainly social.[14]

On 19 December 1944, he told Stathy he was 'hoping soon to be able to go to Egypt, Palestine and Turkey to see for myself how things have been going there for the last six years'. Stathy wrote back about his new girlfriend and further bridge successes. His leg seemed to be improving and he, too, was full of excitement about the future. Only his hairline bothered him. It was receding and he hoped it would stay put.

In April Max told LSE he 'had been made director of an export firm, Fimex Ltd'. It was a rather risky lie since he had listed himself as 'Director of Fimex' on his various forms for the past two years. He said the firm was sending him abroad on a three-month visit which one LSE official told another with disbelief 'was considered of such national importance that he was given priority in obtaining a visa etc'. In later years Max said his visit was for Tube Investments, to check out business agents who might report to the Middle East Supply Centre about which merchants were on the Allies' side. Were his connections and languages finally being put to valuable British use? He was anxious to go because he wanted to get his mother out of Turkey. He bragged to Bertrand Russell about the mission and shipped out the third week of April 1945 in a convoy escorted by a destroyer through the Straits of Gibraltar. He said being hounded by German U-boats in the Atlantic and hearing depth charges explode made him feel he was finally part of the war even though it was almost over.

In Max's account of the trip adventure turned to intrigue at the British Embassy in Cairo where he was told his contact from Tube Investments had died. Would Max go on to Baghdad alone to interview two brothers who might make good agents? He agreed, but before he could leave Cairo the war ended. He celebrated at the Gazira Club with friends from Turkey then went on to Baghdad where he became ill and was put up by Daphne Kendall, a friend whose husband had been posted to the Middle East. He claimed to have no idea what the Embassy wanted to know from the men he was to interview, so he explained to them in French how much help they would be if they passed information on to the British. When one brother abruptly left the room, the other informed him that the absent brother was shifty; he would pass the information on himself for 10 per cent less. Max reported them both to be unreliable and went on to Tehran and then Beirut where he met other well-heeled refugees from Turkey. He skied with them in the mountains in the mornings, swam in the sea in the afternoons, and found the Middle East as international as Constantinople had been in his early years. 'Friendships and connections followed you from one country to another' he said.[15] Through his contacts at the Foreign Office and a friend in the Passport Office at the British Embassy in Istanbul he secured visas for Frieda, Richard and Anya to travel from Turkey to Palestine.

They met in Jerusalem. Now very much the man of the family, Max settled them into the King David Hotel where they 'lavished in their reunion'. Jerusalem was 'a paradise in those days, quiet and restful', he said. 'The only soldiers there were on leave.' It was agents the city was full of. 'People were circulating all the time on some kind of mission. One never asked [what] because it was indiscreet – and anyway, they didn't answer.' When he made himself known to British Intelligence he discovered that many agents were authors. One was Arthur Koestler. Max found him arrogant. 'He had a kind of cruelty about him. He was conceited and in love with his own opinions. He was on some sort of mission.'[16] Was Max too? Did he report on Koestler? Koestler on him?

Max took many post-war trips to the Levant with official approval and said little enough about them and his wartime activities to make both sound slightly mysterious. Like most good storytellers he arranged his anecdotes to serve his purpose. There was never any mention of the Holocaust, of survivors in Palestine or elsewhere. And there was no mention of himself as a Jew. He put all that behind him. What is certain is that as an enemy alien he felt useless to the country he wanted for his own and when he became a British citizen in 1946 and took his place among the men who had actively fought Hitler, he effectively played down his part in the war. His story of it ends in July 1945 with him bidding farewell to his family. As he waits for the flying boat to return him to England he floats on the Dead Sea sharing newspapers with customs and immigration officers.

* * *

Max arrived back in England between the election on 5 July and the surprising announcement on 26 July that Labour had trounced Churchill's Tories. Molly was at Kensington Close, Ralph away with the Old Vic touring liberated Europe; the New Theatre productions were slated to begin in September. London had been devastated. The smell of charred wood lingered over great gaping holes and jagged walls. Millions were without housing; blown out windows in the remaining buildings had been covered with plywood or opaque R-Glass; tarpaulins hung over damaged roofs. There was no electricity and food rations had been tightened. People were exhausted and after years of sacrifice wanted a government that would provide proper health-care, housing, education and opportunities for ordinary people.

Max was not an ordinary person. Despite many sadnesses, his family's wealth and connections had protected him well from the upheavals in Turkey and from Hitler. The war had been more a frustration than a serious hardship for him. Perhaps that was why he bragged at LSE about the 'national importance' of going to the Middle East. He now hurried to

Cambridge to tell Bertrand Russell about people Russell had asked him to look up. But Russell tempered his exuberance by telling him to 'calm down. Don't be excited. Talk more slowly so as not to get confused; think first; express yourself clearly.'[17]

When Labour's victory was announced Clement Attlee came to LSE to tell Laski they had won. Attlee was very nervous at the sudden turn of events, Max remembered. Laski explained to the students at length why Churchill had lost, and the significance of what had taken place. Max had always thought it important to support the government, although even during the war his political views were 'never very strong' and Churchill's politics interested him less than the fact that they shared the same birthday. To be politically left Max had believed 'rather treacherous' but on that day he said Laski's lecture turned him a 'little bit to the left'. Laski understood the distance an immigrant must travel and Max was 'touched by the care he took of his students and his devotion to Labour politics. He was a marvellous human being and I was very grateful to him. He was a sensitive and caring man. He introduced me to people and guided my thinking. He taught me what mattered in England, how to fit oneself into a completely new society. He made me feel at home in London.'[18]

Laski nonetheless failed to get Max through his degree. In October 1945 when he re-registered for the autumn term Max told the dean: 'I will not be able to devote as much time to my academic studies as originally mentioned. The reason is that I am kept more busy with my present employment.' Eight months later he admitted that from 'May 1945 onwards my work at my office kept on taking more and more of my time (I even had to go abroad for a while)' and on Laski's and Manning's advice he asked for permission to postpone his degree until 'this pressure of work at my office clears (it is caused by a certain amount of reorganisation)'.[19]

Business at Fimex was picking up and the work came with interesting introductions – at one luncheon Max was seated beside Lady Churchill – but he was restless for change and overwhelmed by the magnitude of London's destruction. He helped Laski 'in practical financial matters, on occasion banking for him, and taught him about business'.[20] He procured jobs for Laski's demobbed students and friends through his connections in the City. Laski was grateful and Max needed to be appreciated. But Ralph was worried 'most genuinely about [him] and [his] state'. Molly had taken a job in Australia. 'Better to be quiet than quarrelling [Ralph] suppose[d] – but so much life is running away every hour that one deplores waste. Still, your work is going better than before, and that is most satisfying. But you are such a dear <u>good</u> fellow that one would like some dear good creature to complement you.'[21]

In July 1946 LSE gave Max permission to interrupt his degree on the understanding that when he returned he would have to put in an extra year. He left for the Middle East at the end of the month intending to come back in September but stayed away until November then left again on 10 December for Turkey. Stathy had been moved back to Europe for more surgery and died during the operation. This was the worst blow. Laski's final comment in Max's LSE dossier said that Max had 'been handicapped by absence from England. But he had plenty of brains and a first rate intelligence.' Max said simply: 'I began with Laski as an enemy alien and ended as a British subject, and that is what I wanted to be.'[22]

3
The Accountants and George Bernard Shaw

The war left Britain strapped for cash, deeply in debt and increasingly unable to meet its international commitments. The winter of 1947 was one of the coldest in British history. Coal and fuel supplies had run critically low. There was little electricity and heat. Food rationing was worse than it had been during the war. Even bread was rationed. Nonetheless, throughout the winter Max and Ralph continued to play squash, sometimes with Anthony Quayle, and to have supper afterwards. Tony brought his fiancée Dorothy Hyson, and Margaret Leighton came. Max missed family life and Margaret took him home with her to Birmingham where her parents, her siblings (Hazel and John) and her grandmother lived under one roof. They all liked Max.

But it was at the theatre watching Margaret that he slowly fell in love. During his brief return to London in November 1946 he had seen her play Roxane to Ralph's Cyrano at the Old Vic; in January 1947 he watched her rehearse *The Alchemist* with Ralph and hoped his mother would come to London in March to meet her. He moved himself into the flat he had bought from Daphne Kendall at the top of the hill in Ladbroke Grove so Frieda could have Kensington Close. Through the winter business continued to improve but Ralph thought Max 'still a bit lost' and put him up for the Savile Club. He wrote Max's name in the candidates book thinking that was all he had to do, but without a seconder Max was overlooked.

Friends at Spicer and Pegler were more practical in watching out for his interests. The firm had a high reputation as accountants, auditors and tax advisers. They also published textbooks, mostly written by the senior partners, for a prosperous accountancy correspondence college they owned named after H. Foulks Lynch, the accountant who had established it in 1884. By 1947 the college had been sold to another firm of accountants who used the textbooks and kept them up-to-date. These books were suddenly in heavy demand by demobbed service men who wanted to become accountants, and they were in short supply because there was little paper. When Richard Pegler suggested to Ernest Evan Spicer that since Max was 'so interested in collecting books why doesn't he buy our little publishing company' Max jumped at the chance.[1] Mary Wraith's son Gavin remembers Max arriving in a handsome pre-war Alvis at their house in Leicestershire to celebrate with champagne.[2]

The deal was that Max could have HFL (Publishers) Limited for £5000 on condition he take with it the Stellar Press, Spicer and Pegler's then money-losing printing works at Barnet. Copyright to all Spicer and Pegler books came with HFL. R.H. Code Holland, the managing director of Pitman, who distributed the textbooks, told him he could get around the paper quotas that had troubled publishers throughout the war by obtaining extra paper available for essential books through the Moberley Pool – an additional supply of paper released by the government to the Publishers' Association from 1941 until 1949 to be shared among its members. Max went to his trusted Stanley Whitbread at the Westminster Bank for money. A recently demobbed friend, Winston Drapkin, added more and agreed to run the Stellar Press. Code Holland then suggested that Max could increase profits with larger runs of certain books, such as *Spicer and Pegler's Income Tax*, which the Institute of Taxation subsequently adopted for many years as their choice text. Other popular titles on the list were *Bookkeeping and Accounts* and *Company Law*, both still in print in 1984 when Max sold the publication rights in HFL's books in print and under contract to Butterworth, keeping the name as a trading company for himself; this he changed on 26 November 1985 to Reinhardt Books, which became his last publishing house.

In 1947 when Max bought HFL he left the editing of the accountancy and law books to his correspondence school partners who were qualified accountants and experienced editors, and concentrated on the financial end of publishing the texts. By 1949 he had increased the turnover from £2000 to £14,000 a year. Although he did not know it at the time, he had underpinned his future publishing enterprises. It was an amazing accomplishment given that it was achieved when the country was on the brink of financial collapse.

* * *

Ralph now widened Max's view. One Sunday after squash he suggested that he, Tony Quayle and Max should publish books on the theatre.

Max agreed. He would form Max Reinhardt Ltd and Tony and Ralph would advise him on what to print. Max had just read the 1931 Constable edition of the correspondence between George Bernard Shaw and Ellen Terry. It began in the early 1890s when Terry was already a grandmother and had been Henry Irving's leading lady in a long procession of Shakespeare's plays. Shaw was in his mid-thirties at the time, a drama critic and socialist active in St Pancras affairs. He was trying to establish himself as a great dramatist in the face of hostile critics and to win Terry for his plays. They rarely met yet their letters were candid and often extravagantly affectionate.

Shaw's ninetieth birthday had recently been celebrated with the Shaw million – Penguin's reissue of 100,000 copies of each of ten of his works. The lot had sold out in six weeks. So Max thought a reprint of the Shaw-Terry letters germane and they had a wonderful preface by the old dramatist himself. Tony suggested they ask Sybil Thorndike if she knew who took care of Shaw's copyrights. She must have asked Lewis Casson, who wrote to Shaw on Tony's behalf. The reply came back: 'Tell Anthony to write me direct, and not to try to get round me by bothering you. My shop is open. He must be a d. young f. GBS.'[3]

Undeterred, Max went about forming the new company. Again he headed to the Westminster Bank for money. 'Ask for more than you need', Alexander Korda advised. 'The larger the sum the more likely that the decision will be made by someone at the top.'[4] Richard Pegler's brother-in-law, Adrian Evans, had been a pilot with the RAF and was without work. Pegler wondered whether Max might give him a job. Adrian was the brother of Dwye Evans, a director of the publisher William Heinemann, and the son of Charles Evans, who had headed Heinemann before A.S. Frere became chairman in 1945; Frere had been with Heinemann since 1923, and managing director since 1932. He had published all of Graham Greene's novels and was his close friend. He also published Somerset Maugham and J.B. Priestley.

Max took Adrian Evans in and changed the new firm's name to Reinhardt & Evans; to thank him Dwye Evans joined Tony Quayle and Richard Pegler on the board. Ralph became a member later; he was filming *Anna Karenina* at Shepperton Studios at the time and was then to play Baines in Graham Greene's *The Fallen Idol* and go on tour to Australia. The Heinemann connection would be indispensable to Max although he would buy Adrian Evans out within a few years and revert the imprint to Max Reinhardt Ltd, keeping Dwye Evans on the board. In 1947, he rented an office at 66 Chandos Place where the publisher Dent was housed, and hired Laura Coates, daughter of the architect Wells Coates, to run it. Max then moved from his flat in Ladbroke Grove to H4 in Albany, where Frere had a set of chambers. From there he could walk to his new office and to the New Theatre.

Tony and Dorothy Hyson married on 3 June 1947 and Max and Margaret Leighton on 16 August. According to Max it was Margaret who wanted to marry. She also wanted the wedding to be in St Mary Abbot's Church in Kensington High Street, which meant that Max had to be baptized. He agreed to repeat his baptism lines but said he was 'not very happy' delivering them. 'I didn't feel any different after what I said. Religion had never played any part in my life. I still had no religion.'[5]

Of course to be an atheist is not the same as to deny being Jewish. A couple of decades later when he was dining with James Michie, his chief editor at The Bodley Head, someone said 'I presume you're a Jew Max', and Max replied, 'Not that I know of.'[6] While this is more a measure of British anti-Semitism in the circles Max moved in than it is of his honesty (he had after all officially become an Anglican), his answer showed him as uncomfortable about acknowledging his Jewishness twenty years later as he was about uttering his baptism lines in the summer of 1947. After the wedding he and Margaret had a quick lunch. She went to her matinée. There were three happy days in Brighton with a proper reception and lots of flowers. Then it was back to Albany and work.

Max thought the Shaw-Terry correspondence should be the first in a series of theatre books which Tony could edit. They hoped James Agate's *English Dramatic Critics* would follow. Max suggested they do Hazlitt's *Review of the English Stage*. Tony suggested Stanislavski's *Building a Character*. They wanted to include Max Beerbohm's *Around Theatres* in the series. It was a Heinemann publication and Tony asked Dwye Evans to tell Beerbohm they wanted to bring out in a uniform edition a series of major works on the theatre by the very best authors. Beerbohm insisted on wide spaces after full stops, decent spaces between the lines, and plain notes of exclamation and interrogation. Max suggested they 'omit some of Beerbohm's essays so as to make one volume out of the present two'. They would meet his 'requirements with regard to printing' but the royalty he wanted was 'a bit too high. Could he reduce it to 15%.'[7]

* * *

By 7 September they felt ready to approach George Bernard Shaw. Tony wrote to tell him that he and his friends wanted to publish the Ellen Terry letters; they would start with a run of 10,000 copies, sell them at 10s each and give G.B.S. 10 per cent. 'You must make your offer to

Miss Christopher St. John [the editor of the 1931 edition]', G.B.S. wrote back. 'She controls Ellen Terry's copyright ... Hurry ... If a book at 10/- cannot afford 15% royalty it is not worth publishing.'[8] On 14 October Max sent him a contract giving him 15 per cent and everything he had told Tony he wanted. The accompanying letter was signed 'Believe me to be, dear Mr. Bernard Shaw, Yours very sincerely, Max Reinhardt.'

'It won't do as it stands', G.B.S. thundered back. 'I will redraft it when I know the following. Have you a publishing business in the USA? What is to be the retail price? I shall supply four or perhaps six portrait illustrations which will greatly enhance the attractiveness of the book.'[9] Max reported that he had no US business but was in close touch with Heinemann and their US organization and that he would go to the US to watch over Shaw's interests. G.B.S. did not reply. Max wrote again on 26 November to say he had hired Alan Keen to do the cover. 'You may recollect his drawing for Shakespeare's First Folio which I am told is in your possession.' There was no reply. On 3 January 1948 Max wrote again to say he had not heard from Shaw for months and was a little worried. 'I'm quite ready to complete our transaction', G.B.S. wrote back five days later.[10] He was willing, he said, to share the 15 per cent royalty with Ellen Terry's rights holders. Max agreed, and reported that he had arranged with the beneficiaries of her estate to lease their rights for five years. G.B.S. answered that he was 'prepared to execute an agreement of which the enclosed is a draft on receipt of your approval'. This was exclusive of US rights. 'My own American publishers, Dodd, Mead & Co. would no doubt be willing to consider a proposal. I should be content with a 7 1/2% royalty; but this is not a contract.'[11]

Shaw signed on 24 July 1948 giving Max copyright until 19 December 1953. Max would publish the book at his expense and sell it 'at whatever price [he] deemed right'. He was so excited that he boldly told Shaw 'the Terry letters are with Putnams not Dodd, Mead' and asked if he could also publish G.B.S.'s letters to the actress Janet Achurch and her actor husband Charles Charrington. Max would call the book *Letters to the Charringtons* and have the Mercury Theatre's director Ashley Dukes, who owned them, write an introduction. 'NO', was Shaw's answer. 'Charrington the actor is unknown now, and the name would be taken to mean the well-known brewer-philanthropist ... The only mentionable name is that of Janet Achurch ... "GBS Counsels A Great Actress" is the sort of title that occurs to me.'[12]

'Certainly a much better title', Max shot back on 13 September. 'Perhaps later.' He was off to New York with a letter of introduction from Frere. He went to Simon & Schuster and told Richard Simon straight

out, 'I want to buy some best sellers.' They sold him the rights to
S.J. Perelman's *Westward Ha!*, which was illustrated by Al Hirschfeld
and had been turned down by Heinemann as too expensive to publish.
Simon & Schuster agreed to do a run-on of 5600 copies at the end of
their own printing to save Max money and paper. He then saw Edward
Dodd and got from him a proposal for a joint edition of a collection of
Shaw's letters. 'No', G.B.S. replied to that suggestion too, and sent Max
instead photos for the Ellen Terry letters with the caution, 'Do not dream
of 13 illustrations. They would add to the cost of the book and spoil it.
Except for the three I have selected and those I sent you, they are rub-
bish, and have been published ad nauseam.' This was 10 December. By
17 April 1949 the photo Shaw had captioned 'The Green-Eyed Millionairess' came into question. 'You have, I think, the portrait of my wife
called "the green eyed millionairess". This is indefensible.'[13]

On 8 June G.B.S. had

> just seen the advertisement of the Terry book, and learnt with dismay
> that you have priced it at 18 shillings. You are behind the times: the
> day of the 18/- book is past: people who pay it now buy Penguins
> and have what they save by it confiscated by Cripps ... Nobody that
> buys a book of mine shall feel that he has not had full value for the
> money, which means that the book shall occupy the whole family for
> a fortnight. My standard volumes contain two full length new plays
> with my prefaces, and one short one. The price is 7/6d and the first
> printing 50,000. That is what my fans expect. You are offering them a
> reprint of an old book for 18/-. If you sell more than a few thousand
> at that rate you will be lucky. And your intention of beginning a series
> of reprints falls through. Don't trouble to reply. I must put myself in
> order for 'I told you so' in case – G. Bernard Shaw.

When he discovered how many copies Max had printed he put pen to
paper again. '5000!!! Have I come down to that? You have thrown away
£4750 by not making it 7s.6d and printing 25,000. I have received the 6
copies, thank you ... GBS.'[14]
'A miraculous collection of letters', John Connell reported for 'The
Critics' on the BBC on 26 June 1949. 'The tenderness, the wit, the kindness, the high and worthy spirit, the charm and fun.' Tony Quayle, who
by then had become Director of the Shakespeare Memorial Theatre in
Stratford, read the reviews – all laudatory – and wrote 'My Dear Maxie.
I do think it is a magnificent achievement and it gives me great pride
to think that I am a sort of Godfather to your first publication.'[15] Ralph

agreed that they had chosen well. These letters established Max as a literary publisher and as Shaw's publisher.

But Ralph had been less happy than his two friends. On 19 March 1948 he had written Max from Los Angeles: 'I miss you terribly. Sunday evenings are a California desert ... no squash at all.' Max and Tony had sent books. 'You should visit', Ralph had written on 28 September. 'We have a nice little house right on the beach with a spare room and a pretty good cook and lots of gin.' There were problems at the Old Vic, but Tony and Max were too busy with their own affairs to do more than send a lively if unsympathetic telegram. 'Father Quayley and Godfather Maxie lunching inadvisably well together in London but safeguarded by subsequent squash game. Miss Godfather Ralphie and send him loyal loving greetings.'[16] At the end of 1948 the Old Vic was reorganized and Ralph, Burrell and Olivier lost their jobs as heads of the company. Ralph was 46. By February 1949 he was at the Haymarket playing Dr Sloper in the Goetzs' *The Heiress*, and would make a film of the play the next year but he did admit – Gary O'Connor said 'with his usual self-containment'– to feeling 'rather badly treated' by the Old Vic.[17]

* * *

In publishing there was no quick return to pre-war conditions. The paper quota remained until 1949 and there was a shortage of manpower and raw materials in printers' shops and binderies. Since war economy standards of book production continued (British war paper was made from straw and looked dirty, rationing kept type small and margins tight) American books remained more attractive and durable by comparison. They were also cheaper until the pound was devalued in the autumn of 1949 from $4.03 to $2.80. Yet the turnover of books rose slowly in Britain, from just over £10 million at the end of the war to £37 million in 1950, of which 30.7 per cent represented exports. By the turn of the decade publishing was becoming a complex business and only the smallest publishers could continue without sales, production, advertising and subsidiary rights managers.

Reinhardt & Evans was small but had technical benefit from HFL. Max still tabulated figures by hand as he had done in the Darrs' office in Istanbul. On New Year's Day 1950 he listed as sold 3800 copies of Billy Rose's *Wine, Women and Words*, 3000 of Margaret Cooper Gay's *How To Live With a Cat*, 600 of Ruth and Augustus Goetz's *The Heiress*, and 5300 of S.J. Perelman's *Westward Ha!* He slated for March publication Joseph Jefferson's autobiography *Rip Van Winkle*, Walter Stokes's

Modern Pattern for Marriage, Stanislavsky's *Building a Character*, William Nicols's *Words To Live By* and F.E. Loewenstein's *The Rehearsal Copies of Bernard Shaw's Plays*. Giles Playfair's *Kean: The Life and Paradox of the Great Actor* was in the planning, although without its original introduction by Olivier who had said he did not much like the book and refused to have his part of it reprinted. Alan Dent's *A Century of Dramatic Criticism*, Stephen Potter's *Sense of Humour*, some poetry by Roy Campbell, a book by the Portuguese writer Eça de Queiroz, and *Shakespeare Memorial Theatre 1948–1950* (with forewords by Ivor Brown and Tony Quayle) were scheduled. Max still had Shaw's letters to the Charringtons in mind. He wanted to do Esmond Knight's *Down At Unkers* but thought this book for children needed better illustrations. And Tony had suggested they do a Stratford edition of Shakespeare with introductions by George (Dadie) Rylands. Max thought the project would require a fair amount of capital but agreed it would be worth finding. He wanted the introductions to give a short history of each play's production, ending with the Stratford version.

Max was pleased with their success but told Tony the firm had been a struggle which he had only survived with 'the financial help of HFL and Fimex. One day the Press will pay us back for all the time and effort we have put into it. For now we have our Sunday squash. That as you know is the greatest joy of all.'[18] But the real cause of his listlessness was not the necessity of using Fimex and HFL Ltd to balance the Reinhardt & Evans books. His accountant John Hews was doing a fine job; while Britain had lived under threat of national bankruptcy and through the difficult years of Attlee's restructuring, Max had not been personally short of funds. On 2 April 1948, soon after the government had been forced to pass an emergency austerity budget that restricted services, increased duties and caused even more rationing of meat, potatoes, bread and fuel, he had bought Send Barns, an Elizabethan house near Ripley in Surrey from Richard Pegler. It had seven acres of land and cost him £14,000. 'Fimex', he had told Tony, 'should have a house in the country where we can all go and relax.'[19]

He had also acquired a second set of chambers at Albany opposite his original rooms where he and Margaret slept and Max had a work room. In the new set they entertained and Margaret slept when she came home late. And here was the real problem: Margaret's schedule was too busy for Max's liking. Ralph had secured her a long-term contract with Alexander Korda. Henry Sherek had signed her to play with Rex Harrison in T.S. Eliot's *The Cocktail Party* and after that to do Philip Barry's *The Philadelphia Story*. At first Max enjoyed the social life that went with her success. He got to know T.S. Eliot, sitting with him at rehearsals; he and

Rex Harrison confessed to one another that they did not understand all Eliot's lines; director Harold French became one of his steady bridge partners; Sherek brought him Havana cigars from New York which Margaret obliged him to smoke although he disliked cigars; there were parties in Alexander Korda's luxurious penthouse at Claridges and Moura Budberg's flat in the Cromwell Road. But as the months passed Max saw less and less of Margaret. It was easier for her to get to the film studios at Shepperton from Send Barns, but when they were there Max had to commute to London. When she was on the stage they stayed at Albany, but then she often turned up very late, sometimes in the morning as he was leaving for the office.

From the day he had seen the theatre Max Reinhardt's name on tram advertisements in Vienna our Max had thought actors the freest of human beings. Ralph and Tony had never seemed restricted in meeting him for games and meals. Suddenly Max found the discipline of the theatre problematic – 'the hours, the diet. I had much more freedom of thought and action than Margaret did', he complained. 'I had to go to the office, but then I could go to a film, or out for a meal. She had rehearsals all the time. Nothing else mattered. She always had to do things for the theatre, and for publicity. We couldn't do things together any more. It was a frustration in my life. She and her friends were under tremendous strain. I didn't envy their lives any more.'[20]

When Max's mother was in London things were worse. Frieda could speak little English and was very unhappy. While Max knew Margaret was busy and had nothing in common with his mother, he nonetheless resented Margaret for not giving Frieda more time. He planned for the three of them to holiday in Turkey so Margaret could meet the rest of his family but she refused to go. Max was used to having things his own way and he wanted domestic stability. As Margaret pulled away from providing it, by his own admission Max became very angry with her. He had joined the Savile in 1950 after Stephen Potter seconded Ralph's nomination and he began to stay there late playing bridge.

Ralph too was a worry. Max had seen him in the Brighton preview of R.C. Sherriff's *Home at Seven* and felt obliged to point out that Ralph was too well dressed for his part. Ralph seemed lost without his Old Vic base, so on 30 March 1951 Max sent him a formal invitation to join the Reinhardt & Evans board. He had studied book-binding as a young man and Max appreciated his professional interest in the finished product. 'I can promise you there will be no duties for you except those you would like or be interested to undertake', he told Ralph. 'It will give us great encouragement to have you.' As if to cheer himself as much as Ralph he added that he had sold some stock making for himself, Ralph and Tony, each '£22.14s.3d, which is a good omen for the first transaction'. In June he got Ralph seats for Wimbledon and effected a scheme he had started in March to import wine by the barrel. Ralph, Tony and Frere each got 70 bottles of Medoc and 70 of Sauterne for £25 1s 9d. He had their names printed on the labels and numbered the bottles 'like a limited edition of a book'.

* * *

When Shaw died in 1950, Max wrote to the Public Trustee to see if he could now publish Ashley Dukes's 62 letters from Shaw to Janet Achurch and her husband. While he was trying to arrange a joint American edition with Dodd Mead, Dukes decided to sell his letters directly to Appleton-Century Croft because he needed quick money. Then out of the blue on 25 April 1953 Max was informed by an American collector, T.E. Hanley, that he had a larger stash of 191 letters and cards which he considered the real Achurch collection.

Hanley had bought the letters from Joseph Schwartz, a dealer who promised to make him famous for owning them. In the summer of 1952 Edward Dodd wrote in the *Antiquarian Bookman* that Hanley had offered him the letters for a collection Dodd Mead intended to publish. That, Hanley told Schwartz on 18 February 1953, was 'nothing but a damned lie. Neither he nor anybody connected with his publishing firm ever got in touch with me in any way, and he merely used my name as a "pitch" for other possible Shaw letter owners and their cooperation. In view of Dodd's use of my name without my consent or permission, I will not co-operate with him in any fashion.'[21]

Max liked the cut and thrust of commerce but this deal was becoming scabrous. He tried to get Hanley to let him publish the two caches together, which Hanley said he would consider if Max could arrange for him to buy Dukes's 62 letters first, and for a lower price than Dukes had wanted from Appleton-Century Croft, who by then had backed away from Dukes's proposition. It took Max until the autumn of 1953 to convince Dukes to sell his letters to Hanley and when Hanley's cheque arrived on 15 September it was for only half the agreed $1400. Hanley told Max he would pay the rest later; he had paid the third quarterly instalment of his federal income tax that day and was temporarily short of cash.[22]

Dukes left his letters in sealed envelope No. 3982 marked 'contents unknown' at the Notting Hill Westminster Bank on 2 October and sent

Hanley a letter saying he was now part owner of them. In due course the rest of the money arrived but in February 1954, as Max was leaving for New York to see Hanley's part of the cache, he received a letter saying Hanley would be in Florida; he was planning a trip to London in December and would meet Max then. That trip was duly cancelled because, the elusive Hanley said, his wife was sick and she was no longer sure she wanted the letters published. If she changed her mind, Hanley assured Max, he would be the first publisher they would approach.[23] Max was by then used to the sometimes strange and often humorous stories that accumulate in a publishing house. But he had had enough of this one. On 3 January 1955 he replied: 'I can assure you that, in the past, every time an important collection of letters was published, they enhanced the value of the originals.' Hanley's collection was sold a few years later to the Harry Ransome Humanities Research Library at the University of Texas, and on those rich shelves he became famous for it.

* * *

From the time he had published the Shaw-Terry correspondence Max had doggedly followed the trail of Shaw's other letters. In December 1951 there had been another setback to his desire to publish more of them. 'With the authority of the Public Trustee and as the principle publisher of Bernard Shaw's works in Great Britain' Constable elicited letters for 'a definitive selection' they wanted to publish. Max responded quickly with a second edition of his Shaw-Terry letters. It appeared on 2 June in a new double jacket selling for 25 shillings. On the inner flaps were sketches of the Lyceum in 1890 and on the inner front an empty plaque. On the outer acetate jacket the five-lined title *Ellen Terry/and/Bernard Shaw/A/Correspondence* was arranged to be placed over the inner plaque. Elizabeth Bowen's review of the earlier edition was quoted from *The Tatler*. The book was printed by Wm Clowes & Sons Ltd and the new double jacket at Max's Stellar Press. A thousand copies were bound in cloth boards, 2000 kept for later binding. Max instructed his printers to 'please cut from the relevant brass the words "and Evans"'. He was once again master of his company.

His wife had been less easy to control. When Tony signed Ralph for the 1952 season at Stratford and wanted Margaret to play *Macbeth* and *The Tempest* with him, Max encouraged her to take both parts and suggested that the summer be a trial separation, to which she agreed. According to Gary O'Connor, in Stratford Margaret quickly began an affair with Laurence Harvey. One story had Max arriving earlier than expected from

London to give Margaret a party and Harvey making a quick exit through the back door to return an hour later through the front with the other guests. Another had Ralph also in love with her and adrift all season because of it.[24] Max, who was intensely loyal and private, said only that he became so angry with Margaret after a dinner party at Albany one night in 1952 at which she was extremely rude to their guests, including her sister, of whom he was very fond, that he went to the Savile for two weeks and never returned home.

Max moved into a maisonette above the flower shop that former Tory politician Thelma Cazalet (Keir) had run in Sloane Street since 1945 when she lost her seat in Parliament. Max and her husband, the writer David Keir, were Savile friends who fished for salmon together in Scotland. Cazalet hired a housekeeper named Mrs Tucker to cater for Max's parties and soon Tony sent Diana Fowles (then Oldland) from her job at the Shakespeare Memorial Theatre to 'look after Max because he's a bit sad at the moment'. She found Max 'very, very deeply hurt by Margaret',[25] who continued to telephone. 'She always agreed to things and then did the opposite', Max grumbled.[26] Fowles became Max's personal assistant for close to ten years, shopping for his clothes, driving him around first in his Fiat and later in his Jaguar, and doing his secretarial work at the office. 'He was sad but charming,' she said, 'generous with his friendship – although not with my salary – and always appreciative.' He threw himself into his work, which meant very late hours for her.[27]

In March 1953 the Keirs took Max with them to Jamaica to cheer him up. Ten years later he told Rex Warner, 'I arrived there terribly tired and thrilled to have some sun and be able to bathe in March. As soon as I got better I got terribly irritated with most of the people I met there who were all escapees, either from taxation or from editors or from socialism or from the bomb, and the whole conversation seemed to be how ghastly things were at home. I was thrilled to get back to foggy, wet London.'[28] The Royal Court Theatre was near his new flat. He had an attractive roof garden off his sitting room for entertaining his bridge friends in the summer. There were his Sunday squash games (now played at the RAC) with Ralph and Tony. The rest of the week the Savile provided companionship and the safety of English manners. There no one asked him about himself.

4
Nonesuch

In the late summer of 1952 Sir Francis Meynell suggested that Max join forces with him to revitalize The Nonesuch Press. They had met at the Savile through Ralph and Stephen Potter, who was being paid 200 guineas a year by Max Reinhardt Ltd for general editorial advice. Nonesuch had been founded in 1923 by Meynell, his second wife Vera Mendel (who had provided the firm's working capital of £300) and David Garnett (whose empty basement at 30 Gerrard Street in Soho, where he had an antiquarian bookshop with Francis Birrell, had served as its first office). Meynell had named the press from a tapestry in the Victoria & Albert Museum which showed the Tudor palace of Nonesuch; he liked the word because it meant 'unlike anything else', and because 'nonpareil' was the name of a rarely used minute type he favoured. He thought of himself as an architect of books, whose job it was to coordinate the talents of the best editors, illustrators, printers and binders. His aim, he told Max, was to have fun experimenting with designs that would produce beautiful and long wearing books.

To have fun as a publisher was also Max's desire and he admired The Nonesuch Press. From its first book of John Donne's love poems edited by Meynell himself, Nonesuch had set new standards. Max collected the books and knew the backlist. Among its highlights were *The Week-End Book*, which Meynell and Vera Mendel had first edited in 1924, Blake's *Pencil Drawings*, selections of De Quincey, Dante, John Evelyn – the list went on. They were carefully edited, easily readable (the various printing firms Meynell used had given him access to a vast choice of typefaces) and reasonably priced (machine composing and printing had enabled Meynell to reduce costs). He had close publishing connections in America and Max appreciated that Meynell's books had been sold there by Bennett Cerf and his partner Donald Klopfer, who had formed Random House.

The press had had financial problems after the Wall Street crash when sales had fallen drastically, especially in the USA; from 1931 Meynell had been able to work as a publisher only part time, earning a living primarily in advertising. He had sold the press in 1936 to George Macy, who had started a Limited Editions Club in New York in 1929, but had stayed on as a designer. Macy had issued debentures to the printers and binders to settle Meynell's trade debts, then moved the press to Russell Square, near Faber and Faber, who handled some of its work. He had kept Nonesuch alive during the war by offering discounts to shift stock, and by printing in France and the USA. Now that the press was profitable again Macy had redeemed the debentures and generously returned the unencumbered title to Meynell because he wanted him to be 'Mr. Nonesuch again'. In *My Lives* Meynell wrote, 'I had no money to finance any new Nonesuch venture and no means of distributing or accounting. These needs Max Reinhardt was ready to supply.'[1]

And so the business proposition was put to Max, he said, over a game of snooker. Meynell wanted to reissue Herbert Farjeon's seven-volume Nonesuch edition of Shakespeare, which he had published between 1929 and 1932, and he needed help. The new edition was to have only four smaller volumes, although each would probably have over a thousand pages. He wanted to use two kinds of paper, a thicker one for the poems (to become Volume Four) and something thinner for the *Tragedies*, *Comedies* and *Histories*, with the title page of every play in the thicker paper so the book would open invitingly at the beginning of each. It sounded exciting to Max and they agreed to form The Nonesuch Press Ltd with Meynell as managing director, and his son Benedict, Pamela Hayman Zander (his secretary/assistant) and Max as directors. The Nonesuch Library of compendious books, which had a separate existence under Sir Robert Leighton and was distributed by Faber and Faber, was not part of the original deal.

They began work even before signing the contract. Their first problem was to find the paper Meynell wanted – India paper that was thin, opaque, with a minimal roughness to prevent sticking, and capable of taking the smallest typeface legibly. This was solved by asking Imperial Tobacco if their mill, Robert Fletcher & Son, could produce it. Max got Townsend Hook (owned by *The Times*) to make the heavier Japon Vellum for the title and half-title pages. It took five tons of paper and four different mixes before the colour matched the India paper, leaving Hook's with a huge surplus, which Max claimed they accepted in their excitement about the project. Wm Clowes printed and bound the volumes and generously gave Max three years to pay for the work.

By August 1952, and with their contract still unsigned, he and Meynell were aiming 'publication for soon after the coronation ceremony, or even before if possible' and planning to incorporate 'Coronation Edition' in the title or sub-title. Meynell hired Reynolds Stone for 100 guineas to engrave a full page dedication to the queen, along with five new headpieces and the zincos. The dedication would read: 'By her gracious permission this edition is dedicated to Her Majesty Queen Elizabeth II by her dutiful and devoted servants of The Nonesuch Press in the year of her Coronation.' Meynell was pleased with the progress and on 21 October told Max he had found in his previous edition 'a delightful fact that in one instance a speech is ascribed in the text not to the fictional character but to the actor chap who made it. All this means that the job is enormously worth doing because without this kind of list the reader of the Folio text could easily be befuddled.'[2]

But things between the two were not always so buoyant. It seemed the younger Max still had a few lessons to learn. When on 20 November he sent Meynell a letter he had drafted to 'Dear Mr. Macy' in New York suggesting Macy would be the best person to handle the Coronation Shakespeare in America, Meynell's response was corrective. Max's letter must start 'My Dear Sir' and the address at the bottom of Max's paper needed to be changed: '"Messrs" must not come in the name of a firm when it is a "Limited" – or indeed at all when the letter is being addressed to an individual in that firm.' After his signature Meynell penned the further lesson that '"Messrs" is correctly used only for a partnership.' On 1 December another letter arrived questioning Max's letterhead. It had 'Max Reinhardt Ltd/The Nonesuch Press/HFL (Publishers) Ltd' in large print on three lines centred at the top of the page followed by the 66 Chandos Place address in smaller letters off to the right. Meynell suggested that only Max's own firms be listed at the top, that 'Max Reinhardt Ltd act also as publishers for The Nonesuch Press' be added and 'either taken to a side panel at the top or placed below the Director's line' at the bottom, which was where Meynell had assigned Max's role as distributor on his own Nonesuch paper. Max corralled his ambition and was cautious in his next letter. 'With your permission', he suggested on 20 January 1953, 'the Stellar Press can print 30,000 prospectuses within 2 weeks.'[3]

Their contract was finally signed on 5 February. In it Max Reinhardt the man, Max Reinhardt the limited company, and HFL (Publishers) Ltd agreed to finance and publish Nonesuch books, which Meynell would design and Max would sell at prices agreeable to them both. Max said that Meynell's solicitor, Martin Zander, was so concerned there be no misunderstanding that he made them go over the twenty-page contract point by point. Max was used to contracts, but he was more used to doing business on mutual agreement and given how far along the project had advanced on that basis he found the attention to legal detail amusing. When they signed Max took out a bottle of champagne to celebrate but there was such explanation and initialling to be done that before the final signatures were fixed they had emptied several bottles. In the next twenty-three years Max and Meynell changed how they worked many times but never again referred to the contract.[4]

A week later Meynell reported he had received 'the following pleasant though in one respect disappointing' letter about the dedication page they had sent for approval to the queen. Her private secretary had replied that the queen was pleased with the dedication page of the Nonesuch Shakespeare and looked forward to receiving the book but that the summer would be so busy there was little chance she would be able to receive the volumes personally from Meynell. Had he himself expected more? At the bottom of his letter he cautioned Max not to 'be too disappointed if you don't get a large initial order: if the book is good, as we think it is, it will build itself up'.[5]

Max felt in no way defeated, and he certainly needed no one to tell him about selling books. He immediately issued a press notice saying their Shakespeare would be 'dedicated by gracious permission to Her Majesty the Queen'; it would be 'in the original spelling and capitalization and punctuation, not for archaism but for visual and vocal significance, in the exact text of the First Folio, with all the Quarto variants and one, but only one, choice of modern readings given in the margins'. In a subsequent release he explained the differences between the new and old editions: *Pericles* and *The Poems* were included in the text (though they were not in the First Folio) as well as six Quartos which were radically different from the First Folio text and three non-canonical plays in which critics had discerned the hand of Shakespeare. The books would have linen sides with no spine text. Goudy Modern type would be used. There would be a readable and scholarly introduction by Ivor Brown, and the set would occupy (and this Max knew Meynell was very proud of) '234 cubic inches as against the 720 of the old'. As to the other problem, by late May, Max had arranged for Thelma Cazalet 'to write to the Queen Mother and suggest that we offer to do either of the following: (a) give a small party, say in a private room at the Savoy, to present her with a copy, or (b) offer to go to Clarence House or Buckingham Palace and give it to her there, whichever would be most convenient to her'.[6] Eventually the very bohemian Meynell did put on his morning coat and go to the palace with the books.

They had decided to sell the edition at £7 7s but during the printing Max heard that someone else was bringing out a different Shakespeare and he and Meynell quickly agreed to cut their profit to compete. So the price was £7. Before the books were even bound, Max had sold over 2000 copies, including 750 to Random House in New York. When the edition was launched on Meynell's birthday, 12 May, 4500 copies had been sold; when Max watched the coronation from the Athenaeum Club with Ralph, Mu and their young son Charles, his second Nonesuch publication, *Gloriana's Glass* was ready to sell for £1 7s 6d in a limited edition of 1250. A tribute to Queen Elizabeth I compiled by Alan Glover, *Gloriana's Glass* played on the popular notion that the young queen's coronation signalled the start of a new Elizabethan age. By October all the bound sets of the Shakespeare were gone and Max had paid the printer. 'It is shattering to think that the investment was over £20,000', he told Tony Quayle but 'by the end of the year, I think we should have recovered all our costs and started making a profit.'[7]

In 1954 he produced for Meynell 1650 copies of *The Verse of Hilaire Belloc* and 1100 of Gerard Manley Hopkins's *Selected Poems*. The publication of the limited editions is 'small business ... to Francis and me', he told George Macy. 'We can only afford to go ahead with them because we are fortunate enough to get our main income elsewhere. But we have fun and love publishing them, and for my part it is a pleasure to work with Francis and a thrill to reintroduce into the market attractive books in the Nonesuch tradition.'[8] In 1955 they issued for 15s a new unlimited, more profitable edition of the Nonesuch pre-war bestseller, *The Week-End Book*. To celebrate the end of food rations and acknowledge that even most upper-class country houses were now without a cook, it had a new food section. Max's major editorial contribution was more serious. He replaced the old 'Starshine at Night' with a brilliant exposition of the universe by Fred Hoyle, who had just delivered the first Reith lecture.

5
The Bodley Head

Max had meanwhile continued to publish theatre books on his own and had also gained a reputation for books of humour. He had added to his Reinhardt list Paul Jennings's *Oddly Bodlikins,* S.J. Perelman's *The Ill-Tempered Clavichord,* books by Peter Arno and Leslie Stark, several by Stephen Potter including *A Humour Anthology* and *Sense of Humour,* collections of David Low's cartoons, Michael Ayrton's *Tittivulus* and Vicky's *Meet the Russians.* Along with his Nonesuch *Gloriana's Glass,* the latter two were among 86 selected from 650 submissions as the best designed British books in June 1954.

Although in the mid-1950s Max was having a problem getting £45,000 owed to Fimex out of Turkey, money seems generally to have moved easily between his firms to pay expenses and maximize profits. He was always on the lookout for new challenges. In 1949 he had incorporated the Endeavour Press to publish thrillers, but he never used the company and after trying unsuccessfully to sell it to Meynell for £35 in 1953, he would add it to The Bodley Head agreement in 1957. There was the Good Food Club, an association started by Raymond Postgate in 1949. Membership was secured by buying a guide which Max tried to get the licence to publish in 1953. Then in January 1954 he went to the Board of Trade with the idea of moving the Stellar Press to a development area where he could build a new factory. Although these ventures were not realized, business was profitable, variable and loosely organized. In the early 1950s letters from Max's lawyers often read, 'My partner considers [so and so] to be a decent fellow', and from Max in reply after a new company had been struck, 'You will no doubt keep this letter in a safe place.'

He had intended to divorce Margaret amicably on the gentlemanly grounds of desertion, which could be done after a five-year separation.

47

'Money was not a problem for her', he insisted. 'She was earning more than I was and she had Albany to live in with Laurence Harvey.' But she kept telephoning Max and before the five years had passed turned up injudiciously one evening at his Sloane Street flat to say 'she had changed her mind and wanted to come back'.[1] Because she then refused to divorce Max for desertion as they had agreed, he sued her for adultery. The divorce was granted in 1955, two years earlier than Max had scheduled.

Soon afterwards he bought the lease of 14 Trevor Square, hired a decorator from John Lewis to put it in order, and took Mrs Tucker with him to run the house and small garden; he was pleased to tell people that Harriette Wilson and Rochfort had lived at number 16 for a couple of years in the nineteenth century. Then in July 1957 he moved his office to a renovated building on the corner of Earlham Street where it leads into Shaftesbury Avenue. It had three floors, a basement which could be used for packing, and a terrace on which Ralph sat in the sun to write him a cheque for the £2500 ready cash he needed to secure and equip the property. In return Max gave Ralph 2667 shares in Max Reinhardt Ltd along with a letter stating he would buy them back by 15 April 1961 with £70 a year interest. While Ralph had spontaneously given Max the money, Max had insisted on this formal arrangement, and the situation embarrassed them both. Ralph returned Max's IOU saying he would keep the shares 'by me' and Max cleared the debt as fast as he could, on 4 May 1959. He later said repaying Ralph quickly was one of the proudest moments of his life.[2]

No sooner were HFL and Max Reinhardt Ltd in the building than Ralph intervened again in Max's publishing life by introducing him to Boy Hart. After the war Ralph and Hart had continued to paint together, in a studio off Harley Street. Hart was a director of the merchant bank, Ansbacher, one of many financial institutions looking at the time for businesses in need of capital loans in return for tax exemptions. Derek Verschoyle, the *Spectator*'s literary editor in the 1930s, including the years Graham Greene was its film reviewer, had suggested to Hart that Ansbacher's might buy the old and prestigious publisher, The Bodley Head.

Founded in 1887 by Elkin Mathews and John Lane, who had chosen as a symbol to hang outside their shop the head of fellow Devonian Sir Thomas Bodley, founder of the Bodleian Library at Oxford, The Bodley Head had quickly made its name with fine editions and *belles-lettres*, publishing Oscar Wilde, Aubrey Beardsley (including *The Yellow Book*) and Max Beerbohm. Mathews had left in 1894 and Lane ran the company himself for the next thirty years. His list grew to include H.G. Wells, Anatole France, Arnold Bennett, Stephen Leacock, Saki (H.H. Munro),

Agatha Christie and C.S. Forester. As is now well known, John Lane's nephew, Allen Williams, changed his name to Lane and began working at The Bodley Head in 1919 straight from school. Learning the business from the bottom up, he became a director in 1924, managed the firm after his uncle died in 1925, and was its majority shareholder after the death of John Lane's widow a year later. The firm was by then in financial trouble and Allen Lane worked for the next ten years to keep it from bankruptcy. He launched Penguin Books in 1935 – the first 80 titles carried The Bodley Head name – and transferred some of his Penguin profits to shore it up. In 1936 he boldly published a limited edition of 1000 copies of *Ulysses*, but the firm was in such poor financial shape by then that he had to put it into voluntary liquidation, keeping his Penguins and breeding them into the series, periodicals and sub-brands that quickly became a national institution. In 1937 The Bodley Head was rescued by Sir Stanley Unwin (who owned Allen & Unwin), Wren Howard (part owner of Jonathan Cape) and W.G. Taylor (of Dent) and operated successfully under Sir Stanley's watchful eye.

Verschoyle and Hart had gone as far as to discuss the possibility of Ansbacher's buying the firm with Graham Greene. Verschoyle's idea was that he then be put in to manage The Bodley Head with Greene as adviser.[3] But Hart quickly struck another agreement with Max who wrote to Sir Stanley on 14 August that 'some banker friends of mine who have not approached you before, have asked if I would be interested in joining them to make you an offer for The Bodley Head, which I know you have been considering selling'. He introduced himself as the owner of 'HFL (Publishers) Ltd., who publish all the Spicer & Pegler text books' and Spicer & Pegler as 'my closest friends and advisers on all financial matters'. Sir Stanley would have known about Reinhardt Ltd and Nonesuch, but in not mentioning them Max evidently wanted to appeal to him as a business man, which is no doubt how he still thought of himself. He assured Sir Stanley that 'these people are extremely serious' and asked him to ring if he was too.

They met the next morning. Max came away with an account of The Bodley Head stock, work in hand, plant, goodwill, rights, copyrights, furniture and cash and the same afternoon suggested to Hart that an offer of £70,000 would be in order. Hart, who knew nothing about publishing, was concerned that the commercial advantage of the firm due to its reputation (the goodwill) which Sir Stanley had estimated at £12,000 was perhaps too high, but he sketched out a plan whereby Ansbacher's and Max would form a holding company to buy Sir Stanley out on a fifty-fifty basis. Ansbacher's would loan the holding company £70,000;

Max would sell Max Reinhardt Ltd to it, which would serve as collateral for the holding company's loan to Max of his half of the payment to Sir Stanley. Hart cautioned that in this deal Max would lose a half interest in his own business, but would in return gain a half interest in The Bodley Head, the purchase of which would be financed by Ansbacher's, which meant in effect that Ansbacher's would have a prior charge on Max's half of the new company.

Such a risk seemed to further excite the 40-year-old Max who pressed Hart to proceed. The offer was made on 20 August, less than a week after Max had spoken to Sir Stanley, subject to further financial examination and to the new company not being committed to any long-term agreements of an unusual nature either to its staff or otherwise. Max valued his own company at £15,000 and detailed its assets in three categories: books already published by Max Reinhardt Ltd, already published jointly with Hodder & Stoughton, and works in progress. These he valued at £13,095, £86 and £4598 respectively. His cash in the bank he listed as £4.

He then suggested a change to Hart's proposal. He agreed that Ansbacher's should loan the holding company whatever price was to be paid for The Bodley Head, but that he would loan whatever he got from the bank for his company (which he suggested should be £15,000), rather than sell it to the holding company. That way there would be repayment in interest from the holding company, which he thought should be made from part of the profits of both companies and repayment in proportion to the amount of the two loans. He said he was prepared to guarantee that within three years of purchase he could realize a minimum of £35,000 from The Bodley Head stock and £11,000 from the Max Reinhardt Ltd stock, providing a total of £46,000 even if the amounts he could realize from the individual companies might need to be rebalanced.

This seemed fine to Hart, but Sir Stanley wanted £80,000, which Hart was unwilling to pay. A month passed. Then on Monday 17 September Max played his trump card. He confessed to Sir Stanley who was 'getting tired of these non-conclusive negotiations' that he felt the same way. He had spoken to Hart who was not willing to raise the offer beyond £72,000, Max said. There was nothing he could do about that but he assured Sir Stanley he 'would be happy to receive The Bodley Head into [our] group, and take good care of all that is inherent in its rich tradition'. Then, against what Hart had originally proposed, he promised the company's staff would be well looked after, and offered Sir Stanley 'out of my own resources [an additional] 10% less tax of the net profits of The Bodley Head for 1956 as a fee for your valuable services to the company for that year. The decision must now be yours,' he told him, 'I am off to the Frankfurt Book Fair on Wednesday midday.' He wanted the company badly and timed his letter to arrive just before he was to leave town, as he had his 1948 retort to Shaw when, puffed with a young man's success at getting the great man's signature on the Ellen Terry deal, he was hungry for the Charrington letters. He needed, he told Sir Stanley, to plan the future of Max Reinhardt Ltd and the tenancy of the new building in Earlham Street according to whatever his circumstances would be when he returned.

His tactic worked. On Tuesday morning he reported to Hart that Sir Stanley had agreed to their offer but 'wanted a little extra which he would ask us to pay, in due course, to the Booksellers' Benevolent Fund'. Max had therefore agreed to pay him 10 per cent of the 1956 profits 'up to the limit of the 1955 profits. Anything above that [of 1956 profits] we would divide equally.'[4] And so he left for Frankfurt.

* * *

On his way back Max stopped at St Jean Cap Ferrat to visit Tony and Dot Quayle at the Hôtel Voile d'Or, an informal set-up in a villa that the film director Michael Powell had inherited from his father, and which Powell's wife, Frankie, ran. Since Quayle was still a director of Max Reinhardt Ltd there was The Bodley Head purchase to discuss. In turn the Quayles had another proposition for Max. A young New York casting director they knew named Joan MacDonald would be passing through London soon and they wanted Max to meet her. That was fine with Max, but at the moment business was more pressing.

On 8 November Max suggested to Ansbacher's that he split Max Reinhardt Ltd. He would rename his inactive Endeavour Press, Max Reinhardt Ltd and the present Max Reinhardt Ltd would 'in due course go into liquidation'. The new company would 'take over as well [as the whole Bodley Head business] the work in progress of the old Max Reinhardt Ltd', while The Bodley Head would 'take over the old Max Reinhardt Ltd stock [and] sell it, less a commission of 20%'. He guaranteed that the old Max Reinhardt Ltd would produce not less than £15,000 a year and on 27 November 1956 he asked Francis Meynell if there were any objection to his transferring their Nonesuch contract to the new Max Reinhardt Ltd; splitting the company, he said, 'was necessary for tax purposes'.

Meynell had no objection. The arrangement made no financial difference to Ansbacher's and it left Max with his own press to be used separately from The Bodley Head in the future. He suggested that his salary as managing director of John Lane The Bodley Head and the new Max Reinhardt Ltd be '£3000 per annum, to be drawn partly as salary and partly as expenses'. The directors of both firms, he said, should be those of the old Max Reinhardt Ltd – himself, 'Richard G. Pegler FCA, Anthony Quayle CBE, A. Dwye Evans, Sir Ralph Richardson, plus any number that Messrs Ansbacher & Co. wish to appoint'.[5] They were Hart and the chairman of Ansbacher's, George Ansley (an anglicized version of the name).

Max then added Meynell to the board and a week later told Hart that J.B. Priestley wanted to come on as literary director. Max had spent the weekend at Priestley's house on the Isle of Wight and his wife, Jaquetta Hawkes, had suggested Max ask him; Heinemann was Priestley's publisher but The Bodley Head had done his first book and he had been a reader and adviser for the firm for years. Max thought '£500 a year plus a share of the profits of any proposition that he brought us and which was successful' would make him happy 'particularly if some payment could be made either in kind or tax free'. Max also wanted to hire as 'editor a first class literary person, not as eminent as either Jack or Graham Greene, who could work for us and execute all the suggestions that the literary directors would make. The ideal person,' he told Hart, 'and Priestley agrees – would be John Raymond, the present assistant literary editor of the *New Statesman*, who does exactly the same job for Eyre and Spottiswoode. If he would come to us I think it would be a perfect arrangement. He could put into execution any ideas, brilliant or otherwise, which Priestley, Greene or anybody else would give him. I feel he might come for a salary of about £800 or so a year.'[6]

Max was pleased with himself for engaging Priestley and gave a dinner party to further impress Hart at Trevor Square. But the Richardsons could not attend as it was 'the eve of their departure and they will both have quite a lot of packing to do. Besides, they are dining with the Priestleys on Thursday night so they'll be talking about this then and I am seeing Ralph on Wednesday before our dinner party (we are playing our last game of squash).'[7] Ralph was to be General St Pé in Jean Anouilh's *The Waltz of The Toreadors* in New York. As it turned out Joan MacDonald's sister Pat would also be in the production.

Making connections had always been easy for Max. Dealing with Ansbacher's proved more complicated. A letter to Hart on 7 November 1956 after Price Waterhouse had gone over his company's finances left him explaining that he 'had never given importance to the appearance of the accounts of Max Reinhardt Ltd for, as you guessed, I used the company, which I own one hundred percent, to suit my purpose'. He admitted that 'inter-company transfers were made to suit our small group as a whole. If for instance, the sale of a particular book, even if very successful (take *The Week-End Book*), had not covered its costs of production because of a large printing, then we would be showing a fictitious loss, for on its sales we would be paying Book Centre and travelling commission.' What he had done may have been standard business practice, but he nonetheless felt it necessary to affirm his good intentions for the future. 'I want to make it clear', he told Hart, 'that I do not intend to burden Max Reinhardt Ltd with new and unexpected expenses. HFL will not charge them any rent until they can well afford to pay their share, and you will find that the other companies with which I am associated will be generally very helpful.' He suggested the rent he would charge the new firm be calculated a few months after the move to Earlham Street and promised Hart it would not be more than The Bodley Head's present rent. Max was not compromised by the audit but he did acknowledge that 'it is a useful corrective to find one's activities scrutinised by an impartial observer'.

Hart accepted Max's explanation but in mid-November he was still worried about 'the goodwill' they were buying from Sir Stanley. When he asked for a guarantee that George Allen & Unwin would not steal The Bodley Head's authors Sir Stanley was rightly offended. He had already agreed to sign an undertaking not to publish a few authors they would list in the contract. Having spent more than twenty years in building up the John Lane business he thought the idea that he would entice away its authors humorous were the implications not so serious.

Max explained to Hart that while The Bodley Head owned a few copyrights, like those in Chesterton's work, most were licensed under contract which was normal publishing practice, and there was no risk of losing them. He also sensibly pointed out that in his experience

> you can never keep an author if he wants to leave a publisher. In fact, the author-publisher relationship is a delicate one, and works only if based on mutual trust and benefit ... The publishing trade is a small one and all that happens within it is quickly known ... If [Sir Stanley] did [what you suggest] it would do him and his firm infinite harm ... Although he may not be liked in the trade and has got a reputation for being rather mean, he is not dishonest and he prides himself on the work he has done for the trade generally. He would certainly not want to prejudice that.

In any case, Max added, not 'boastfully but only as a further assurance ... if authors have stayed with The Bodley Head under this present management they will be more likely to stay when I am in charge. For I think our reputation as publishers is not a bad one and our authors have always been contented and given us a good report.'[8]

But Hart persisted. Lawyers letters were exchanged. 'If what you want is an undertaking that I will do nothing to impair the goodwill of the firm I have laboriously built up, I will gladly give it, ridiculous as such a request seems to me', Sir Stanley agreed. 'If an undertaking is wanted that I will not during the next five years publish any novel by a John Lane author other than Bertrand Russell and my son David (Severn) I will gladly give it, though the request is superfluous because George Allen & Unwin is not interested in fiction. I will gladly include Lane's most profitable authors, such as Helen Dore Boylston and John Everard.'[9]

Max thought that would be the end of it but Hart then complained that Sir Stanley was lecturing him and Max had to intervene again. This time he advised Hart to consider Sir Stanley's

> nature and upbringing (he is a stanch pillar of his Church), and ... an elder statesman of the trade. There cannot have been any imper-tinence involved ... He is well over 70 and has been a publisher all his life; he is a past-president of the Publishers' Association, and on the whole he has done an enormous amount for publishing, partic-ularly regarding copyright and overseas rights ... He has written the standard book on publishing and whenever there is a crisis he is the one to take up the battle for the trade. He would not cheat us over goodwill ... I am certain there is no commercial risk involved for The Bodley Head.[10]

Hart remained firm. Sir Stanley told him he 'obviously knew nothing about publishing' and 'he regretted having agreed to sell this business ... Whereupon [Hart] pointed out that if this was the case, [he] was quite prepared to withdraw.' Luckily Wren Howard and W.G. Taylor continued to want to sell and somehow Max, who was in awe of Sir Stanley and very anxious to buy the company, was able to smooth things over. The contracts were finally exchanged at 2.30 p.m. on 11 December with the agreement that there would be no 'detrimental action against The Bodley Head or its authors, at least for a five-year period' and 'at least as long as Max Reinhardt manages the business'. Sir Stanley later told his son Rayner, who eventually became chairman of Allen & Unwin, that 'Max was the only man with whom he had done substantial business for whom he retained real respect'.[11]

During this confrontation, Joan MacDonald had been in London for ten days. She and Max had gone with the Quayles to Peter Ustinov's *Romanoff and Juliet*. Max had given them supper afterwards at Trevor Square then taken Joan to the Embassy Club and the Four Hundred. They had danced all night, watched the sun rise over the Thames and seen each other every day until she returned to New York. Joan was tall, slim and beautiful and by the time she left Max was in love again. But arrangements within the holding company needed finalizing before he could ask her to marry him. There was the possibility of adding to The Bodley Head package T. Werner Laurie Ltd which Sir Stanley's uncle, Fisher Unwin, had managed before making his own imprint. With the exception of Winston Graham's Poldark novels Max thought the backlist not worth much but there 'was the possibility of making a profit on selling some of their books without responsibility for us', he told Richard Pegler.[12] Into the new group he also brought Max Reinhardt (Canada), a company he had formed in November 1954 to sell his own and Nonesuch books there.

As things stood on 21 December, 'The Bodley Head shares would be owned by Max Reinhardt Ltd and that company would borrow from Ansbacher's the amount required to pay for them.' Hart felt 'that so long as the loan is outstanding, [Ansbacher's] should have the maximum security, and therefore, we require to hold 51% of the Max Reinhardt shares. We shall of course agree that as soon as the loan is repaid, Max Reinhardt can buy from us at cost sufficient shares to equalise our holdings ... The Bodley Head would pay a management fee to Max Reinhardt, which would provide that company with the funds necessary to discharge its interest obligations to Ansbacher's.' Max could wait no longer. Operating as he always did on trust, he left for New York the same day without a contract or formal guarantee from Hart that when he reduced the loan to less than £15,000 he could buy back for £1 that crucial Max Reinhardt share. Ansbacher's, he discovered later, insured his life for 'a large premium for the flight'.[13]

*   *   *

Joan MacDonald was born in 1924 in Paris where her father, Carlisle, was the *New York Times* correspondent; her mother, Dorothy Allen, was the descendant of a conservative New England family. By today's standards she gave Joan and her younger siblings little maternal attention. Joan was turned over early to French nannies and when her lack of interest in English became worrisome she was sent to friends in London for long holidays. Carlisle eventually returned to New York to set up a public relations department for the US Steel Corporation. This was a far more lucrative occupation than journalism and he built the department into a huge concern within the company. Joan and her siblings enjoyed a very comfortable upbringing, which included the best private education, for Joan at the Chapin School. Perhaps predictably her brother, who was the middle child, got the university education she and her sister were not offered. Joan went instead to the American Academy of Dramatic Arts for a year, then worked in radio publicity until after the war when she became an assistant at an advertising agency. In tough competition with men she worked her way up to become casting director for ABC, then for NBC.

In late December 1956 *My Fair Lady* was the rage of New York; only with her theatre connections was Joan able to secure two tickets. To her astonishment Max had obtained two more through a New York contact, and he continued to surprise. Within a couple of days he had won her parents over despite her concern they would disapprove of him because he was Jewish. He spent Christmas with them, then flew Joan to Toronto for an evening with her sister Pat, who was on stage with the Richardsons.

Joan was 'swept off her feet'. Max knew how to do everything and after two weeks with him in London and two in New York she was happy to let him. He was handsome and full of initiative. 'He exuded great warmth and his smile was irresistible. His presence filled the room.' At the old Metropolitan Opera he whisked her through the intermission bar-crush to a reserved table where champagne awaited them. He graciously handled having Margaret Leighton and Laurence Harvey unexpectedly seated next to them at Sardi's. He even knew how to propose marriage in the most New York of ways – over hamburgers and cheesecake at Lindy's. Thinking herself 'a big fish in a small pond' and sensing that for all his *savoir faire* 'Max needed a partner not someone with a competing career' Joan decided to give up her career and marry him. She felt he was 'isolated in himself and so was I. We were a good team – and that's what marriage is.'[14]

Ralph pronounced Joan 'one of the most charming girls one has met about two continents lately'[15] and Max returned to London triumphant. On 7 January 1957 he was officially appointed director of The Bodley Head for a term of three years at the salary of £3000 a year plus expenses. T. Werner Laurie had been added to the deal and he and Winston Graham, whose Poldark novels were the plums of that list, soon became friends. Judy Taylor, who was then The Bodley Head's assistant to the children's editor, Barbara Ker Wilson, remembered Sir Stanley Unwin turning up one day in their old office in Little Russell Street with a youngish, dark-haired man who was good looking, smartly dressed and had well polished shoes – in an early *Who's Who* entry a whimsical Max admitted he liked polishing shoes. There had been rumours about the firm being sold. Richard Hough, who Taylor would later marry, had been running it until 1955 when he left for Hamish Hamilton because of the uncertainty. Barney Blackley, who had then taken charge of the firm, had been told by Sir Stanley there was no pay rise coming; he should 'ask the new owner'. Blackley remembered Max as 'pipe-smoking . . . diffusing quiet panache [with] an air of cosmopolitan worldliness, a sense of flourish without ostentation'.[16]

With an air of affable command, Max soon returned to interview each person individually and began in his mind to integrate the present staff with his own people to shape his team. Britain's average weekly wage in the mid-1950s was £10 5s; it was lower in publishing, and much lower at The Bodley Head. While thrifty with salaries, Max was ready to pay for what he wanted. He gave small rises to most, larger ones to a few, and enthusiastically assured everyone that he would solve any financial problems the firm faced. He had not come to The Bodley Head (Allen Lane had agreed to his dropping John Lane from its name) to impose a new vision but to run more efficiently what he and Ansbacher's had bought – respected publishing experts and an imprint that matched his own traditional, although from some of his new staff's point of view, exotic, international sensibility. They would soon learn that Max was an enabler. He would demand loyalty and return it; over the years he would honour people with small tributes, with directorships, and some with larger favours. He was free of pomposity but he had a deep-rooted egotism which gave him his authority. He was no egalitarian. Everyone knew who owned the company. It was Christian names all around; Max was MR. While his even temper, graciousness and desire for fun would help him attract and keep the best people in every part of the publishing process, he was a businessman who liked the feel of books and the company of authors more than he liked to read. He would help his staff get on with making the books they wanted to – books that would make him a profit.

Barney Blackley was to remain chief editor of the adult list, Barbara Ker Wilson to continue as head of the children's list. In quick recognition of the growing importance of books for children, Max raised her salary to a startling £1000 a year.[17] Judy Taylor would remain her assistant. When Wilson soon left to marry, Taylor would take over that department and become one of the first women (along with Eunice Frost at Penguin and Norah Smallwood at Chatto & Windus) to rise to the top of British publishing.

Iris Taylor, who had been assistant to the chief accountant, was to take charge of royalties and subsidiary rights; Max's own accountant, John Hews, would handle the new company's finances. Leonard Lake, who had been at The Bodley Head since 1928, was to head production. Will Carter, who had very successfully designed the Max Reinhardt Ltd books, decided he needed help with the additional load and suggested Max approach John Ryder, who had worked at Phoenix House and was looking for another job. Ryder was a fine typographer who had written two books about printing and design, *Printing for Pleasure* (1955) and *A Suite of Fleurons* (1956). Max offered him £1000 a year to design the Bodley Head style (together with letter designer Michael Harvey); it would make Max's books elegant, durable and easy to hold and read. Max knew the value of his backlist; one of their first projects would be a new edition of *Ulysses*. And Max knew the value of distinction; by 1961 John Ryder had restored The Bodley Head booklets, a tradition started by John Lane before the turn of the century of preparing a gift booklet for friends at Christmas. The first booklet Ryder designed celebrated the twenty-fifth anniversary of the first publication of *Ulysses* by The Bodley Head in 1936. Twenty-four of these limited Christmas editions would be printed over the next three decades, each containing an excerpt from one of Max's current bestsellers and many being illustrated by Bodley Head artists – Edward Ardizzone, Mitsumasa Anno and Maurice Sendak among them.

'Glad to hear things in business are humming at such a pace', Ralph wrote on 9 March. 'It will be most interesting to see how The Bodley Head looks say in one year from now.' He had met Joan's parents and while cautioning Max about the 'perilous path of marriage', reported that Joan was 'looking very pretty and spoke of course of her journey to London'. Boy Hart had asked Ralph's opinion 'about adding more guns and powder to the publishing business' and Ralph had replied that the deal would be fine so long as Max could find assistance. Jack Priestley would not 'solve the problem of day to day steam power on the buying side or the ideas side', he confided to Max. 'I hope you do find someone though; it is a headache.'

The Bodley Head kept Max busy, so his marriage had to take place in London instead of in New York. Max planned a quiet wedding at Caxton Hall Registry Office in Westminster with his mother, who was to come from Paris, the Quayles and, since Joan's parents were unable to attend, close family friends Anna and Christopher Purcell *in loco parentis*. But public curiosity about Margaret Leighton followed Max and when the party left the registry office on 14 March photographers mobbed them; 'Silent Max Weds' was one newspaper headline. So discreet had Max been that even his close friend Thelma Cazalet, who relied on him as an extra man for her parties and country-house weekends, was surprised when she read the news. Frieda was at Trevor Square when Cazalet rang to find out why Max had married: 'Is she wealthy'? With her limited English Frieda heard 'healthy' and said 'I think so.' 'Oh that's why', Cazalet replied.[18] Cazalet and Joan became good friends but this misunderstanding of Joan's circumstances followed Joan to Max's bank where the manager, who thought she was the daughter of a steel tycoon, was visibly taken aback when she handed him $50 to open a account. Max loved to tell both stories but the retelling never changed anyone's impression that Joan's father was a steel magnate. Certainly from the first the Reinhardts exuded a wealthy glamour that was perhaps more familiar to their theatre friends than to Max's conservative publishing peers.

After the ceremony there was a small luncheon at Trevor Square. Then Max and Joan headed to Paris where Charles Ritz (whose *A Fly Fisher's Life* Max would publish in 1959) gave them the best suite in his hotel and kept it stocked with flowers and champagne for the next four days. When Ritz himself married he told Max 'you and Joan looked so happy on your honeymoon I thought I'd try it myself'. On their last night Max invited George Ansley to dinner. The story he recalled in *Memories* about Ansley arriving with two Parisian girlfriends and instead of congratulating the newlyweds being angry that he himself had never been offered the same suite conceals the fact that even on honeymoon Max was not away from business. When Priestley sent Max a 'picture as a little present' on 20 March 1957 it came with the suggestion that *The Bodley Head Leacock* begin a series that 'wants a format design [of] 100,000 words – bigger than the American Portables but not too big, nice looking and solid as they can look for, say, a guinea a book. [It will be] a good bread-and-butter line for the firm, and pleasant occasional work for me.' In future years Priestley would look at the oval watercolour and remind Joan 'It's good. Make sure you appreciate it's good.'[19]

* * *

At the beginning of Max's thirty-year reign at The Bodley Head Britain was still pulling itself out of the war and his exuberance about what he and his team could do was infectious. Max brought glamour, the famous Nonesuch books and HFL Ltd; he was a small conglomerate in himself.

He soon moved the staff into his newly prepared triangular building at 10 Earlham Street. On the wall as you entered were the names of his expanding empire: Fimex, HFL (which The Bodley Head people jokingly tagged High Finance Ltd), The Stellar Press, Max Reinhardt Ltd (which now owned The Bodley Head although most of the staff did not realize it), and The Nonesuch Library (through which Max administered The Nonesuch Press although he did not own it outright until 1986). The three floors were connected by stairs on which new linoleum had been glued; Priestley told Judy Taylor it smelled 'like a giantess painting her nails'. The main street window was soon adorned with a huge photograph taken by theatre photographer Angus McBean of The Bodley Head's books on shelves. In front of it John Goodwin, who had come from the National Theatre at Stratford to do publicity, had arranged such an inviting heap of recent publications that people banged on the door thinking them for sale. The street was a colourful clutter of book, flower and fruit stalls. Number 10 was cramped from the start so when the second floor of the building across the road became available Max rented it for the children's department. Below that office was a shop that sold trumpets and trombones, and a few doors down there was a boxer's gym.[20]

Max was persuasive and his enthusiasm made The Bodley Head attractive to unusual and talented people. Not all stayed but those who left remained friends. Within a few years John Goodwin had gone to work with Peter Hall at the Royal Shakespeare Company. Goodwin found Max 'a joy to work with, friendly, encouraging, very ambitious. The Bodley Head was an exciting place to be, and had the "offer I couldn't refuse" not come I'd have been very happy to stay at BH.'[21] Colin Haycroft who had worked and reviewed for the *Observer* would move on to his own publishing house, Duckworth. Christopher Hollis's son, Nigel, would eventually become a director at Heinemann. Guido Waldman started in 1958 as American paperback and book-club rights manager, took over foreign publications, and stayed for thirty years. He found 'Max an affable, genuinely friendly soul [who was] happy to give avuncular advice to his younger staff while trusting them to use their own discretion and common sense in fulfilling their tasks – and quite philosophical when it turned out that the only way a young person could learn his trade was by making mistakes'.[22] Euan Cameron, who came in 1965, left for a short term with Michael Joseph, returned in 1968 as publicity manager, became a director of the firm in 1973 and added editorial work to his load in 1978, said Max was protective and easy to work for.

Max's method of determining salaries was to ask people 'How much can you manage on'? Cameron shook hands on £800 a year as Max rose from his 'impressive swivelling leather arm chair, exuding a hypnotic charm and smelling faintly of some rare and aromatic hair lotion'.[23] Most settled for less, and while Max took a paternalistic interest in his staff, Judy Taylor thought he really had no idea how any of them lived. She never forgot the morning her Hoover broke and when she arrived in a distressed state was told by Max to go and buy a new one. 'I don't have any money', she said. 'Well go to the bank', he replied. 'But I don't have an account,' she answered and when he looked askance, 'I don't have any money, Max. I live on what I earn.' Like all the staff she was paid in cash and thought the fact that she lived on her wages was beyond his imagination.[24]

Perhaps that is one reason salaries at The Bodley Head remained low in comparison with those at other publishing houses. When Taylor left to marry at the end of the 1970s after building up the finest and most lucrative children's list in London and acting for some time as Max's deputy managing director, she was making only £10,000 a year. Yet Max championed her in every other way; he appointed her a director of the company in 1967, was instrumental in having her elected to the Council of the Publishers' Association (both then rare honours for a woman and a children's book editor) and helped get her an MBE in 1971. Max was generous of heart but chary with money. He told his authors 'you do the writing', his staff 'you make the books you want', and both 'I'll do the paying and worrying.'[25]

In 1957 Max was hungry for success and part of the reason The Bodley Head prospered was because of his tight financial control. Ansbacher's were interested in what they had financed, and Max was lucky to be working with Boy Hart who was full of helpful suggestions and respected Max's business acumen. HFL was making such a nice profit that within a couple of years Max had lifted his holding in The Bodley Head to 80 per cent.[26] He had a large expense account which suited his generosity as a host. Joan was at home. Everything seemed possible as husband and wife began their new life together.

6
Enter Director Graham Greene

At the beginning of June 1957 Ansbacher's gave a luncheon to which they invited Graham Greene. He had supplemented his war income by serving as a director for Eyre & Spottiswoode then worked there as editorial director from 1944 to 1948, inventing a Mrs Montgomery, whose manuscript was supposedly lost at the press to amuse himself. Greene told Max he missed publishing and was looking for something to do after he had written his 500 words a day so Max asked him to join the board of The Bodley Head and help revamp their list. Like Priestley, Greene's own publisher was William Heinemann. Greene did not much like Priestley, but he liked Max immediately and permanently, in part because Max was so affable. Max's first letter to 'Dear Greene' was an apology sent 5 June, two days before Greene's official election to the board. 'I'm so sorry that you so very much disliked the first page proofs that we sent you. The book was accepted by the previous management and as we took over the list as it was we just went ahead with the production of all the books on it ... I am postponing publication ... I am most grateful for your advice.' Within a week Greene had glanced through the catalogue and suggested

> combining Rex Warner's translations of Euripides, of which [The Bodley Head had] published three, into one volume at a reasonable price ... What is the position today of Kenneth Grahame who was an idol of one's childhood? ... I remember Norman Dale as a very good writer of adventure stories for children ... Barbara Comyns. She's a crazy but interesting novelist whom I started when I was at Eyre & Spottiswoode ... George Bernanos. The Diary of A Country Priest ... Marcel Aymé. If we still have rights in his books I do think some concerted drive should be made to put him over in English.[1]

In 1957 the letters came two or three a week. Greene suggested republishing Nathaniel West's *Miss Lonleyhearts* and *The Day of the Locust*.

> Is anybody in your office watching the LONDON MAGAZINE? ... There is a story which seems to me quite up to the, shall we say?, Salinger level called <u>The Dormouse Child</u> by A.E. Ellis. Apparently Ellis has never published anything before outside undergraduate magazines but he has completed a novel ... Shouldn't we write and ask to see it? ... Another contributor ... is Shevawn Lynam who is attached to the Press Section of the British Embassy in Paris. Her first novel has been published in America and France 'but has not yet appeared in Britain'.[2]

It was Greene's connection with Anita Björk that made it possible for Max to do an English selection of her late husband Stig Dagerman's writing, which the Anglo-Swedish Literary Foundation subsidised and bought 3000 copies of. 'Here', Max told Greene 'is a book with lots of prestige on which we really cannot go wrong.'[3] In the late fifties Max made the same arrangement for Gunnar Haggloff's *Swedish War Trade Policy during the Second World War* and for Nobel laureate Selma Lagerlof's biography. Greene suggested the unknown and 'fascinating Judge Dee mysteries written in English by a Dutchman called Robert van Gulik who [was] an authority on the Far East', and an Arsène Lupin omnibus with a possible preface by T.S. Eliot, a great admirer of Lupin. Heinemann was watching the *London Magazine* closely for new writers and perhaps trying to prove his loyalty, Greene said they 'may well slip up and I think we should keep a very careful eye on the magazine'. Max did. 'If I write to you many more letters you'll regret ever having taken me on our Board' Greene wrote in the autumn of 1957 to which Max instantly replied, 'Dear Graham, Many thanks for your letter. From my point of view the more I get from you the better, so never hesitate to write.'[4]

For the rest of Greene's life he suggested books and Max followed them up. Greene was a superb scout. He knew the foreign and British publishing scenes well; he read reviews and met authors everywhere he travelled; he suggested British editions; he checked translations for what he called 'translator's English' and thought up better titles; he picked out interesting scholarship which might be republished, scholars who might be of use as ghost writers or editors of particular editions; he supplied quotes for jackets and sent lists of people he thought publicity copies of books should be sent to. He helped Max get books, often telling him what to say to encourage a writer; he passed along the latest literary gossip and his own hunches about what was worth printing; he knew children's books, read manuscripts, replied to even the most recalcitrant authors.

And he took on Priestley, who persisted in spelling Graham with an 'e' and who was becoming troublesome on the board.

> Dear Max, On second and third thoughts I wonder whether we dismissed the possibility of including [Ford Maddox] Ford in The Bodley Head editions a little too lightly. I am aware of course that Priestley [who as a reader for John Lane years earlier had recommended Greene's first novels for publication] is not very enthusiastic about the idea, but it seems to me an admirable volume could be made from the Good Soldier followed by extracts from his admirable and amusing autobiographies, his topographical books and his criticism, with about twenty pages of poetry perhaps at the end. I admit I am a fanatic on the subject of Ford and would like to see a revival of his work, and it seems to me that an inclusive volume of this kind might well lead up to an omnibus edition of his historical Trilogy of the Fifth Queen. Anyway can we consider the idea a little more carefully?[5]

On the republication of Ford, Priestley lost to Greene. Or perhaps it was Max who won, for he persuaded Greene to edit the four volume *Bodley Head Ford Maddox Ford* and to write introductions to the first and third volumes, published in 1962 and 1963.

On 28 April 1958 *My Fair Lady* opened at the Drury Lane Theatre to thunderous applause and rave reviews. Max had published the text of the musical with Cecil Beaton's illustrations of the costumes and had a special copy bound and delivered to Buckingham Palace. The queen was to attend a benefit performance on the second night, and Max was invited by the assistant lord chamberlain to join her for a drink, along with the American producers. He said he would be honoured, but could he bring his new wife? When told only the Americans' wives were invited because of limited space Max replied seamlessly 'but Joan is an American' and they were taken up the back stairs into the little green anteroom behind the queen's box.[6] Max had 'arrived'. The production broke all box office records, running until the film was released by Warner Brothers in 1964, and Max's book was a huge financial success.

* * *

It was not long before the possibility of publishing *Lolita* arose. Because no one in Britain or America would touch it (Roger Straus had told

Nabokov not even to publish it pseudonymously), the novel had been released in English by Maurice Girodias at the Olympia Press in France. There were no reviews but in December 1955 Greene had named it one of the three best books of the year in the *Sunday Times* and then been denounced by John Gordon, editor in chief of *The Times*, for recommending pornography to the public. Knowing that Gordon nonetheless strongly disapproved of censorship, Greene had some fun by forming with John Sutro the John Gordon Society against Pornography. They then held a meeting where publishers suggested schemes to cleanse the language, the zaniest of which was to include a pledge in Scrabble games that had to be signed on purchase, promising never to use in play words that were not in the Oxford Dictionary. *Lolita* became an instant *cause célèbre*. So many letters were received by the society's fictitious secretary that Greene invited John Gordon to give a lecture on the necessity for censorship. Gordon then retaliated by challenging Greene to a public debate on pornography. Anita Loos said it was one of the funniest evenings she ever spent in London. Walter Minton of G.P. Putnam was also in attendance and, realizing the book's value, took a chance and published it in America in August 1958.

When the possibility of publishing it in England came up Greene was ecstatic. Priestley said that 'if Grahame [adding the 'e' by hand to his typed letter] insists that Lolita has great literary merit then you feel entitled to publish it ... I shall have no unfriendly feelings about it but I shall feel it my duty to resign.' He felt so 'strongly that its publication could have some unpleasant anti-social effects'[7] that he waived his director's fee for six months (for part of which he was in any case to be in America) and convinced several other board members that prosecution was a real possibility given the climate in England against pornography. Hundreds of thousands of books including novels as innocuous as *Moll Flanders* and *Madam Bovary* had been recently destroyed under the old 1868 law, and customs officers regularly confiscated books from travellers' luggage.

Max sided with Greene. An offer was made to Nabokov in October but in November Max discovered there were contractual problems, he suspected between Nabokov and Olympia. Not only were Weidenfeld & Nicolson to publish the book, it 'MUST be published [in collaboration] with another publisher'[8] Max told Greene, and insisted he was only interested if he could do the book alone. But Greene continued to believe that Nabokov wanted The Bodley Head to have the novel because of what he had done to make it famous. 'I wouldn't be surprised if we got LOLITA yet if we keep a firm stand against collaboration', he wrote back on 5 November. On 8 December he wrote again to say Weidenfeld had consulted counsel and were going to cut several pages from their American edition. 'One doesn't know whether Nabokov realizes this or has given his consent to it.'

In early January Priestley finished editing and introducing *The Bodley Head Scott Fitzgerald* and Max paid him in part in his favourite cigars, as he was asked to. 'I would not have done as much work as I did on the Fitzgerald for a fee of £100 from any other publisher',[9] Priestley grumbled. He knew Max had renewed the offer to Nabokov and that because the law against pornography did not allow publishers to defend themselves by arguing the merits of a book if prosecuted, Greene was going to sign the contract on behalf of the firm; if he were sued he would be allowed to argue the novel's literary merit in his own defence. It was a generous and courageous offer on Greene's part. To Priestley's delight, Nabokov's reply was neither. Claiming to have preferred The Bodley Head and insisting the book would not be cut by Weidenfeld, Nabokov told Max it was too late. George Weidenfeld had in fact sent a copy of a small first printing to the director of public prosecutions in a campaign orchestrated by Gerald Gardiner to outwit its director, Sir Theobald Mathew, and had been told that *Lolita* would not be prosecuted. Greene had wanted The Bodley Head to test the law, and was personally wounded. 'The way we were treated was very unsatisfactory', he told Max privately. 'We were right not to publish with them.' Greene had also figured they would get *Lolita* if they refused to publish jointly; Max later added that he had not wanted in the circumstances to appear nervous and in need of support from another publisher.[10] It was an expensive gamble they lost; when the novel was published in November 1959 it was a quick bestseller of over 200,000 hardback copies.

By then Priestley had decided he was ready 'to earn my keep' again 'if you would like me to come back on the Board'.[11] He tried to arrange more lucrative terms for himself but Max took the view that Priestley had only threatened to resign over *Lolita* and, since they had not published the novel, if Priestley wanted they would resume their original arrangement. Priestley stayed on, continuing to edit, suggest books and complain about his payment. His attitude tightened Max's friendship with Greene. The firm had already exceeded its target of £180,000 turnover for the year, and Max had other projects in mind. He told Ralph he wanted to revive John Lehmann's *New Writing* which Penguin had published very successfully, during the war, but as sales dropped off in the late forties Allen Lane had closed down. Max thought *New Writing* could be restarted in a way that would draw new writers from other firms to The Bodley Head. Negotiations were beginning for *The Nonesuch*

Bible, a complicated publication printed at both Oxford and Cambridge University Presses in three boxed volumes. Rex Warner had brought Giorgos Seferiades (George Seferis), the Greek Ambassador in London, to Max and suggested Max publish his poems, which Warner would translate. Meanwhile Max and Greene were in the process of acquiring Gracie Fields's memoir *Sing As We Go* (1960) and, far more interesting, Charlie Chaplin's autobiography.

7
Charlie Chaplin: The Great Coup

In September 1957 Greene had seen in *The Times* that Charlie Chaplin was writing his autobiography. Max contacted Chaplin immediately on the telephone and on 13 September sent him The Bodley Head catalogue with a letter repeating 'what I said last night: that we would be delighted, honoured and grateful if we had the chance to publish your autobiography. It would be a universal book and I promise you we would try our outmost to do full justice to it.' He got no reply. Before Christmas Greene sent a telegram – 'Am now connected with publishing house The Bodley Head and would be delighted if allowed make competitive offer for your autobiography'– and Max an appreciation of Chaplin and an offer for £10,000. There was no reply. Greene had met Chaplin in Hollywood and in 1952 had defended him in the *New Statesman* when Chaplin fell victim to the McCarthy Act. He felt he could send another telegram: 'Shall be in Switzerland end of February. Could I drop in on you and seriously discuss your autobiography?' Still no reply came.[1]

In the spring of 1958 Max tried again. He and Greene were to dine in Paris with André Maurois on 15 March and since they would be in the neighbourhood he asked Chaplin, if they could take him to dinner and discuss his autobiography? This time there was a reply. On the16th they flew to Geneva, drove to Vevey and took Chaplin out. Chaplin said he had just begun to write, was finding the process slow, and if Max wrote again to make sure he put his name on the front of the envelope; Chaplin evidently never opened mail unless he knew who had sent it.

On 20 March Max put his name prominently on the front of another envelope. He and Joan were going soon to a publisher's conference in Vienna after which they were meeting Greene. Could they stop in to see him on their way back to London? This time Chaplin took them to a restaurant up in the hills near Vevey. Joan and Chaplin's wife Oona discovered they had attended neighbouring schools in New York. They were invited to stay the night and when the women retired, Chaplin read what he had written to Max and Greene. As he read about the poverty of his childhood, his half-brother Sydney and especially about his mother, he cried. Next morning Greene told Max the autobiography was going to be wonderful. He told Chaplin he did not believe in many things, but he did believe in good writing, writing which conveys the right kind of emotion, and what Chaplin had read to them was first rate. Chaplin agreed that Max should publish his book and because Chaplin was uneasy about contracts, Max agreed there need not be one until the writing was finished.[2]

By 3 November 1958 Max had offers for publication from Simon & Schuster for $10,000 and from Norstedt in Scandinavia for £14,000 and he had urged Chaplin on with a much larger advance. Chaplin liked the advance but worried about taxes. Max telephoned Vevey every few weeks to say he was going to St Jean Cap Ferrat, or somewhere close by. Could he stop in? He sent books from The Bodley Head and the Coronation Shakespeare from Nonesuch. Then he figured out how to solve Chaplin's tax problem, and he hoped his own contractual one. Chaplin could make a gift of his incomplete manuscript to a trust company in Lichtenstein from which The Bodley Head would buy 'from the trustees copyright of the book for £50,000 (in effect an advance on royalties and estimate of earnings)'. To 'provide for the probability that the book will earn over £50,000' they would 'have another agreement that you will complete the manuscript and we will pay you royalties and other amounts earned in excess of £50,000'.[3]

Years later Max explained this arrangement to Greene's niece, Amanda Saunders, as in part Greene's idea.

> He thought it would be an interesting experiment to form a small company which would acquire the world rights of books, and I suggested we call it Solitas (Société Litteraire Anglo-Suisse), which name appealed to Graham immediately. The partners were Graham, Oona Chaplin and a relative of mine [Oncle Richard]. The first books we bought were Graham's four children's books, and we appointed Verdant [Greene's holding company] as our agent. Solitas then instructed Verdant to sell them to The Bodley Head, and the Swiss company made a small profit on the deal which was distributed to the three parties. We had great fun over the whole project, which proved profitable, and my memories of it are all of joy and pleasure.[4]

In 1959 all Chaplin had to do was sign below the clause 'I will deliver the manuscript by the end of June 1960.'[5] The arrangement did not make Chaplin write any faster and despite it Max still had only a gentleman's agreement with him. There was to be no regular contract until the book was finished and Max knew that Chaplin's agent was getting daily offers for it from other publishers.

That August Max and Joan holidayed as usual at the Voile D'Or on Cap Ferrat where Greene brought Yvonne Cloetta to meet them. He had met her in March in Douala after gathering material for *A Burnt Out Case* and she would become his de facto spouse for the next 32 years. Max had replaced his rubber dinghy with a small cabin cruiser he called *Maximilian*. It had an international passport and he would ask the *douanier* at Nice to come aboard, give him a drink and a tip, and load up with duty-free liquor to replenish the hotel's cellars. The Chaplins came for a day and the three couples picnicked amiably on the boat. But by February 1960 the wait for the book became tense again when Max learned that Charles Chaplin Jr was writing a ghosted biography of his father which Random House was to publish in New York in May, Longmans in London in October. 'We need to talk', he wrote to Greene.[6] After worried conversations with Bennett Cerf and Chaplin himself they concluded the book would not compete with theirs, and Max used its publication to secure his own position by placing a large advertisement in the *Bookseller* on 18 March announcing that Chaplin's autobiography was in preparation for The Bodley Head. As a result he got even more handsome translation bids from all over the world.

But publication was still years away. Chaplin refused to use a secretary; he said he preferred to write in longhand. He also preferred to work with Max directly so Max went to Vevey more frequently. In spite of Chaplin's promise to get up early when Max was there he never worked before lunch after which he read to Max what he had written and they discussed it. 'He was very touchy', Max said. 'He didn't like being criticised.' Afterwards they walked down to Vevey to get the foreign papers. Sometimes Chaplin stopped outside a bank to read the share prices and tell Max how much he thought he was worth on that day.[7]

* * *

While Max was fond of Chaplin, and very keen for his book, other things occupied him that spring, the most important of which was that Joan was pregnant. Trevor Square would have to be sold and a move made to a larger house, 9 Alexander Place just off Thurloe Square. Because The Bodley Head's profits were still low, Max was considering the publication of a series of quality paperbacks which would be sold at 7s or 7s 6d in bookshops, in competition with the cheaper ones available from news-stands. A similar series of these larger 'B' format paperbacks had been successfully started in 1952 by Jason Epstein at Doubleday in New York and profitably copied there by Random House and others and now English publishers were following suit. Max was anticipating paperbacking The Bodley Head's books in house rather than licensing the paperback rights to a third party, like Penguin, which reduced his royalties and might eventually lose him authors to vertical publishers. He figured if he issued twelve titles to start with and kept at least two dozen in production at a time he could make money.

Some books that might fit the series had been sent to a few chosen people in April – a manuscript by Jack Lindsay about ancient Britain had gone to Jaquetta Hawkes for her consideration along with twenty of her favourite Dunhill cigars – and booksellers were being canvassed for their opinion. The general consensus was that Max should not start the series because in addition to libraries buying well known works in hard cover, the market was already glutted with exactly the sort of quality paperbacks he had in mind.

Alexandra was born on 28 July 1960. She was a beautiful baby and Ralph happily became her godfather. But in September she had to be rushed to Great Ormond Street Hospital with a dangerously low red blood cell count. She was given a transfusion and the consultants thought she would be all right. So on 3 October Max wrote to Chaplin that he and Graham had 'some business to attend to in Geneva, and we would be delighted to motor down to see you and Oona at Vevey. Your son's book just appeared, and although the reception has not been bad, many reviewers expressed the wish to read your autobiography.' Chaplin was entirely compliant; Max and Greene arrived at the Trois Couronnes to find their bill had been paid in advance, and left the next day with half the book. The rest of the typescript arrived in London soon after. It was about 250,000 words, which Chaplin said he would reduce to 150,000. Chaplin had been reassured that Max's trust scheme (which by then had become more detailed and included far larger payment) would give him maximum financial advantage.

Then in late November Greene became profoundly worried. Arnoldo Mondadori was pressing for the Italian rights and Greene, Max and the rest of the board knew Chaplin had still not formally assigned them to The Bodley Head. Max calmly reassured Greene by telegram that 'increasing firm offers [were] still pouring in but no commitments yet made. STOP. Impossible for us to lose financially.' He boldly told Mondadori his 'offer had been entered in our records with all the others that we have from all over the world, but Mr. Chaplin does not wish to commit himself at the present to the sale of any rights except the British book publishing rights'.[8]

Greene read Chaplin's book at the beginning of December. 'I treated it quite cavalierly', he told Max. 'It took about a fortnight to get through and I have only made rough corrections, but I find that I have shortened it by about 15,000 words. I'd like to talk about these to you in general terms, and how best we should make suggestions to Chaplin.' Max congratulated him on his 'editing job; I had not realised you had worked so much on the typescript and how very much you have improved it. I have added a few more corrections and I hope that Charles Chaplin will accept our recommendations. I have seen a number of press reports that he has been invited to go to Russia in the Spring and that he might go after finishing his memoirs. He may, therefore, be in a mood to finish them quickly.'[9]

Chaplin continued to rewrite. He readily agreed to Greene's cuts but in mid-June 1961 Max had to return to Vevey to get him to promise to stop revising by the end of the year. On that occasion they agreed the book would be approximately 180,000 words and have 32 full pages of photographs (these turned into 48 pages) but Chaplin still preferred not to sign a contract until he was finished because, Max told Greene, 'he needs to talk to his tax people'.[10]

On Chaplin's word that The Bodley Head had world rights to the book, Max began to arrange for serialization in the *Sunday Times*. He then told the board they should make a final offer to Chaplin of half a million US dollars. Only Greene was not shocked by the amount. Loyal Ralph tried to jolly everyone by reminding them of the importance to sales of the cover: 'You do judge a book by its cover!' The board agreed to the enormous sum, but not until Max had agreed to borrow it from his own bank, Ansbacher's being unwilling to underwrite it without a proper contract. Even Chaplin realized the impossibility of any bank agreeing to so huge a sum without his signature, so on 25 November 1961 he wrote for Max what he considered to be sufficient evidence of his intent: 'Dear Max, For your business convenience, this is to confirm our verbal agreement whereby you will have the world publishing book rights of my autobiography on the conditions we have discussed, subject to contract. This, of course, does not include the stage, film and serial rights. Yours, Charles Chaplin.'[11]

A few weeks later during a check-up the Reinhardt's baby was found to have an alarmingly low red blood cell count again and was eventually diagnosed with a rare life-threatening disease called Diamond Blackfan Anaemia. There is still no known cure for this congenital failure of bone marrow to produce red blood cells. At the time no one knew what to expect since Alexandra was Great Ormond Street Hospital's first case of the disease, and the first to be documented in Britain. But it was clear that Alexandra's life would not be ordinary. She was put on steroid therapy and Joan and Max spent Christmas at her cribside, shocked by the news. Greene came to Max's rescue with Chaplin, urging him on with the work at every opportunity. By the beginning of 1962 Simon & Schuster had raised its offer for the American rights to $100,000 and were sharing their editors' corrections on the existing chapters with Max, who was leaning on them for American place names and people's identities, as they were on his editors for the British equivalents. By 22 May Greene was reading 'the proofs of the first part of your autobiography with enormous pleasure', as he wrote to Chaplin. But Chaplin was still not satisfied with the rest. 'It has been very interesting to see how the rumours of the book have got about and the number of references which appear from time to time in the press by people who obviously know how good the work is', Greene added. 'Don't let's leave them impatient for [it] for too long!'

Then Max had another problem; he needed a new editorial director. Again Greene came to his rescue. 'Steal James Michie from Heinemann', he told Max. 'He is an extremely intelligent and nice person with a great many contacts among young authors, and he has experience in travelling in the USA.' Michie had been Greene's editor at Heinemann and Greene plied him with dinner at Albany and the offer to stay in his villa in Capri if he would join Max. What Michie wanted was six weeks holiday a year, never to have to go to Frankfurt again and the freedom to take on whatever books he liked. When he asked Max if The Bodley Head would publish Henry Miller's *The Tropic of Cancer*, Greene instructed Max not 'to discourage [him] at this point and I personally would be all for publishing Henry Miller. At the same time I imagine that the Americans have been a bit cagey in choosing The Tropic of Cancer which is several degrees less pornographic and less interesting, as far as I remember, than The Tropic of Capricorn. The courageous thing for us to do would be to publish in one volume both Tropics. I will get the books sent to you from Paris.'[12]

James Michie came and Max sent him to Vevey. Chaplin was 'impossible, a monster of egotism', Michie said. They argued all day over whether a bush was 'luxurious' (which Chaplin thought sounded 'much more like a bush') than 'luxuriant' (which Michie suggested), and whether Douglas Fairbanks Jr 'came into rooms' (which was in the text) or 'entered them' (as Chaplin insisted he always did).[13] Two days later Michie was sent back by Chaplin who told Max if he ever saw 'that bloody poet' again the deal with The Bodley Head was off.[14] Greene took over to urge Chaplin on. Max stopped off and insisted Chaplin use a typist who used to sneak into the village to telephone Max. Then the telegrams began. 'I am really at the end of my tether. I am leaving for a holiday on Friday 21st Sept. and hope I do not have a breakdown before I get there. Please come to my rescue and arrive as soon as possible, and stay as long as possible.'[15] Max returned to Vevey within the week. In April 1963 Simon & Schuster sent Max $25,000 as a first payment of the advance for the American rights, and in May Peter Schwed went to the Museum of Modern Art in New York to choose twenty-one pictures for the book, but it took Max until October to get Chaplin to agree on paper to the sale of the serial rights. 'I have just come back from Frankfurt exhausted', he wrote to Greene on the 16th.

> I took to my bed for forty-eight hours. The place is getting grimmer every year. The trip to Charlie was quite successful. He has now given us the world serial rights and I am on the point of selling the American rights to McCall's Magazine for $300,000. We have also nearly reached the end of Charlie's revisions and the best sign of all is that he is starting to write the music for The Kid which he plans to reissue when the book comes out. At Frankfurt I sold the German rights for $62,500 to Fischer Verlag, which is good.

But when, soon after in the south of France, Max was explaining the deal to Chaplin, Chaplin suddenly got up from the table and said he was leaving, which he and Oona did, without their luggage. Max was furious that Chaplin expected to control his book as he did his films and when the telephone began to ring repeatedly (Max presumed from Chaplin) he refused to answer. A few days later Chaplin's lawyer Maître Paschoud arrived at the hotel and said he had 'just come from Peter Ustinov. They're all the same.' Evidently Chaplin had not understood a particular line in the contract. 'Tell him to cross it out', Max replied and the matter was settled.[16]

* * *

There were four sets of galleys and Chaplin kept changing one while another was in progress. But as Max told Greene on 24 February 1964 after another 'long session with Charlie, [he] is now getting frightfully excited at the thought that the book will be printed fairly shortly'. They were finally down to typos and minor changes like clarifying references. Then came the serialization proofs with Chaplin making corrections on the telephone: one day 'Vicky becomes Victoria'; next day 'Victoria becomes Victoria and Josephine'. There seemed no end to it until finally on 30 April Max got from him 'a corrected copy which is approximately 30,000 words. Without false modesty', Chaplin wrote, 'I think it is a good redaction.'[17]

Max arranged for them all to meet in high summer when he planned to hand Chaplin an advance copy of the book. He, Joan and Alexandra would have the Frere's villa at Cap Ferrat until mid-June, then move to a rented one until the end of July. Max wanted to discuss various promotion problems with Chaplin and he hoped Greene would 'be there too to help me a little'. He looked forward to the holiday. J.P. Donleavy's *A Singular Man* was subscribing well although Max was not sure it would pass the censors in New Zealand, Australia and South Africa. And Eric Ambler had sent in his new novel, which Max thought 'absolutely first rate and one of the best things he has done for a very long time'. The Bodley Head was having quite a good year, and he told Greene they 'ought to have a few extra days on the boat'.[18]

Then in May there was a quick change of plans. Fischer Verlag had authorized a radio reading from Chaplin's book without permission. Because of the breach of contract, Max had to start legal action which 'is going to be time-absorbing, boring, jolly expensive and a great nuisance', he told Georgette Heyer, who had just given him *False Colours*, her first Bodley Head novel. 'We do have to protect our authors, don't we.' To Greene he wrote: 'it is simply maddening for I really needed a bit of sun and a holiday and I was so much looking forward to our little trip together'.[19]

Max sorted the problem out. The broadcast went ahead in June. The Reinhardts made it to St Jean in July and on the 19th Max gave a dinner party for the Chaplins, Greene and Yvonne Cloetta, Eric Ambler, his wife and the Freres. 'It was a beautiful evening and we ate under the olive trees', Joan remembered. But even as they celebrated Chaplin needed assurance from Max that his rights were well protected. Then on 13 September when the *Sunday Times* published the first serial instalment, Mr Arzubei, the editor of *Izvestia* rang Lord Thomson, who owned the *Sunday Times*, to ask if he could publish 1000 words from the second segment, which was to appear on the 20th. Russia was not yet part of the International Copyright Agreement. So having assured Chaplin that his rights were protected, Max now had to tell him that he could not stop *Izvestia*. Chaplin paused only a second before replying: 'Get them to pay us in caviar, Max. And make sure it's beluga.' *Izvestia* added 'a token payment' of £5 5s a few weeks later because, they said, of their respect for Chaplin. But Max insisted it was because of the four kilos of caviar that The Bodley Head became the first company in the annals of international publishing to receive copyright payment from Russia.[20]

When the shipment arrived at Heathrow he sent Chaplin half a kilo with a note saying 'Let me be your caviar bank and when you have finished I will send you some more.' He kept a kilo and a half at home and the rest went to the Savoy for the big publication party on 30 September. Letters of thanks arrived for days thereafter and none was more welcome than that from Chaplin's wife.

> What a success ... your beautiful party. We rehashed it next day at lunch with Paul-Louis, Diana Cooper and Noel Coward; they talked about it at such length we almost missed our plane. [It was] the best of a formal party – beautiful table, delicious food, wine, beautifully dressed women – as background for a terrifically gay and amusing informal evening. I am convinced no one else living could have managed to deal with Charlie through these past years as you have. It's a pleasure that such a difficult relationship as publisher and author has ended in a real friendship.[21]

That Christmas the Chaplin's card had a photo of *mère* and *père* on a sofa surrounded by their children each reading *My Autobiography* in a different language. By then it had sold over half a million copies.

8
The Reinhardt-Greene Team

For several years Max had been having disagreements with his chairman, George Ansley, who liked to meddle in Bodley Head literary affairs rather than confine himself to financing. In March 1958 just before Max and Greene saw Chaplin together for the first time, Max had arranged a small party for André Maurois, one of his inherited writers. Ansley got wind of the arrangement and insisted he would give the dinner at the house he had rented in a cul-de-sac off the Avenue Foch in Paris; it had been Anatole France's home and Mme Maurois had lived in it as a child. Max and Greene made fun of Ansley's intrusion in their plans, but the evening went well and Maurois, who had served as a liaison officer with the British army in the First World War and was a well-known Anglophile, suggested they publish a new English translation of Balzac's works. Rather than leave the project to Max, Ansley set up a luncheon to which he invited M. Basdevant, the head of the literary department of the Quai d'Orsai (the French Foreign office). Max had been taught by Basdevant's father at HEC, and Ansley thought the connection might get them money for the translation. When Basdevant said there was none to be had, Ansley then decided he would advance their interests by organizing a larger, Anglo-French literary luncheon at the Plaza Athénée Hotel in Paris to which he invited Sir Gladwyn Jebb, the British Ambassador. The affair was rather pompous and it further convinced Max (who was still in debt to Ansbacher's) and Graham (who thundered at Max that he was dead against any control by the board of the choice of books) that Ansley had to go. But Ansley seemed unstoppable.

By 18 May 1961 Ansley and his friend Lionel Fraser, chairman of Thomas Tilling, the industrial conglomerate that had acquired full control of Heinemann Publishers Ltd in April, were negotiating a merger between Heinemann and The Bodley Head. Heinemann Publishers (the parent company of William Heinemann) were to purchase a 51 per cent interest in Max Reinhardt Ltd (of which The Bodley Head was a subsidiary along with Werner Laurie, The Nonesuch Library and Max Reinhardt, Canada). Max was to receive 60,000 Heinemann ordinary shares in exchange for his 50 per cent interest in The Bodley Head. Half of these Heinemann shares Max was then to transfer to Ansbacher's who would retain them as security if he was called upon by the bank at any time within the next three years to find a purchaser for 24.5 per cent of the share capital of The Bodley Head group. If Ansbacher's did not exercise this right, Max could then require the return to him of the Heinemann shares free of charge, or require the bank to transfer 24.5 per cent of the capital in The Bodley Head to anyone he designated, at which time the Heinemann shares would belong to Ansbacher's. Tilling agreed to pay The Bodley Head's and Ansbacher's loans and interest.

Max and Peter Ryder, the managing director of Tilling's, were to be joint managing directors of the concern, Ryder replacing A.S. Frere as chairman of Heinemann. Max was to take over the general coordination of the activities of Heinemann Publishers, to be paid £5000 per annum (£1000 coming from The Bodley Head, which would then be a subsidiary of Heinemann with Max remaining as managing director), and to 'devote his whole time and attention to the interests of Heinemann Publishers Ltd' with the exception (he penned into the 29 May 1961 draft agreement) of 'an occasional interview or a few board meetings a year of the active companies of which I am a director such as HFL Publishers Limited and the Stellar Press Limited'. Dwye Evans was to remain managing director of William Heinemann Ltd and to become a member of the Heinemann Publishers board along with Frederic Warburg and Rupert Hart Davis (whose companies Secker & Warburg and Rupert Hart Davis Ltd were also by then subsidiaries of Heinemann Publishers). Greene was to join the new board as literary adviser, Frere was to become the president, which meant that although he would continue his contact with authors and generally assist in the development of the business, he would lose control of the firm. The draft announcement said that expansion of the Max Reinhardt group would be assisted in Britain and abroad by its association with Heinemann's many valuable and specialized departments, and that Heinemann would acquire under the arrangement 'excellent back lists and an interesting future programme'.

Max did not like the deal. Like Allen Lane who had turned down Tilling's offer to buy Penguin from him in 1957 for £400,000, Max did not want to lose control of his operation. But unlike Lane, Max had little choice and Greene thought the deal might be beneficial. So on Sunday 28 May the Reinhardts, the Quayles and Greene went to the Brompton Grill to celebrate, Greene toasting what he considered their success with champagne. But by Tuesday everything was off. Max said the Heinemann directors had never been told anything about the merger and were rightly hostile to it, and that Fraser got scared and backed out. Fraser told Ansley on 2 June that while he liked the possibility of the merger, it would have affected too many people. Ansley shared Fraser's regret that the talks failed and wondered if it was because of a clash of personalities or the result of a misunderstanding of intentions.[1]

Frere was bitter because by the agreement he would have lost control of the firm, and he soon retired to the south of France although he remained close friends with Max and Greene. On this occasion Greene wrote him formally

an arrangement was discussed with Heinemann's and accepted in principle one Sunday [May 28] afternoon . . . that I and Max Reinhardt should join the board of William Heinemann as part of a general reorganisation which would have included The Bodley Head. On the Monday I received from Lionel Fraser a copy of the announcement he proposed to give to the Press and I approved it. On Tuesday I was informed that my presence on the board was considered undesirable by other members of the Heinemann group. This personal rebuff could have been laughed easily off if I had not become more and more aware of the fact that I no longer had any personal contact with anyone in the firm and that – to speak frankly – I could no longer depend on you to look after my work; from my agent and the rumours circulating in the publishing world I had learned that you were no longer in a position to do so.[2]

Did this rebuff come primarily from Dwye Evans? Evans, Fred Warburg, Rupert Hart-Davis and Alan Hill were the key people on the Heinemann board when Fraser backed down. Dwye Evans had been on Max's boards since the beginning and his brother had been the Evans of Reinhardt & Evans. After missing several meetings in 1960 Dwye Evans had unexpectedly turned up that December when everyone at The Bodley Head was very nervous about still not having a contract with Chaplin and told the board it made no difference how they proceeded because in the end the autobiography would go to Heinemann. 'In that case, you shouldn't be on this board', Greene had replied, and Max had made sure Evans no longer was by paying him £250 from his own Endeavour Press and an equal amount from The Bodley Head 'as compensation for loss of office'; done this way he told Evans, the pay-off was not taxable. It meant that Evans was 'resigning from the Endeavour Press as well, for otherwise their payment would not be made to you in this way'.[3]

Greene, Max and Frere, who continued to help Max with publishing matters, remained close friends. Greene moved his books to The Bodley Head. Within a few weeks of the collapsed merger he had supplied the blurb for what became *In Search of a Character: Two African Journals* (1961), the first book of his that Max published. When he got the revised proofs he did not like the title page, which had already been changed to his specifications. 'It remains awfully heavy', he told Max. 'This may be partly due to the necessity of balancing the rather large colophon of The Bodley Head. I notice that if one eliminates the author's name the balance is much better. What does this mean?! Do you think it would be an improvement if the colophon and publisher's name were dropped a couple of lines or so?'[4] Max dropped them.

'Authors are not factory hands, nor are books to be compared as commodities with tobacco, beer, motor-cars and automatic machines', Greene wrote to the *Observer* on 17 July 1961, when his reasons for moving from Heinemann were publicly questioned.

> A novelist ought certainly to hesitate long before he deserts a publisher who has helped him when help was most needed, in the long years of poor sales, but does he owe loyalty to a board which changes from year to year and may, in this new phase, include directors with no experience of publishing and with little interest in books save as a 'quality' commodity less liable than others to depreciate in value at a period of economic depression?

Max was no such publisher and as Greene told Frere 'a publishing firm to an author means a personal contact, a personal sense of confidence reciprocated'.[5]

Max and Greene trusted one another completely. Max provided the kind of publishing freedom few modern novelists had. Greene was able to control every aspect of the design and sale of his books, had complete freedom from editorial intrusion (or the best of editors if he wanted suggestions), and since he had a decided hand in what Max printed, he wielded huge influence in publishing and often in political circles. When he moved from Heinemann he brought with him Eric Ambler (whose *Dirty Story* won a third Crime Writers' Association Award for him in 1967), George Millar, and the very profitable Georgette Heyer; and he paid even more attention to acquiring other authors for The Bodley Head. In April 1962 he heard that Mario Soldati was no longer happy at André Deutsch and suggested Max write to Arnoldo Mondadori in Milan to 'put in a claim for him. To my mind he is incomparably the best living Italian novelist and much more interesting than Moravia.' In September he told Muriel Spark: 'I do wish you would come to The Bodley Head with your novels. I am very fond of Max and I think you would find us a progressive firm.' A few years later he wrote to David Cornwall: 'A rumour has reached me that you are contemplating leaving Gollancz; otherwise I would not write to you, as I have no wish to poach . . . I have taken my own books to The Bodley Head and Ambler with me.'[6]

In February 1964 when Max was offered Mauriac's *What I Believe*, Greene advised him to publish it in order to get *The Life of De Gaulle*, and wrote to Mauriac to tell his French publisher to give Max both. That August he suggested Max reprint Claude Cockburn's paper *The Week* with a long introduction by him about running it. In September he brought in R.K. Narayan, telling Max that one day he might receive the Nobel Prize. All Narayan's books were out of print in England; Max bought *The Teacher* and *The Guide* and for £500 secured his next novel. Max wrote to Marlene Dietrich at Greene's suggestion at the beginning of 1965: 'Rumour has it (I am afraid that the book trade is very gossipy) that you are writing, or thinking of writing, your Memoirs. If this is true I would be thrilled if we could publish them. We have a reputation for publishing biographies and books on the theatre and films. Our most recent world success was Charlie Chaplin's autobiography.'[7]

If Greene liked someone's book, as he did Andrea Newman's *Mirage*, he wrote to London's major reviewers individually to say 'I am anxious that it should not be lost in the vast tide of Library novels. Do read it, even if you disagree with me.'[8] Even on his travels he looked out for The Bodley Head's interests, as on 8 April 1965 when he reported having read David Halberstam's *The Making of a Quagmire* 'with extreme fascination and respect. [It is] an extremely important book by a man who does not take at all the conventional line about the American presence [in Viet Nam].' Max published it that autumn with a quote from Greene on the cover.

In return Max performed many small personal favours for Greene. In June 1962 Greene asked Max to 'be awfully good and send as a present from me your Doctor Spock books on small children to my daughter Caroline . . . I was reminded of this by seeing Dr. Spock on television, and he seemed to be talking a lot of sense' (*Baby and Child Care* was a Bodley Head bestseller). In June 1963 Greene requested 'please [underlined twice] no photos in advertising in journals. The whole point of life is not to be recognized by people.' In February 1965 Greene could not 'imagine anything more dreadful than being a centre piece at the Adelaide Festival of the Arts! You will know how to refuse politely.' In May he needed Max's 'name for my Cambodian visa'. In October 1967 he reported he would 'be in Paris on the 26th. Please bring 2 pair of pyjamas if the makers have got them ready.'[9]

Perhaps more importantly Max and Oncle Richard advised Greene on his complicated financial arrangements. When Greene needed money, Max shifted it from one place to another for him, or changed a contract for a given book and sent a cheque. 'Just send me a telegram whether you agree', was their arrangement. When Greene was writing *Travels with My Aunt* and thought the franc in danger of devaluation and the pound to follow, he told Max to 'make a contract and advance now'.[10] If Greene did not understand something Max had done, Max explained it in the clearest way. He was able to simplify the most complicated financial and legal matters. 'Now this is what we have done', so many of his letters began. And being the good businessmen both he and Greene were, they knew how to recycle everything – stories into editions, editions into collections, collections into selections – the possibilities for profit were as many as they could imagine.

In January 1968 Greene 'heard the Penguin cover of *The Comedians* had Daladier instead of Duvalier', and demanded that 'if true the book should be withdrawn and the cover reprinted'. Max knew it was true 'but the edition is sold out and the new jacket is correct. I didn't see the edition as they were hurrying to sell it in Europe before the Americans. The jacket will raise the book's second hand value', he sensibly told Greene. He and Greene both paid particular attention to selling books second hand. First editions were kept for later sale, often through Bertram Rota. Pages were sent to Greene to be signed, then returned to Max to be bound into books and sold as numbered, limited editions. With one such package of papers Josephine Reid, Greene's secretary, sent a note saying, 'I hope the sheets have not been too crumpled – I did them up as carefully as possible – but of course I'm not an expert packer!'[11]

* * *

When Greene moved to The Bodley Head, Priestley stubbornly told Max, '[Heinemann] made me. I must stand by them now.' He did write an introduction for a new edition of *The English Comic Characters* published in 1963, which The Bodley Head had originally published in 1925, and signed a contract with Max for *The Bodley Head Anatole France*. But Max wanted a larger sign of loyalty. 'What thrills me is the possibility that one day we may do a new book of yours', he wrote to Priestley 10 December 1962. 'I do not think you will have difficulty about a contract with me.' Priestley would not budge. When he was sent his usual cigars he growled 'that they seem to burn rather more quickly than most Havanas, and, a deliberately slow smoker, I do find this rather a defect'. When he signed the Anatole France contract he complained that he would never again agree to 10 per cent on exported copies or giving the publisher 50 per cent on reprint copies. And when on 30 April 1964 Max sent him £80 3s 11d for *English Comic Characters* and a cheery note saying 'it is selling nicely and everyone seems pleased that it is back in print', Priestley grumbled 'I do not think I have seen a single review of it, but then I never have press cuttings and must depend upon the newspapers I happen to read.'[12]

Then Priestley got into a row with Greene about *Candy*, Terry Southern and Mason Hoffenberg's Rabelaisian satire based on *Candide*. It had been published pseudonymously in France, banned, and reissued under the title *Lollipop*. Greene wanted to publish it. This time George Ansley agreed with Priestley – *Candy* was a very naughty book they must not touch; if they did Ansley said he would be the laughing stock of his Travellers Club in Paris whose members he had so tried to impress with his past literary manoeuvres.[13] On 29 April 1964 Max returned the novel to Greene sheepishly saying he 'was a little disappointed until the later part. The Candide-like experiences didn't quite come off. I doubt in any case that this is a book that we could publish.'

Roy Jenkins's 1959 Obscene Publications Act had been tested successfully in 1960 in the Lady Chatterley trial but publishers were still cautious. Max's counsel told him that if he were prosecuted for *Candy* the penalty was unlikely to exceed £1000 plus costs so long as no copies had been sold, and that he was unlikely to have to sit in the dock like Frere had to when Heinemann published Walter Baxter's *The Image and the Search*. But just because William Burrough's *Naked Lunch* (published in a limited edition by John Calder) had not been prosecuted, counsel suggested Max should not assume *Candy* would slip by. If Max went ahead he was advised to present the novel as an amusing and satirical American bestseller which the British public are entitled to read. The Bodley Head should announce it would mass-produce the book and sell it at a price everyone could afford. Max was further advised to have well-known authors and prominent critics ready to support it. Frere had had Malcolm Muggeridge and Greene waiting outside the court to give evidence. In suggesting Priestley be kept in the wings for this purpose, Max's counsel could not have suggested a worse author to speak for the literary merit and benefit to the public of *Candy*.

Greene would not let *Candy* go and by the end of the year Max had made an arrangement to publish it with the Putnam imprint, which had come under his umbrella in 1962. Ansley was furious because of the possibility of prosecution and a war broke out over literary control of the firm. In what appears a coordinated attack, Greene wrote a fierce quasi-public letter to Max on 23 November 1964:

> It would be impossible in my opinion to carry on publishing if the choice of books were not left to the discretion of the Editorial department...I would not be prepared to remain a member of the board of The Bodley Head if the Board were to take editorial decisions. I would go further and say that I would not be prepared to remain an author of The Bodley Head if any book which I wrote had to be judged by the Board of Directors. My next might well prove for different reasons just as 'difficult' as <u>Candy</u>.

He was bent on changing public opinion and considered Priestley's and Ansley's stuffy ideas to be holding The Bodley Head back. Hart was so concerned they might lose Greene that he replied to the letter himself.

Evidently satisfied, Greene then began a battle to move his Heinemann books to The Bodley Head. This included having Max exercise his option to buy back the share in Max Reinhardt Ltd which his original contract allowed when his loan to Ansbacher's had fallen below £15,000. In a statement not unlike Greene's to Frere on leaving Heinemann, Max told Hart on 18 March 1965 that he wanted control of literary matters because Ansley's interference over *Candy* had been 'an unwarrantable piece of dictatorship'. What had happened had made him apprehensive

> about the future and about being at the mercy of remote and unpredictable control. To me and to many of my friends and colleagues, this business of ours is our way of life and we must have the security of knowing that it cannot be jeopardised by decisions made by others to whom publishing is only a subsidiary interest. It is because my confidence has been badly shaken that I am insisting on security and protection for our authors, our staff, and myself, and all this has nothing to do with the fact that The Bodley Head happens to be doing well now.

Candy went to the New English Library (which brought out an abridged edition), but by June Max had a new service agreement with Ansbacher's in which The Bodley Head shares were transferred to Max Reinhardt Ltd and the Putnam shares to The Bodley Head, giving Max the financial flexibility he needed to build a new factory for his Stellar Press in Barnet and to buy a larger and faster printing machine for it (HFL's books were printed at the Stellar Press and seriously behind schedule because of the old machine). Max's salary was officially raised to £6000 (which he was being paid anyway because of the company's substantial profits that year). More important, Hart was to replace Ansley as chairman of the board.

Meanwhile Greene had asked Sir Geoffrey Eley at Tilling's to tell him 'the amount of money which would be required from me to take back the copyrights'. He argued that Heinemann 'has not in any way suffer[ed] by our association. It would be a graceful act if you were able to let me have back at an agreed price these old books now that the connection had been severed.' Peter Ryder, Chairman of the Heinemann Group, returned an emphatic 'NO' and provocatively invited Greene to add another book to Heinemann's uniform edition of his books. Greene replied to Sir Geoffrey, 'A divorce is never a very satisfactory end to a marriage, but I would have thought a friendly financial settlement . . . a good deal more satisfactory to your shareholders than a life-long wrangle. Such a wrangle could only draw attention in publishing circles to the separation.'[14]

Max suggested Greene ask his agent, Laurence Pollinger, to send someone to Hatchards and Bumpus to see how many titles of the Uniform Edition were on the shelves, and to get from Heinemann a complete account of the stock of his books. They then got Pollinger to complain that *Twenty-One Stories* was out of print. Heinemann replied that a reprint of *Twenty-One Stories* was in hand and that they kept in stock more than 2000 copies of each of Greene's books which were also in Penguin editions (Greene and Heinemann had a deal with Penguin for paperback rights in ten of his novels). Greene demanded an explanation for why Heinemann distinguished between those titles and other editions of his books. The reply was that it was those books that Pollinger had asked about. Greene said there was no reason to make such a differentiation and insisted Heinemann keep the stock of all his books up to the same level. On 21 September he judged 2000 a 'sound figure . . . That you should so flatly disagree only exacerbates a situation which can scarcely stand any further deterioration. The financial owners of your firm already know my views on your policy of holding authors on a list against their will, but I wonder if they know enough about publishing to realize how unnecessarily offensive is your attitude to my request.'

A year later Max offered Heinemann '£50,000 for the publishing rights and stock of all Graham's books', assuring Charles Pick, the managing director, that the offer was not necessarily the final one. 'If you allow him to go, it must be done on terms which will be financially beneficial to you, and I don't think you will find me difficult about this.'[15] But Heinemann was determined to keep Greene and the argument continued until Greene suggested Heinemann and The Bodley Head publish a joint Collected Edition of his work. At first Max was against the idea but he, Greene and Pick came to an agreement whereby the books would be produced by Max, printed at Clowes, sold for 35s and bear the imprint of both firms, with the original publisher's name first. In return Greene allowed Heinemann to continue to sell his paperback licences to Penguin. The first four volumes appeared on 6 April 1970 in the now familiar dark green jackets designed by John Ryder and Michael Harvey, revised and with new introductions by Greene. Max estimated that producing those initial 5000 copies of *England Made Me*, 4500 of *It's a Battlefield*, 7000 of *Brighton Rock*, and 7000 of *Our Man in Havana* reduced his 1970 profits by about £7000.

1. Max aged 2, Constantinople, 1917 (courtesy Joan Reinhardt)

2. Max's parents, Frieda Darr and Ernest Reinhardt, Constantinople, 1917
(courtesy Joan Reinhardt)

3. Max as RAF Aircraftsman 2, London, 1941 (courtesy Joan Reinhardt)

4. Maxie and Ralphie (Richardson), as they were to one another (courtesy Joan Reinhardt)

5. The newlyweds at Versailles: Joan and Max, 1957 (courtesy Joan Reinhardt)

6. At The Bodley Head: Children's Book Editor Judy Taylor being admired by Anthony Quayle and Max. Rumer Godden is in the background (courtesy Joan Reinhardt)

7. Noel Coward and Max, 1964 (courtesy Joan Reinhardt)

8. Charlie Chaplin and Max, 1964 (courtesy Joan Reinhardt)

9. Charlie Chaplin, Francis Meynell (centre) and Ralph Richardson at the Savoy, 1964 (courtesy Joan Reinhardt)

10. (L to R) Noel Coward, Joan, Charlie Chaplin, Oona Chaplin and Max at the Savoy, 1964 (courtesy Joan Reinhardt)

11. Benjamin Spock and Joan at Bepton, 1970 (courtesy Joan Reinhardt)

12. Max with his daughters Alexandra (centre) and Veronica in California, 1982 (courtesy Joan Reinhardt)

13. Max and Joan with Alistair Cooke in Antigua, 1984 (courtesy Joan Reinhardt)

14. Max and Graham Greene in Beaulieu-sur-Mer, 1987 (courtesy Joan Reinhardt)

15. Buying Nonesuch, 1986. Seated (L to R) are Joan, Alix Meynell, Max, John Ryder, and standing Benedict Meynell and John Hews (photocredit: Alexandra Reinhardt)

9
Georgette Heyer

On 1 January 1963 Georgette Heyer wrote 'Dear Mr. Reinhardt: So Frere thinks it a pleasure to deal with me does he? He must have forgotten how broad a view I've always taken of his duties toward me. My own opinion is that all inkies are hell, and ought to be incarcerated.' What was Max to make of this woman who had followed Greene to The Bodley Head? On 24 April she wrote again to 'Dear Mr. Reinhardt' then came to a full stop. 'No: on second thoughts I'll alter that to Dear Max, because now that we have entered into what I hope will prove an enduring association the sooner we abandon formality the better it will be for both of us.'

They began to meet fairly often and one day at Rules she told Max she had been to a luncheon given by the queen who had subsequently gone to Harrods to order several copies of her latest book, and commented to the assistant that Georgette Heyer was quite a formidable person. 'But I'm not formidable am I Max', Heyer boomed at him across the table. 'I don't frighten you do I?'[1] But she did a little. She was forceful and had a very sharp tongue and until her death in July 1974 she wrote Max long letters deprecating him, her own books, the Inland Revenue, typists, workmen, fans – her shot had wide scatter.

When Heyer delivered *False Colours* in June 1963 Max found with it a note saying 'by the way, I don't want the advance royalty at the moment, so do please hold it back! Of course, the IR sharks may suddenly issue fantastic demands, but they haven't done so yet!' Max knew what to reply when it came to money: 'Your advance was available whenever you wanted it, even before starting the book, so it is here at your disposal and for your convenience.' But when he sent her the blurb for *False Colours* a month later she shouted, 'For Christ's sweet sake – ! NO!' When he needed a few words about the book for publicity she could not imagine 'why on earth the Trade should want to know what this book is about … for these dim-wits ought to know by now that my books aren't About anything; and that all my faithful public wants to know is that it is the Regency mixture as before.' Then on 20 April 1964 when Max asked 'have you had the photograph taken and could we please have a couple of copies, one for the Book Fair and one for us', she bawled: 'NO! I have not been photographed, nor have I as yet made any arrangements to be photographed, and if you aren't careful I WON'T be photographed. As for the Bloody Book Fair, isn't it bad enough to be displayed within the covers of Woman's Journal, without the vulgarity of appearing on a bookstall?'[2]

Soon Heyer and her husband, Ronald Rougier, were 'longing to meet' Joan and invited the Reinhardts to dinner at the Connaught along with the Freres. Max usually arranged parties for his authors but Heyer beat him to the pleasantries: 'We ought to celebrate my first appearance under your aegis … We ought to have a nice, comfortable evening. Shall we say black tie, and 7:45 for 8:00?' She was a generous hostess, and it was a well-deserved celebration. By the end of 1964 Max had sold just over 50,000 copies of *False Colours* for her and had been offered competing advances from Penguin for £3000 and Pan for £2750 for the paperback. At the time Heyer was more interested in Max's love of bridge and began to invite the Reinhardts to her flat, making an allowance for Joan, who did not play, by asking her own son and daughter-in-law 'Richard and Susie to join the party. The Rougiers can cut in and out, which will provide Joan with a Companion', she told Max.[3] He appreciated that there was always caviar on her table and that her son, who became a judge and later put Max up for membership in the Garrick where they continued to play bridge together, was particularly good at the game.

He also appreciated Heyer's success and professionalism. She liked to get a book out in time for Christmas and as she had a great international following she would ask Max the date of his shipment to Australia, the most distant of his overseas markets. In 1966 when she was a little behind schedule with *Black Sheep* Max told her that if he had the typescript on 7 July in the morning he would be able to have the book printed, bound and delivered to the boat before it sailed on 25 August. Heyer got the manuscript to him in impeccable shape when the office opened that day, and Max had the page proofs corrected by her, back at the printers by 4 August, and ready for the shipment three weeks later.

In other ways Heyer could be touchy and abrasive. Less than a year after the success of *False Colours* Max reported that her next book, *Frederica*, was 'selling like hot-cakes' and had topped the bestseller list. 'We haven't paid you any advance on the book and the book has earned much,

much more than the advance already. Tell me when you want it', he wrote to her on 9 September 1965. Rather than being pleased she replied that 'Miss Lindsey of Harrod's Book department tells me that Everyone Loves <u>Frederica</u>. Not <u>quite</u> everyone! Her creator continues to dislike her.' When she was made an honorary member of the Mark Twain Society for the novel's success Heyer claimed 'this little tribute has in no way changed my opinion of <u>Frederica</u> – or, I may add, my opinion of the vast majority of my fans. But I do think you're lucky to have me on your list! Well, I mean to <u>say</u> – ! An author who makes outstanding contributions to literature with technically competent bits of tripe like <u>Frederica</u>, <u>must</u> be an asset! Even though it does make that author sick!'[4]

She did acknowledge the book as 'being a little gold-mine'.[5] By then Max had sold over 60,000 copies of it and done a third reprint. But when he said the 'sales of <u>Frederica</u> are already higher than those of <u>False Colours</u> – we are all delighted and so, I hope, are you', she complained about how much tax she would have to pay. 'She was almost haunted by the fear of not being able to pay her taxes', Max said. 'She was constantly looking for ways to pay less and at one point sold several books to a Swiss publishing company to try to avoid them altogether.'[6]

Contracts were made with her 'on signature, on publication or on call, whatever you prefer' and since she watched her financial intake carefully, Max spent a good deal of time reassuring her. In late 1965 Heyer was particularly worried about her books because she thought Heinemann was going under. 'Unfortunately I don't think they will go into liquidation', Max told her,

as their backers, who are bankers, could never allow one of their companies to do that. However, should they ever do so and your books become free, we will take them on and publish them immediately. This is a solemn pledge. There is of course a danger that Heinemanns might be sold to another publisher, but if that were so, it would be purely because their bankers would want to sell them. Unless there were an American group of publishers, I don't think there is any firm here who would give them as good a price as we would. Because to us your back list and that of any other author who had come to see us from Heinemanns would be more valuable than to anyone else. Frere knows this, and I told him to whisper it into the ears of Sir Geoffrey Eley when he sees him. In the meantime if any of your books are out of print, you are perfectly justified in asking them to reprint or let the rights revert to you.[7]

In September 1966 when Heyer needed money because 'we are getting possession of a new flat [at 60 Jermyn Street] on the 22nd and I have to shell over a large sum for the fixtures', Max sent her '£3,600, being the advance on Black Sheep. If you need any more money, don't hesitate to ask because there will certainly be quite a lot more due to you for the royalty.' There was no answer so when the next month Pan offered a £7500 advance to paperback the novel, he asked again if she needed more. 'You haven't bullied Pan into it, have you', Heyer wanted to know. Thereafter he became less enthusiastic when turning over her earnings. On 18 April 1969 when he sent her £12,226 7s 10d for *Black Sheep* and *Cousin Kate*, he added: 'I don't know if this will distress you or please you or whether it will give you too many problems.'[8]

When *Lady of Quality* was ready to be published in 1972 she complained she had had to pay 'the National Drain ... £28,000 [last] year – I can't tell you how MUCH I enjoy working myself to a standstill for the privilege of Educating the masses, subsidizing the cost of strikes, and all the other things public money is squandered on.'[9] Her husband suggested Max loan her £10,000 instead of paying it to her as an advance for the new novel and he obliged, dividing her next royalty payment into £18,219.50 and the loan. By November she was again top of the bestseller list issued by Smith's *Trade News*, and subscriptions from Book Club memberships totalled almost 100,000. Max was pleased; Heyer mumbled about forthcoming taxes and paid Max's secretary, Belinda McGill, the £7.33 she owed her for having proof-read the novel at home after working hours.

Heyer was a top-selling writer but some critics wondered about the importance of her work and this may have led in part to her own denigration of it. If she were taken 'simply as a novelist for women whose only novel-reading was popular romance she would deserve the highest praise', Marghanita Laski wrote in *The Times* on 1 October 1970 when *Charity Girl* was issued. 'As the genre goes her books are better than most, and more complicated: it often takes a couple of chapters to guess who will finally marry whom. The Regency element is pleasantly novel and the props, if limited are genuine period pieces.' But Laski could not understand the appeal of Heyer's historical romances unless in 'these dandified rakes, these dashing misses, the wealth, the daintiness, the carefree merriment, the classiness, perhaps even the sexlessness'?

Much as Max respected Laski – and her father – he disagreed. Heyer's liking for male conversation, he said, was reflected in the male dialogue in her novels. He had sat on a West Indian beach beside a Canadian mining tycoon who carried half a dozen of Heyer's books in his beach bag and when he discovered that Max knew her asked him to tell Heyer of the enormous pleasure she had given all his tough mining colleagues over the years. Heyer was able to describe battles and combat well, and she knew her military history. She rarely paid attention to her fan mail, which was voluminous and mostly eulogistic, but one day a letter came from an elderly gentleman who wanted to know what part his great-grandfather's regiment had played at the Battle of Waterloo. Heyer knew the battle so well that she recognized the regiment as the only one to have fled the field. Max said she did not have the courage to reply to the letter.[10]

Max's interest was to keep Heyer on the bestseller list. In their early hard cover editions he sold between 70,000 and 100,000 copies of the seven books he published of hers, and well over 1,000,000 of each in paper in the Commonwealth market alone. He also enjoyed her company. He thought her 'one of the most charming, affectionate and loyal friends anyone could have had'.[11] His literary questions to her were simple. 'Does it have a hero?' he asked about *Cousin Kate* in 1967 to which Heyer rightly replied, '<u>Really</u>, Max, how can you be so dumb? <u>Of course</u> there's a hero! Do you think I was born yesterday? He may look like the Villain of the Piece, but he's no such thing.' In May 1972 Max pitched his comments more carefully when she sent him part of *Lady of Quality*: 'Joan and I both read part of the nine chapters and her opinion, which is much more valuable than mine, is that it is very good vintage Heyer.'[12]

When Heyer died in 1974 her husband and Jill Black, then editor for the authors closest to Max, finished her uncompleted manuscript of *My Lord John*, which Max published the following year. Three years later the Georgette Heyer Historical Novel Prize was set up in her memory, her son putting up a third of the £2000 award, The Bodley Head and Corgi Books the rest, with guaranteed publication by both houses. Rhona Martin's Tudor novel *Gallows Wedding* won the first year. The prize so enhanced the reputation of the genre that by 1981 when Valerie Fitzgerald (Norah Lofts), won it for *Zemindar* she was paid an American advance of $250,000 dollars for the book. So Georgette Heyer continued to bring in plenty of money.

10
The Bodley Head Books for Children

Barbara Ker Wilson was children's book editor when Max arrived and she was about to do something new – sell the rights to the first of John Ryan's Captain Pugwash stories in five languages, printing all editions, just changing the black plate for each language. This would greatly enlarge the print run and therefore cut the cost of each copy. Unfortunately for Max the pound was devalued between the costing and the printing and he lost money on the venture, but Captain Pugwash showed him one way to increase profitability in children's picture books. When the currency stabilized almost all full-colour picture books for children in Britain were printed in this way, which meant that a substantial portion of the manufacturing cost of the books was paid to the originating publisher early, providing working capital.

Wilson had been producing about 34 books a year for The Bodley Head in runs below 6000 except for a few picture books. On the backlist were an edition of Hans Andersen's fairy tales and legends, illustrated by Rex Whistler, and Kenneth Grahame's classics *Dream Days* and *The Golden Age*, introduced by Naomi Lewis. The current list included 21 career novels, C.S. Lewis's *The Magician's Nephew* and *The Last Battle* (which had won the 1956 Library Association's Carnegie medal), John Buchan's *John Burnet of Barnes* and *The Magic Walking Stick*, Marcel Aymé's *The Wonderful Farm* and *Return to The Wonderful Farm*, Marjorie Flack's successful *The Story About Ping*, Amabel Williams-Ellis's best selling scientific biographies, Josephine Kamm's biography of Gertrude Bell, *Daughter of the Desert* (which carried a Book Society recommendation), and other steadily selling non-fiction.

The Bodley Head had no children's catalogue and there was no specialist children's traveller. But there was twenty-five year old Judy Taylor; when Max learned she had recently been interviewed for a job in the children's books department at Gollancz he said simply, 'Oh, you stay here. I'll take care of you.'[1] After three years at St Paul's School, Taylor had spent a year in Toronto as a mother's help and on her return to London had been hired by Richard Hough to mail catalogues at The Bodley Head. This had turned into a permanent office job in 1951, although her step-mother had had to add 10 shillings a week to her salary of £3 so she could pay her rent. Mainly by listening to what was going on in the small, almost one-room Bodley Head office, in the next few years Taylor had learned the then invaluable nuts and bolts of publishing – how to lay out text, scale illustrations, choose typeface, prepare plates, even pack books in corrugated cardboard and flatten the sides with wooden blocks before wrapping each bundle in brown paper and tying it with a slip knot. Because she was the youngest member of staff and probably because she was a woman, she was asked to read manuscripts of books for children, and here was her chance.

When Wilson left in 1958 Max considered Taylor still too young to take her place but he had already decided she would head the children's department the following year. It would be one of his wisest and shrewdest publishing decisions. He split the list for that first year, bringing in Antony Kamm as senior editor and letting Taylor take charge of the picture books. Then he found Taylor the best mentor in the business. This was Canadian-born Kathleen Lines. Trained as a librarian under Lillian Smith at the Children's Library in Toronto Kathleen Lines had come to England before the war to work with Humphrey Milford at Oxford University Press. At a time when poaching was frowned upon, Lines brought with her to The Bodley Head two bestselling authors, Lucy Boston and Rosemary Sutcliff. She immediately recommended to Max that he hire Jill Black, a historian, to take over non-fiction for older children, and in 1961 he hired Margaret Clark, who had worked for Eleanor Graham on Penguin's Puffin Books and been misled by Allen Lane into thinking she would take them over. Clark was a very fine editor; she soon took over fiction for older children and eventually in 1972 Judy Taylor's job as children's head. Black too was a fine editor and she soon added to her responsibilities editing those adult authors Max looked upon as his own.

Kathleen Lines imbued in this team of young editors the maxim that only the best books were good enough for children and Max gave these talented women every support in publishing them. In 1961 he sent Judy Taylor to New York – by boat so she could rest from recent surgery. Joan was so worried about her being alone in New York that she insisted Taylor stay at the Vassar Club and Taylor was so frightened of being in New York alone that she holed up there until Richard Hough, who was also in the city (on behalf of Hamish Hamilton), showed her how to get around. She was soon very comfortable in New York and for the rest of her tenure as children's book editor spent three weeks a year there both buying and selling books. Max was enormously generous with travel funds and there was never a budget. In the years before credit cards, Taylor took hundreds of pounds in travellers cheques and did the accounts when she returned. The only economy in the early years seems to have been in long distance telephone calls. Taylor hired a typewriter on arrival and sent a carbon report to 'Dear Mr. Reinhardt' by air each evening. If a quick move was in order Bow Street rang her back.

Carrying a briefcase full of early proofs and manuscripts to sell, she met the American heads of children's books – Ursula Nordstrom, Margaret McElderry, Susan Hirschman. She met as many artists as she could, visited the NY Public Library to see what New York children were reading, and the American Children's Book Council run by John Donovan in the Flatiron Building to see what had just been published. Early on she bought Eve Titus's *Anatole* series, Paul Galdone's books of nursery rhymes and folk tales, and Roger Duvoisin's books about Petunia the illiterate goose, and Veronica the hippopotamus who longed for fame. She continued to publish the *Happy Lion* books by Duvoisin's wife, Louise Fatio, the first of which had been acquired for The Bodley Head by Richard and Charlotte Hough in 1955. All of them became minor classics.

Many of these books were by artists who had come to the United States from Europe; Taylor found their books more appropriate to post-war British children who were still seen and not heard than American writers' books featuring brash children. *Eloise* was one such fictional child she refused to add to The Bodley Head's list. She thought Kay Thompson's creation 'not an attractive child, prancing about in ridiculous clothes and showing off'.[2] Max got very cross with inefficiency, but never when an editor refused to publish what he wanted to. He simply transferred *Eloise* to his own Reinhardt imprint using The Bodley Head staff to do the work and its catalogue to advertise the book with a simple MR in a bracket after the title. Perhaps to prove his point, he sent *Eloise* to Buckingham Palace and received an enthusiastic letter back from a lady-in-waiting in which she said the queen had read the book to her children.

In the years before consumerism and the media homogenized everything, Taylor's other problem with American-based books was the language; it was costly to change trucks into lorries, kids into children, stores into shops, cops with guns into bobbies in helmets. American towns did not resemble English towns and cars drove through them on the wrong side of the road. She quickly learned that animals crossed the

Atlantic more cheaply than children, although Crazy George had had to be renamed Zozo by Chatto & Windus in its British edition as it was thought bad form for a monkey to share the name of the king. Apart from the cost saving, Taylor continued to prefer picture books that were not robbed of their recognizable settings and distinctive spellings.

In 1964 when Edward Ardizzone offered Max *Diana and her Rhinoceros*, Taylor immediately said yes and only after she had published it discovered that political correctness had hit the book trade. Diana, who took her pet rhinoceros around Richmond, had emptied a pot of aspirin into his mouth when he caught cold and publication was followed by complaints of irresponsibility from librarians and parents. Did The Bodley Head not realize the danger of having Diana dump unmeasured aspirin down the rhinoceros's throat? Although she had been concerned not to expose young Britons to the ill-manners of American children, Taylor had not thought about the danger of Diana's cold remedy. In the next edition the story was changed. Diana had to go to her mother to ask for the medicine cabinet key and then to say how many aspirins she would give her rhinoceros, a dose no doubt safe for herself.

The 1930s edition of Ardizzone's *Lucy Brown and Mr. Grimes* had been even more politically incorrect. The wonderfully wheezy Mr Grimes who had so delighted children for decades was now seen as a dirty old man who had to be refashioned into a family friend before Lucy's grandmother could grant him permission to take the child to the recreation grounds. Tided up, Mr Grimes proved a great favourite again, but he was not Taylor's Mr Grimes. Taylor knew a child's love of the grotesque and mischievous. When she was offered Maurice Sendak's *Where The Wild Things Are* she stood her ground. Jill Black and everyone else in the children's team were set against the book. But Max could spot a winner and backed Taylor. He figured Sendak would do for their children's list what Chaplin had done for the adult one. The book was one of the fastest bestsellers of all time.

* * *

In 1967 at huge expense Taylor and her team printed hundreds of thousands of copies of The Bodley Head's first complete children's catalogue and sent it to every school in the country. Schools were looking for new class and library books and the orders came in fast. For several years there had been an increased willingness of publishers to work together; shops had begun to have sections for children's books; book shows were being held around the country; schools were holding book weeks and associations for parents proliferated. Taylor used the increased contact with librarians, teachers and parents to help change social attitudes. In the early 1960s children's books had mostly white faces, no one was disabled, the roles of women were old fashioned. By the end of the decade black and Asian children had been added to stories and a series about children with disabilities had been launched, in part to show normal children how to help the disabled. There was a child in a wheelchair, a hearing impaired child, another with thick glasses, one who was adopted. The series sold well in English and in translation, especially in Japanese.

By then a separate fair for children's books had been set up in Bologna and Taylor had made contact with children's editors from all over the world. She was travelling to Australia and the Far East as well as to New York and Toronto. She had published some books with Australian backgrounds, like *A Seaside Christmas Tree*, and after seeing Greek words pasted over the English texts of books in Melbourne (where by the end of the decade the largest Greek population outside Athens lived) she had begun to publish some books in different languages for the English and Commonwealth market.

In keeping the young attracted to the printed page her team confronted many technical changes in the early years. By the mid-1960s when *Diana and her Rhinoceros* was printed with American photolithography, getting colours right was easier than with the earlier methods which combined only magenta, yellow, blue and black; at first each was printed on a separate sheet so artists had to imagine how they would look combined, then a method called Codatrace put the individual colours on transparencies so they could be overlaid. Layout was also important. Taylor insisted that The Bodley Head's books for small children should not use italics, should have little bold type, few words in capitals and proper quotes around speech. There were full stops at the end of lines because she knew little children read by the line even if the stop was in the centre. She kept pages uncluttered and used a typeface to match the writing children would learn in school.

Other changes were occasioned by the necessity to cut costs as overheads rose. At the beginning of Taylor's reign publishing prices were usually fixed at three times cost to cover various discounts; by the early 1980s that figure had risen to seven and a half times. In the late 1950s a children's book sold for about 5 shillings; by the beginning of the 1980s it was close to £2. Laminating covers saved the expense of dust jackets – even of having two, one to take the wear and tear in the shop, the other so the buyer had a pristine book, a fairly short-lived experiment copied from the United States. As paper and binding became more expensive

Taylor turned to stitching and then to stapling full colour books at the centre to reduce costs even further and offered Penguin her idea and the exclusive licence for half her picture list if they would produce the books in large volume. At first Kaye Webb said no because of the difficulty of marketing books without a spine. But within a year her people had invented racks to display the books face forward, making it feasible for shops to sell them and the project went ahead. The first twelve of this new series of Puffin Picture Books were Bodley Head books.

To help (and entice) buyers Taylor and her team branded their books in series which targeted different ages. The Acorn Library suited children who had just learned to read. The Natural Science picture books under the advisory of Dr Gwynne Vevers, Curator of the Aquarium and Invertebrates at the Zoological Society of London, were designed to attract young children. The Study Books, Career Guides and Career Novels were for junior and secondary modern school children.

One of Jill Black's special contributions was to get experts to write for older children. Eric de Maré's *London's River* (1964), a history of London and the Thames illustrated by Heather Copley and Christopher Chamberlain, is one example of the benefit of her decision. Christopher Headington's *The Orchestra and Its Instruments* (1965) is another. Illustrated with photographs of the National Youth Orchestra and drawings by Roy Spencer, this book served as a guide to the modern symphony orchestra through many reprints.

In 1972 Black launched the bestselling Bodley Head Archaeologies with Magnus Magnusson as general editor. He won the *TLS Educational Supplement* Information Book Award for *Introducing Archaeology* (1972), which anchored the series. *The Archaeology of Ancient Egypt* was by T.G.H. James, the keeper of Egyptian antiquities at the British Museum, and was published the same year, along with Ronald Harker's *Digging up the Bible Lands*. In 1973 John Hay's *Ancient China*, Ronald Higgins's *The Archaeology of Minoan Crete*, and Magnusson's *Viking Expansion Westward* were added to the series. Paul Johnstone's *The Archaeology of Ships* was published in 1974 and Barry Cunliffe's *Rome and the Barbarians* in 1975. The archaeologies of Anglo-Saxon England, Ireland, early Scotland and world industry soon followed.

Monographs under Kathleen Lines's editorship gave short critical accounts of children's writers and were later joined on the list by the memoirs of Lucy Boston, Naomi Mitchison and Rosemary Sutcliff. There was a series of study books for upper juniors, which provided simply-presented research material on topics such as farming, maps, markets, oil, paintings and railways, each listing further reading on the subject. There was another series of the work of established poets specially for children. And there were the Nonesuch Cygnets, which originated when Francis Meynell was planning his Nonesuch Bible and was sympathetic to the idea that the detailing and discipline of it should be carried over into children's books. The Cygnets sold profitably until the mid-1970s, when the market could no longer support them and Max agreed to the suggestion that they be produced under The Bodley Head imprint on cheaper paper by photolitho. The first Cygnet was *Fifty Favourite Fairy Tales*, edited by Kathleen Lines with illustrations by Margery Gill. Meynell's *By Heart* soon followed along with Defoe's *Robinson Crusoe* and E. Nesbit's *The Bastables*.

Through the changes Max gave Taylor full rein. When she was building up the list she took risks. 'Don't worry', Max would tell her over a large Cutty Sark in his office after 5.30 closing. 'If you fail I'll come down on you like a ton of bricks.' He never did, even when she lost money.[3] In return her team gave The Bodley Head a distinction unmatched in children's publishing, its books winning prizes in many categories.

* * *

In 1967 Max made Taylor a director of the firm. Jill Black and Margaret Clark would follow. 'It was a huge honour to be on the board', Taylor said, 'to have your name on the note paper.'[4] While other children's editors were begging for money to develop their lists, she became party to the finances of the whole company and in a position to make sure her list was remembered in discussions about turnover and sales.

In 1971 she was awarded the MBE in recognition of her services to publishing, an honour she still thinks Max had something to do with. Then in 1972 when Margaret Clark was approached by Collins to be their children's editor and Taylor suggested to Max, 'the only way to keep her is to make her our children's editor', he said, 'OK. Then I'll make you deputy managing director of The Bodley Head; that gives you status in the company.'[5] Although she did not know it at the time, it also signalled Max's intention to groom her to take over the firm; a further indication of his intention was that within a couple of years he had made sure she was also in possession of 1000 shares in the company, becoming, along with John Hews, the only working member of the board to be a shareholder.[6]

Taylor had just been elected to the Publishers' Association Council for six years to sit with, among others, Jock Murray, Alan Hill (Heinemann), Graham C. Greene (Cape) and Rainer Unwin (Allen & Unwin). The association acted as spokesman for the industry, negotiating and liaising with the government and various economic commissions, and giving advice to its diverse members. Taylor was the first and then only woman on the Council, and the only children's editor there. She felt the responsibility of her position heavily, and was constantly aware of being 'odd man out'. At a weekend meeting she felt she annoyed her colleagues behind their newspapers when she wished them good morning as she came into the breakfast room. At meetings over buffet lunches she had to master sports metaphors to enter the conversation. Even on her own turf at The Bodley Head there was a general feeling that the adult list was superior to the children's one. When her list out-earned the adult one for some time Max was amused but 'it didn't go down very well with the others and the adult list had to be brought up so the proportions were kept right', she said with humour.[7]

As if to confirm that women and children should know their place, when she was awarded the MBE a long article about her appeared in the *Times* as a 'Feature for Women'. In it Taylor modestly claimed her MBE collectively for her team, who worked closely together, and for The Bodley Head. But like Max she respected honours and was rightly proud of her role in making children's books prominent. As chairman of the Children's Book Group she had been responsible for turning the autumn Children's Book Show into a large event. Her efforts had encouraged the Design Centre to add children's books to exhibitions of household necessities, and the *Sunday Times* and *Observer* to carry reviews of children's books every week. Taylor would advise *Play School* about how to use books creatively and suggest children's titles and match readers for *Jackanory*. She would write four books herself, the texts for several picture book illustrators, and become the world's expert on Beatrix Potter. In 1988 she would also start a new children's list for Max at Reinhardt Books.

11
From Bow Street to the World's Bookshops

From the time Max took the reins in 1957 and T. Werner Laurie was added to the original deal, The Bodley Head group had grown. In early 1962 the Catholic publisher Burns & Oates had been added along with Hollis & Carter, its lay affiliate, who published biography, history and well-known books on sailing and navigation. In June that year Max had bought the complete shareholding of Putnam & Company, including the interest in it of G.P. Putnam's Sons of NY. The British company was owned by Percy Lubbock's nephew, Roger, who continued as managing director; John Huntington, the nephew of the previous owner Constance Huntington, took over sales. The Putnam list included the work of Washington Irving, Mikhail Sholokhov, Erich Maria Remarque, Dylan Thomas, L.P. Hartley, Marie Stopes, Karen Blixen (Isak Dinesen), Bernard Berenson, and the music critic Ernest Newman. With Putnam came Bowes & Bowes, the academic publisher from Cambridge (whose directors were Roger Lubbock, Dennis Payne and Michael Oakeshott), and Nattali & Maurice, a specialist publisher that brought an almost complete set of copperplates for William Daniell's *A Voyage Round Great Britain* and a renowned list of aeronautical books. Soon Lubbock and Huntington resigned and Max reorganized the companies, bringing Putnam staff members in to The Bodley Head. Rene Antink became his orders clerk, and Fred Miller took charge of distribution and was soon called by Max 'my computer'.

In the shuffle Max found a way to get Priestley off the board. On 4 May 1965 that great champion of the little man whose very name had helped Max through his early publishing years complained that The Bodley Head's new books, which he had 'always regarded … as a kind of quid pro quo for allowing you to keep my name on your list of directors', had not arrived. It was the day the Reinhardt's second daughter, Veronica, was born and Max was otherwise occupied. He sent Priestley 'a lot' by return mail with the lame excuse that because of the Putnam take over there had been an office slip up. Then in September he drafted another letter which he had approved by Hart and Ralph (who reworded the ending). In it he said that since Putnam had joined the group, more working directors had been appointed to The Bodley Head board 'to encourage the senior staff, directors who are personally involved in the affairs of our group'. As Priestley had not come to a meeting for years Max wondered if he 'might care to let [his] place be taken by a working director of the firm'. Priestley's reply was curt. Referring to *Lolita*, he reminded Max that he had 'asked to be dropped from it several years ago, and you begged me to keep my name on. So please take me off now as soon as you can. I do suggest however that you send me (as several other publishers do) any books that you think might specially interest me.'[1]

Greene was pleased and continued to press Max about Ansley, but with the new service agreement in place and Hart in the chair Max wanted to leave things as they were for the moment. He and Joan had just moved to 16 Pelham Crescent, a handsome Regency house of five floors which an architect at the Savile had told Max was a good investment. Four years later a serious case of dry rot was discovered and the top floor had to be gutted and rebuilt, but in 1965 Max trusted his Savile friend and without having the house properly surveyed hired Mrs Tucker's husband, who worked for a firm of builders, to supervise the huge task of modernizing the place. Almost as soon as the work started Tucker told Max he was being cheated by the builders so Max sacked them. In turn they sacked Tucker. Max hired new builders and out of guilt, Tucker as chauffeur. Eric Ambler had owned the house after the war and written some of his thrillers (including *The Mask of Dimitrios* and *Journey into Fear*) in the ground floor study which became the kitchen.

Soon a maid and a cook moved in. Alexandra and Veronica had a nanny with them in their top-floor nursery. Add two poodles and the family home was complete. It was not, however, untroubled. Alexandra had by then been diagnosed as profoundly deaf. She now had to carry two large, cumbersome hearing aids in pockets sewn onto her bodice and to have daily speech lessons with Mary Courtman Davies, whose invaluable book *Your Child's Speech and Language* Max would later publish.

But the major reason Max had not responded to Greene's pressure about Ansley was that Ansbacher's had played a large role in his acquisitions and Max needed money for a larger building to house his growing enterprise. He had found one at 9 Bow Street in Covent Garden and suggested to Ralph that they might form 'a small properties company – The Bodley Head Properties Ltd. and Boy, you and I will put up £12,500 each – total £37,500. That company will then sign a long term lease with The Bodley Head at a rent of £12,000 a year which is income for the properties company. Bodley Head Properties Ltd then on security of the freehold building, will borrow say £90,000 from either Ansbachers or Westminster or whatever.' He thought they could get the loan 'at 1% or maximum 2% above the Bank rate' which was then 8 per cent. 'On £90,000 the interest would be £7200 per year (maybe more, but over the years this will become less). The difference between our income and our outgoings after payment of tax could be used to re-pay the loan. This would mean that eventually (hundreds of years afterwards) BH Properties would own the building. It would be a good investment.' By the beginning of December 1965 he had raised the money among his friends but 'the tax experts', he told Greene, 'finally advised me against buying it for under the new Finance Act, buying and selling property can be particularly heavily taxed … and the shareholders might have to pay capital gains tax twice, so I have agreed that an insurance company buy it and give us a 42 year lease.'[2]

At the end of 1965 Max had another equally pressing problem. *The Comedians* would soon be released. It was Greene's first major novel with The Bodley Head and Max was keen to prove he could match Heinemann's sales. While Greene had been doing his final revisions in Anacapri in July, Max had stipulated that the plot not be divulged to anyone. A run of 60,000 had been ordered for January 1966 publication with proof copies to be sent only to the literary editors he trusted. The secret was kept until the *Yorkshire Post* badgered Euan Cameron and the book's setting became news. Cameron said 'Max called me into his office. He was not amused. Graham Greene, he said, had taken a very dim view of this leak.'[3] No wonder. The MGM film of the novel was already in the works and its director Peter Glenville wanted to get quietly into Haiti to snoop around with his camera before Papa Doc knew what *The Comedians* revealed. When the American edition of the novel appeared 18 days earlier than scheduled, Glenville was in Haiti and the *tontons macoutes* were reading the *New York Times* review of the book. As Greene told the Viking Press in protest, Glenville was in an 'uncomfortable and not a little bit dangerous position'.[4]

On 1 January Greene was made a Companion of Honour and the next morning he took the 10 a.m. train to the Gare du Nord. The night before he had given a farewell dinner at the Connaught with his secretary Josephine Reid, Max and Joan, John and Gillian Sutro. 'The Cheval Blanc was worthy of the occasion' Max wrote in thanks the following day. According to Norman Sherry it had become a tax necessity for Greene to move to France. His accountant, Thomas Roe, had operated a tax-avoidance scheme through a holding company that Greene hoped would save him from paying heavy British taxes. Instead, Roe had been arrested in July 1965 and unlike two of Roe's other clients, Noel Coward, who had special tax dispensation until he could set up residency in Switzerland, and Charlie Chaplin, who was already a resident there, 'Greene resided in England and was in danger'.[5] Once in France, Max put Greene in touch with Chaplin's lawyer, Maître Paschoud, who looked after many foreign residents and acted for the Bank Pictet, Chaplin's and Oncle Richard's bankers.

Publicity surrounding Greene's departure and the film's production raised the sales of *The Comedians* and The Bodley Head's prominence as it moved to Bow Street in June 1966. Covent Garden was still a real market and the street was full of lorries, barrow-boys, men carrying boxes on their heads and retired market people. Staff arrived as the lorries were leaving in the morning and the drivers saved them parking places. Judy Taylor paid an unofficial shilling each week for a spot and in return often found a few vegetables under her red Mini to take home when she left.[6]

Originally a warehouse, the building was easily redesigned. Large windows on both sides brought full light into the new offices and gave views of roofs, a courtyard, and the edge of Covent Garden and Bow Street Magistrates' Court. The creamy white walls were soon hidden with pictures and books; somewhere on a shelf there was a file copy of everything The Bodley Head had published. The first floor was covered with linoleum tiles and the others with beige carpet. Max had antique furniture, but everyone else's was new and as in all publisher's offices constantly cluttered with books, transcripts, proofs, letters, estimates, review clippings and seasonal catalogues. The entrance at the Long Acre end of the building had a large display window to its left. A lift took you from one floor to another.

From the basement Fred Miller and his team packed and distributed their books in the London postal area. Penguin distributed them elsewhere, for which Max paid 8 per cent up to the £300,000 turnover he guaranteed a year, and 7.5 per cent above it with an additional 2 per cent commission for invoicing the books he sent out. In return, he kept about 2000 copies of 50 Penguin titles at Bow Street every December for Christmas sale, which he distributed on their behalf. On the ground floor was the computer room. Rene Antink took charge of sales, invoicing and shipping. On the first floor John Hews topped the financial hierarchy; Iris Taylor looked after foreign rights payments; others kept the accounts and totted up authors' royalties.

The second floor housed both the editorial and publicity offices of the children's department. Judy Taylor's office overlooked the street at the Opera House end of the hall. Margaret Clark's, Jill Black's and Josephine Reid's (Greene's indispensable secretary) looked onto the narrow court-yard at the back of the building. On the third floor with the other publicity, design and production people were Euan Cameron and John Ryder who, working with Michael Harvey and Ian Bain on design and topography, continued to give The Bodley Head books their outstanding design.

The adult editors' offices were on the top floor. James Michie edited Greene until they disagreed over punctuation, Michie using 'a logical system' and Greene preferring his own. Not that Michie thought it right to change an author's work. 'That's not what an editor should do with authors of stature', he said. When he edited William Trevor, for whom he had a close personal affection, he would simply ask ' "are you sure?" and Trevor would reply "you're right or you're wrong" when he sent his answer'.[7]

With Michie was Barney Blackley who took charge of the general adult list and lighter fiction. It was Blackley who guided Dan Laurence through the long and rewarding Shaw project, which Max was able to finance by having the Shaw estate reimburse The Bodley Head and Dodd Mead from their royalties. 'No editor could possibly have hoped for a more rapturous critical reception than Shaw and I received from reviewers and readers of the first and subsequent volumes of The Collected Letters', Laurence wrote in his introduction to the final volume in 1988. Guido Waldman looked after foreign rights, supervised translations and did many himself from French and Italian. He arranged paperback and book club editions and helped Max place books with American publishers. Soon the Hollis & Carter nautical list was turned over to him; it won 'the Sunday Express Best Book of the Sea Award on two occasions; sales however, were insufficient to give the imprint a long-term future'.[8]

Max and his secretary, Belinda McGill, had adjoining offices overlook-ing Bow Street on the same floor. Between them were double doors that McGill opened for the parties Max gave when a book was finished, an author dropped by, or someone new was hired. Max told Francis Meynell 'I can offer you a variety of chairs to sit on, all very comfortable or you can recline on my sofa (gold brocade), which makes my room look more like a drawing room in some palace than an office.'[9] It was here that Max conferred with his top editors over whisky in the late afternoon, and here that The Bodley Head board meetings were held. 'It was a beautiful office', Taylor said. 'Max would be in his armchair at the top of the table.

We never voted on anything. Max did what he wanted anyway as it was his company. He would just tell the outsiders what was going on. Ralph was particular fun because he would turn up in whichever character he was playing at the time and ask innocently what was meant by some technical publishing term he knew very well, which made us rethink things through simply.'[10]

There was one secretary for each adult editor in the office and they did everything from fetching light bulbs to scrutinizing the unsolicited manuscripts that arrived daily. Anything that looked promising was given to the editors but, according to McGill, no great book ever came to the press that way. McGill waited on Max hand and foot: when an author needed a train or theatre ticket, she got it; when Max needed a driver to take him to a conference in Scotland, she drove. She was paid £15 a week and like the other secretaries considered herself lucky to be at The Bodley Head.[11] Euan Cameron said Max made it clear that 'everyone should feel very proud to be working for such a "distinguished" list ... among such "distinguished" colleagues'.[12] That established, he left them all alone to do their work. Inspiring trust was one of Max's gifts as an employer and he valued his reputation for it.

* * *

While never personally short of funds, and always getting maximum use of his tax-free expense accounts, like most publishers Max ran his business on overdrafts because money had inevitably to be paid out in advances and production bills before it was earned back from book-sellers and wholesalers. Income earned from a book's sales was often only a small percentage of the amount spent publishing it. Selling US and foreign language rights provided more. Newspaper serial rights were sometimes even more lucrative. Although publishers and booksellers were equal partners in the trade, they were also competitors; book-sellers griped that publishers did not give them enough discount, that books were not properly packed and were delivered too slowly, that stock was not properly replenished; in turn publishers complained that book-sellers did not stock enough books and that they displayed them badly.

To many booksellers publishers seemed rather snobby, but while sophisticated and apparently wealthy, Max was never pompous. As he charmed bankers for loans, he wooed the representatives and booksellers who sold his books. He gave cocktail parties for them at area conferences. If they were ill he was flexible about their payments, although his own interests always came first – when he discovered that one rep's wife had without consulting him opened a bookshop, he let the fellow go on the grounds that he was bound to become more heavily involved with her business than with selling Bodley Head books.

Certainly Max had built himself into an establishment figure: cars picked him up and dropped him off; secretaries and editors did his bidding; hotels knew him; many publishing projects originated over roast beef and wine at the table kept for him at Rules. But he had a generous manner that set him aside. Every New Year he received personal letters from booksellers all over the country bearing greetings, reports about how things were going and remarking on his 'extreme kindness'. He replied graciously to even the most modest of them: to one which read, '15 sold, but I expect an increased turnover by 25% on last year' Max replied, 'I was very pleased to learn that we have exceeded our target of £s and turnover. It was a great pleasure to meet you when I was there.' Belinda McGill remembered typing 387 such letters for him one year.[13]

Abroad, things were less easy to control and Max's correspondence with his agents in Canada and Australia shows something of the problem. Max Reinhardt (Canada) Ltd had been started in 1954 on $1000 (Canadian). That company was sold to The Bodley Head in 1957, and in 1964 its name was changed to The Bodley Head (Canada) Ltd, at which time the company had 1000 shares, 998 owned by Max and one each by his two Canadian representatives. Books were sold through various Canadian agencies, and blue chip Canadian stocks bought with surplus cash, the share certificates being sent to the National Westminster Bank in London. But as Canada's tax laws changed to protect Canadian businesses things became difficult and by the early 1970s it was costing Max $100 more a year than the firm's dividend income to keep it going. One of the difficulties was that in Canada, unlike in Australia and the rest of the Commonwealth, British and American publishers competed – often viciously – to establish copyright.

In Australia and New Zealand Britain had the exclusive market until the mid-1970s, when books were allowed to be brought in from the USA. People were keen to know what was being published in England and the arrival of a British publisher was something of an event; Judy Taylor used to stop in Singapore to sleep for 24 hours because as soon as she got to Australia she was taken to a TV studio to be interviewed. The Bodley Head in Australia was formed with £100 in June 1963. Max Reinhardt Ltd held 98 of the shares, Max held one, and one was held by Brian Stonier. Along with Geoffrey Dutton (a writer and senior lecturer in English at Adelaide University) and Max Harris (a bookseller and literary magazine editor), Stonier had been working for Allen Lane for two years towards publishing local books (Penguin's first Australian Penguin came out of their Melbourne office in March 1963). Max went to Australia that October to meet Stonier and to arrange for Penguin to distribute his books, but within a few months it became obvious that the arrangement was not working.

Penguin suggested various changes to improve distribution, but on 5 June 1964 when The Bodley Head was close to launching Chaplin's autobiography Max was disappointed that Stonier had not ordered 5000 copies for Australia. 'It is not that one is greedy in asking too much to start with', he wrote,

> but an important philosophy behind the book trade is that if a big initial order is placed, that in itself makes the book more important and this information percolates right through the trade. I was distressed to hear for instance that some of the orders that your travellers were taking were too small, and when a bookseller, however important, places too small an order for an important book, the publisher should refuse the order.

Stonier soon decided on his own account that things were not working out (within a couple of years he, Dutton and Harris would leave Penguin to start Sun Books) and Max got Ken Wilder at William Collins to look after his Australian interests. Knowing full well that nothing in the trade is liked more than books that suggest profit and prestige Max suggested, 'One best seller would help. Last year it was Chaplin, this year it will be <u>Frederica</u> by Georgette Heyer and <u>The Comedians</u>, a new serious novel by Graham Greene.'[14]

Max went to Australia every couple of years and his letters show him an energetic team leader. 'We were all very glad to have had you here at our sales conference', he wrote to Wilder on 10 August 1966, then cautioned him to 'remember that we had fixed a target of £50,000 sterling per year, and this should be our aim. So far our turnover for the first six months is £14,536, but it should be more than that for the remaining six months. Let us see how near £50,000 we can get.' He mentioned several books he was sending, with bits of encouragement for their sale.

> You will do your best, won't you, with <u>The Search For Amelia Earhart</u> ... Do not underrate <u>Rush to Judgement</u>. It will get an enormous amount of publicity both here and in the States, and I don't want you to be short ... Will you make quite sure that you have enough of our children's books for Christmas and I draw your

particular attention to Virginia Haviland's Favourite Fairy Tales ... Lastly do make another great effort for Christmas with The Comedians. A big film is being made ... If you want to spend a little money on advertising the book, let me know and we will support you. I should like to sell another 1500 copies in Australia before the end of this year.

In January 1967 he thought it 'nice to see improvement ... Although we are some way off our target of £50,000, we are getting nearer ... Let's continue with the good work in 1967, and I hope that with the new educational books [started in October 1966], we will be reaching £40,000 at least during this year.'[15]

If his letters to Wilder sounded like lessons from an HFL management manual, he was quick to admit his own problems at home. 'The move [to Bow Street] took quite a lot of organizing and was a major preoccupation for many of us for months ... All is now over and we should be giving much better service to all our friends and associates.'[16] The turnover throughout the world increased by 15 per cent that year.

* * *

On 3 April 1968 a note arrived from Greene saying 'My Paris solicitors in trying to establish beyond question the fact that I am domiciled in France (a matter of great importance for death duties) are anxious that I should resign my directorship of The Bodley Head. I very much regret doing this, but of course it will make no difference as far as any help I can give the firm is concerned.' Max replied: 'How very sad that you should be resigning ... We shall miss you very much, but I do understand, and it is reasonable to follow your solicitor's advice.' One of Greene's last directives was to get rid of George Ansley, who by then Max too wanted off the board. 'To him The Bodley Head is mainly an amusement', he told Greene.[17]

Everything in Max's small empire had been bought with borrowed money – the share of loan capital then was £45,000 lent by Max via HFL, £35,000 lent by Ansbacher's, and there was a £60,000 facility from the Westminster Bank. He was concerned that someone might call in their loan and he wanted to broaden the financial base of his enterprise. On 10 September 1968 he suggested to Ansley that The Bodley Head be provided with an extra £50,000 of capital and the loan facilities made by Ansbacher's and HFL be adjusted. He wanted to issue a hundred more £1 shares to be subscribed for £500 each, and to allow key members of the staff and people already connected with the firm to invest in the company, and while he did not want to destroy the delicate balance between himself and Ansbacher's, he was willing to pay £500 for each £1 Max Reinhardt Ltd share anyone wanted to sell.

There were revolutionary changes in publishing; TV monitors were being introduced in schools and tapes were being used more and more. Records and tapes were frequently having to be packaged with books. Paperbacks were influencing the sales of hardbacks, and it was becoming more difficult to sell fiction except by best-selling authors. Containers were playing a bigger part in overseas shipping and greater use was being made of airfreight. The changes were going to require reorganizing several departments and Max needed the board to 'discuss more publishing matters and possibly fewer statistical ones'. Ansley was not well and only able to attend a few meetings each year, which he did not like to last more than an hour. Meetings, Max said, were going to have to last much longer. 'Would you give consideration to giving up the Chair?' If yes, Max promised to bring in someone who was knowledgeable in publishing or had 'expertise in forms of communication'.

Max had already decided that person should be Greene's brother Hugh, who had known for some time that changes were coming at the BBC, and whose retirement as director general had been announced in July. 'You will be pleased to know', Max told Ralph a few days after he sent his letter to Ansley, 'that George has accepted my offer.'[18] He invited Hugh to lunch on 25 September, and on 2 October sent Greene a telegram saying, 'We celebrated your birthday by Hugh agreeing to attempt autobiography and agreeing to join us as Chairman after the BBC.' Sir Huge, as Judy Taylor and the others used to call him fondly behind his back, fitted in easily at The Bodley Head and soon edited four profitable books of detective stories for the firm.

On 18 October Max left for Japan with fourteen others from the Publishers' Association, including Hugh Greene's son Graham C. Greene, on a mission sponsored by the British Export Council to establish closer ties with Japanese publishers and to increase sales of British books. Max had been a member of the council of the Association and its export committee since June 1963 and he was very proud to be championing Britain in this official way; he took with him copies of Graham Greene's *Carving a Statue*, Hugo Portisch's *Eyewitness in Vietnam*, David Halberstam's *The Making of a Quagmire*, William Trevor's *The Day We Got Drunk on Cape*, Rex Warner's *The Converts* and Edwin O'Connor's *All in the Family*. Like each of the other members of the delegation he also carried three bottles of whisky in his luggage; they had been told to bring them as a favour to the Japanese. Max found the country amusing and befuddling in its manners, but he appreciated the increase in sales that resulted from the trip and the prestige associated with having made it.

12

Alexander Solzhenitsyn and Copyright

Publishing Alexander Solzhenitsyn was a tangled affair at the heart of the business of publishing – the need to control book properties in different markets and in different forms. Until May 1973 Russia was not party to either the Berne Copyright Union or the Universal Copyright Convention by which copyright was established on first publication. In Russia censors controlled the written word and authors who circumvented the publishing process risked imprisonment. They could plead ignorance if their work reached western publishers, and argue that without copyright convention protection they were incapable of stopping western publication if told by the censors to try, but the risk to accused authors within Russia was the same.

One Day in the Life of Ivan Denisovich was first published in London and New York in 1963, a year after it appeared in Moscow under the patronage of Khrushchev, and seven years before Alexander Solzhenitsyn was awarded the Nobel Prize. It was published in competing translations by Ralph Parker (jointly at Gollancz in London, Dutton in New York), and by Max Hayward and Ronald Hingley (at Praeger in New York). Three stories that had appeared in Moscow were then published in America, again in competing translations: 'An Incident at Krechtovka Station' and 'Matryona's House' in 1963, and 'For the Good of the Cause' in 1964.

As Khrushchev's power collapsed Solzhenitsyn had increasing trouble getting his work printed at home. In May 1967 he complained to the fourth Congress of the Union of Writers that *The First Circle* and *Cancer Ward* (the first eight chapters of which had been approved by the Union of Writers and set in type for printing by *Novy Mir*) remained unpublished; *The Intellectual and the Camp Whore* (later called *The Love-Girl and the Innocent*) had been accepted by the Sovremennik Theatre but never produced. Nonetheless, *samizadt* reproductions of his work were circulating in Russia and were often leaked to the west; in March 1965 *Encounter* published some prose fragments translated by Harry Willetts from a Frankfurt publication that had not seen print in Russia.

When Andrei Sinyavski and Yulil Daniel were tried in 1966 for publishing outside Russia things became more difficult for Solzhenitsyn at home, but increased interest in his work in the west. In March 1967 a journalist from Bratislava named Pavel Licko interviewed him for *Kulturny Zivot*. Licko said Solzhenitsyn had given him the first part of *Cancer Ward* to have it published and claimed he would soon give him the second part. Unfortunately for Max, *Cancer Ward* reached the west by other routes too, and competition for it was fierce. In November 1967 James Michie was told about the manuscript by translator Alexander Dolberg (David Burg) who had heard about it from Nicholas Bethell, a talented historian, politician and linguist. Bethell had just met Licko in Bratislava and had been shown three letters from Solzhenitsyn discussing publication of the first part of the novel which Licko's wife, Martha, was translating into Czech. Licko had told Bethell that Solzhenitsyn wanted him to arrange English publication of both *Cancer Ward* and *The Love-Girl and the Innocent.*

Bethell returned to Bratislava and on 22 March 1968 had Licko sign a witnessed publishing agreement with The Bodley Head for both works. The royalties for each were to be 10 per cent of the published price for the first 3000 copies, 12.5 per cent for the next 3000, and 15 per cent for copies over 6000. Licko told Bethell he was going to Moscow in April and would try to get Solzhenitsyn to confirm in writing the verbal authorization he had been given to sell the rights.

That written authorization was never obtained because, Licko wrote Bethell, Solzhenitsyn was living so far outside Moscow that they could not meet. He later said Solzhenitsyn had told him that if he signed anything he risked a five-year prison sentence and if he were pressed by the Union of Writers he might even have to deny the agreement Licko had signed with Bethell for The Bodley Head. According to Licko, Solzhenitsyn had nonetheless affirmed his desire for Max to publish both his novel and play.

Since it would have been impossible for anyone from The Bodley Head to reach Solzhenitsyn without the Soviet authorities knowing, Max decided to go ahead on Licko's word. He contracted Bethell and Burg on 5 April to translate both works quickly. Because of the complicated situation and the fact that other copies of *Cancer Ward* were circulating in the west and might see print before Bethell and Burg's was finished, making their translation unpublishable, Max agreed to pay them a half share in all payments to be made to Solzhenitsyn under the terms of the contract signed on 22 March.

Then the copyright war began. At the beginning of April Licko evidently showed Solzhenitsyn a Russian version of *Cancer Ward* published by an émigré press in Switzerland, then in Milan by Alberto Mondadori as the work of an anonymous author. According to Licko the Italian translation depressed Solzhenitsyn because of its errors and more importantly because he thought the text had arrived via a KGB agent, who he believed had given it to Mondadori in order to compromise Solzhenitsyn. Evidently to protect himself, Solzhenitsyn wrote to the editor of the *Literaturnaya gazeta* on 21 April saying that he had not authorized publication of *Cancer Ward* by any firm and did not recognize as legally valid anyone's publication of it. This was hard news for Max, but since Licko had told him Solzhenitsyn might have to make such a statement he did not change his plans.

Then on 26 April E.P. Dutton and Praeger announced that they had a copy of the Russian text (obtained by Praeger's British subsidiary, Pall Mall Press). They expected to publish it in the summer in a translation by Michael Glenny. On legal advice that the 22 March contract gave The Bodley Head exclusive licence to *Cancer Ward* throughout the world, Max quickly published a token edition of part one of the novel in Russian on 14 May in order to stake his claim, and sold the American rights to Roger Straus. The next day Dutton and Praeger backed down, issuing a joint statement that they were cancelling their plans in deference to Solzhenitsyn's wishes. In July, Max consolidated his position by bringing Licko to London to sign an affidavit confirming that he was Solzhenitsyn's agent and that his agreement with Max was approved by the author.

Meanwhile, there was growing concern in the west about Solzhenitsyn's well-being. Several small émigré presses had sprung up who were using his work for anti-Soviet propaganda, some, as Solzhenitsyn said of the Swiss publication of *Cancer Ward*, supplied with *samizadt* copies by the KGB. In June, just after *The First Circle* was published in Russian by Fischer Verlag, Solzhenitsyn was condemned in Russia for not speaking out fiercely enough about the publication of his work in the west and it looked as if the KGB might be preparing a case against him toward an arrest and trial in the manner of Daniel and Sinyavsky. At the same time, there was an ongoing debate in the western press about whether Solzhenitsyn would be in danger if further publications went ahead. In the *New York Times* Yale's Professor Victor

Erlich said 'that the publishers are playing fast and loose with Solzhenitsyn's personal safety, showing a callous disregard for his expressed safety'; the Institute for Sino-Soviet Studies at George Washington University's Vladimir Petrov wrote that 'the first right of an author is to see his work in print. Solzhenitsyn is being held hostage, to be punished unless foreign publishers collaborate with the Soviet censors.'[1]

In July Roger Straus discovered that Dial and Dell presses were intending to publish both parts of *Cancer Ward* in New York in a translation by Rebecca Frank from a Russian version printed at La Société YMCA Press in Paris. Max's solicitors warned Dial that legal action would be taken if The Bodley Head's rights were infringed and Roger Straus tried to negotiate a joint American edition with Dial to avoid litigation. Both failed.

At Bow Street the rush was on. James Michie found the Bethell and Burg translation in parts unacceptable and asked Max if Belinda McGill could work with Burg to redo them. The summer of 1968 was hot. According to McGill they started at 6 a.m., took two hours off to lunch at a Chinese restaurant in Jermyn Street, then worked through until 8 p.m. every day for six weeks. Michie marked the egregious passages. Burg (who, McGill said, understood English perfectly but did not speak it as well) read each out in Russian and said in English what it meant. McGill (who had French and German but no Russian) typed what she thought a better way of putting it. She remembered ringing her doctor husband late one day to ask where you dispose of an amputated leg and typing 'in a bin' as he replied.[2]

The Bodley Head published the first part of *Cancer Ward* on 19 September 1968 and a token Russian edition of the second part on the 26th. Max then tried to stop the Dial edition by asking the High Court in London to allow him to sue Dial in Britain rather than in America. He was told he was unlikely to obtain damages in Britain for an infringement in America but he wanted to protect Solzhenitsyn by avoiding the publicity his solicitor suggested a New York case would bring, and the expense. Under oath Max gave the history of The Bodley Head's publication, and his foreign agreements with Luchterhand in Germany, Swahlstrom & Widstrand in Stockholm, Tammi in Helsinki and many other companies including Farrar, Straus & Giroux in New York. But, again trying to protect Solzhenitsyn, he refused to give Licko's name and in not making 'full and final disclosure of all relevant circumstances' lost the right to sue Dial and Dell in Great Britain.[3] The case cost him about £7000; Dial published on 15 October, and a year later copies of the affidavits Max had withheld got into the hands of *Private Eye*, so Licko's name became public anyway, causing considerable personal and legal difficulty.

'In their zeal to rush into print they have turned out a rather undistinguished translation and that simply will not do' Max told the *New York Times* about the competitive American edition. The Bodley Head's translation was taken 'from a recently revised manuscript available to nobody else [and] is much more faithful to the Russian and more carefully edited'.[4] He published the second half of *Cancer Ward* in January 1969 in a volume of 279 pages; a 690 page volume of the entire novel followed in 1970, and in a Penguin edition in 1971. The Bodley Head's *The Love-Girl and the Innocent* also appeared in 1969, and was published by Penguin in 1971.

* * *

Meanwhile in Russia the Secretariat of the Union of Writers had accused Solzhenitsyn of writing more dangerous books than Pasternak and again demanded he denounce the use of his work abroad for anti-Soviet propaganda, which he continued to do almost as fast as the émigré presses published it for their own uses. These presses were a continuing problem for Max too – a year later he told *The Times* he would never deal with them because 'Solzhenitsyn did not want his work to be used as propaganda against his country',[5] and he continued to try to protect Solzhenitsyn in other ways.

In March 1969 Max received a letter from the American Academy of Arts and Letters saying that Solzhenitsyn had been elected an honorary member of the academy and of the American National Institute of Arts and Letters; he took care to get the letter to Russia safely, then suggested the honour be announced to the American press. He thought this might help clarify who Solzhenitsyn's official publishers were and 'also help Mr Solzhenitsyn personally . . . The more the Soviet authorities know how highly he is thought of by the West, the better it will be for him.'[6] On 6 August Graham Greene wrote to *The Times* with Max's encouragement calling for his 'fellow novelists to refuse permission for any of our future novels to be published in the USSR so long as work by Solzhenitsyn is suppressed and Daniel and Sinyavsky remain in their prison camp'.

Nothing helped. In late 1969 Solzhenitsyn was expelled from the Union of Writers, which deprived him of his status as a Soviet writer, and on 25 January 1970 in an attempt to stop the unauthorized publication of his work in the west he gave Dr Jur Fritz Heeb, a Zurich laywer and member of the Swiss Parliament, power of attorney to act as his agent. This meant Max had to renegotiate the Licko contract, which Solzhenitsyn now denied ever having agreed to. It was a tricky situation made worse, as Max told Dr Heeb, by 'the press hav[ing] said so many wrong things about these matters that I would advise you not to pay any attention to them'.[7] Not only had Max published and sold extensive foreign rights to two of Solzhenitsyn's books, he had a financial commitment to Licko (the usual agent's 10 per cent fee) and to the translators, as well as to Solzhenitsyn.

In a long letter to Heeb accompanied by all the royalty statements for *Cancer Ward* and *The Love Girl*, his contracts with innumerable foreign publishers and the performing licences for *The Love Girl* with the Tyrone Guthrie Theater Foundation in Minneapolis, Max insisted that by publishing the two books The Bodley Head had prevented the copyrights from 'falling into unauthorized hands and being exploited in a way that would cause embarrassment and distress to the author'.[8] At the time Heeb knew little about publishing and when Max said he would send the royalties he had been holding for Solzhenitsyn as soon as they made a new contract, Heeb's response was fierce. He insisted on changing the royalty arrangements in the Licko contract, paying the translators in a less lucrative way and worse, he denied the validity of Max's original document.

In June Max tore his Achilles tendon playing tennis. Before he went into surgery he telephoned Heeb and, perhaps because of the circumstances, was able to make a financial arrangement with him that got him in return an agreement recognizing the legality of the Licko contract. Max paid Solzhenitsyn the £6738 5s he owed him, and placed in a suspense account the monies owed to Licko and the translators until he and Heeb could work out a new contract. In a later letter to Roger Straus he revealed that the main source of Heeb's anger had been the percentage of Solzhenitsyn's royalties he had been paying the translators.

Heeb came to London on 6 October 1970, two days before Solzhenitsyn was given the Nobel Prize. Max told Straus that he took Heeb to lunch then 'left him with the two translators, but joined them afterwards because they couldn't come to terms about their respective shares in the Minneapolis production of *The Love Girl and the Innocent*. I must say Dr Heeb behaved extremely well.'[9] Two agreements were made, one between The Bodley Head and Heeb on behalf of Solzhenitsyn, and a second one with the translators; Bethell later told Max he and Burg were lucky to get such a favourable agreement, which might have been less generous had the Nobel Prize already been awarded; the prize brought increased sales and by far the larger part of the translators' earnings would come after 1970.

What Bethell did not know was that 'in the future [Heeb] only wants to deal with us', Max confided to Straus. An 'assurance he wanted to have was that if Solzhenitsyn's next book came to The Bodley Head there would be different translators. I agreed.' Max 'had the impression that Dr. Heeb was as relieved as we are that this matter is now settled'.[10] And Licko? He had been arrested by the Czech police a few months earlier and sentenced to 18 months imprisonment for spreading anti-socialist propaganda. Bethel worried especially about Licko's wife who was a fine translator and was reduced to an office job and poverty when her husband was so accused.

That left the Dial/Dell publication. Max wanted to get 'what compensations we can ... from them for pirating the book. They have done so not only in the States, but also have sold the Spanish rights to an Argentinian publisher, and the Portuguese rights to a Brazilian. As we have done the same we are having a bit of trouble with our publishers in these countries.' On 19 October there were more inaccuracies in *Publisher's Weekly* about Max's attempts to stop Dial. 'They have, of course, got it all wrong, and we shall have to issue a statement and I shall have to write to them as well',[11] he tiredly told Straus.

Max's statement, quoting one he had received from Heeb, appeared in *Publisher's Weekly* on 28 December. He explained that he had 'brought proceedings against Dial to get a trial in this country, and the judgement was that we could not do so. We had to take proceedings against them in the USA as they had published the book there and not here. The merits of the case were not on trial.' Then he quoted Dr Heeb's confirmation that The Bodley Head was the 'exclusive owner of the world rights of ... Cancer Ward and ... The Love-Girl and the Innocent' and 'in the position to investigate and, if necessary, take proceedings on behalf of the author against any unauthorized edition of either book' since 'some of the editions published had been presented to the public in a manner unacceptable to the author'. In ending Max repeated Heeb's warning: 'In due course we shall inform the publishers of editions of Cancer Ward and The Love-Girl and the Innocent that have been published without authority what action we propose to take against them. The only authorized publishers of these books in the United States are Farrar, Straus & Giroux Inc.' He and Heeb hoped their combined efforts would stop Dial because the last thing either of them wanted was further court costs.

Max then suggested that he and Straus secure their position as Solzhenitsyn's British and American publishers by issuing *One Day in the Life of Ivan Denisovich*. If they did they would then have published all of the available work except *The First Circle*, which Collins & Harvill had. A film version of *One Day* based on the translation Max had bought from Gillon Aitken was booked for London's Curzon Cinema in March 1971 and he planned to get the book out at the same time. He also proposed a small edition of 1500 to 2000 copies for himself and Straus of *Stories and Prose Poems* (1971), which Michie was arranging for Michael Glenny to translate.

On 8 October 1970 Solzhenitsyn was given the Nobel Prize for literature and sales of his work began to rise. He said he would go to Stockholm and Max told Heeb that he wanted to be there to meet him 'for it obviously will be a unique experience'.[12] Solzhenitsyn was the third Nobel winner on Max's list, joining George Seferis (1963) and Mikhail Sholokhov (1965).

McGill booked flights and a room at the Grand Hotel for the Reinhardts. Max got himself invited to the prize ceremony, the dinner after, and the Russian Embassy in Stockholm where he hoped to be able to speak to Solzhenitsyn alone. But Solzhenitsyn never came.

* * *

In February 1971 Max offered Heeb a £10,000 advance for *August 1914* on condition it was not published in Russia first. Solzhenitsyn's royalties were to be 10 per cent on the published price and 80 per cent of all income from the American and British serial rights, 70 per cent from other countries. Max said he would pay for the translation, and told Heeb that if he could see the typescript before signing the contract he thought he could improve the offer.

But in May, unbeknownst to Heeb, Solzhenitsyn sent *August 1914* to the YMCA Press in Paris and told Heeb he wanted them to publish it in Russian, which they did in June. Heeb then assigned Hermann Luchterhand Verlag general publishing rights and to Max and Roger Straus the English translation, publication and serialization rights to *August 1914* (and later to *November 1916* with options for *March 1917* and various plays), provided no other English translation was published before August 1972. So once again the rush was on. Max hired Michael Glenny to translate the YMCA copy, confidently slated The Bodley Head edition for mid-September 1972, sold the *Observer* pre-publication serial rights, and Penguin the paperback rights for two years later.

Then in July 1971 a man named Alex Flegon who owned a small press in Greek Street photographed the YMCA edition of the novel, bound it in hard covers with pictures of Imperial Russian personalities and wartime scenes, and announced that he would also have his own English translation of the book out by December 1971. He suggested Penguin buy his book since it would be out earlier than his competitor's and be cheaper, and he promised the *Observer* extracts for less than half the The Bodley Head quote.[13]

When Flegon produced his Russian YMCA edition Max issued a writ; when Flegon's offer to Penguin went out he issued a second writ and had three Scandinavian papers (*Aften Postern, Svenska Dagbladen* and *Berlingske Tidende*) publish a letter from Solzhenitsyn (in part in his own handwriting) protesting unauthorized publications of his work in the west and affirming Heeb as his sole agent.

According to the *Sunday Times* 'Law Report', when the case was heard the judge said that Flegon could publish more cheaply than Max because he made 'no royalty payments to the author!' His judgement against Flegon rested on three main points: first, since under Russian law nothing could be published without censorship and *August 1914* had not been approved by the censors, he deemed Flegon's *samizdat* copy never to have been published; second, *samizdat* copies were 'not intended to satisfy the reasonable requirements of the public' and a literary work was only considered published if it had been issued to the public; and third, since under Russian law 'no citizen could trade abroad on his own account because the state had a monopoly of foreign trade', the YMCA copy which Flegon had reproduced could not be considered to have been issued by Solzhenitsyn.[14] So in February 1972 Max won his case and this time he was not out of pocket. Flegon could not pay The Bodley Head's costs but Solzhenitsyn was by then earning large sums and Heeb picked up the bill.

The Swedish Academy arranged to take Solzhenitsyn's medallion to him in Moscow on 9 April and Max and Hugh Greene planned to go there in May, Solzhenitsyn having agreed to meet them in some official place. But neither meeting happened because Solzhenitsyn gave his first interview to western reporters just before the arranged academy meeting and the police intervened. The lecture he had written for the Nobel Prize ceremony was released in Stockholm in August and Max published it in a small pamphlet of 28 pages as *'One Word of Truth...': The Nobel Speech on Literature*.

* * *

Solzhenitsyn was deported on 8 February 1974 and in November Max finally got to meet him in Zurich. He wanted to take him and Heeb something very English and settled on china from Thomas Goode in Mayfair. What did Solzhenitsyn make of it? 'It was a difficult meeting', Max told Roger Straus. 'He ... couldn't understand how we could have been so naive as to accept their [Bethell and Burg's] version.' In *Memories* Max added that when they met Solzhenitsyn had said he wanted to ask a few questions – 'thirty to be precise. The first question went on for half an hour so I said that if they were all as long he had better ask them one at a time. He agreed. My answer to the first question was: "You are wrong on every point. What about the next twenty-nine?" After five hours he agreed that we could continue to publish his work.'[15]

But there were conditions Max failed to mention in his winsome summary, conditions which left him in an invidious position. Solzhenitsyn wanted all connection severed with Bethell and Burg who, however complicated the situation had been, had operated courageously and in good faith and had concealed nothing from Max. He insisted that Max not pay them any further royalties and that he be compensated for the royalties Max had paid them for the translations of *Cancer Ward* and *The Love-Girl*, including all foreign language commissions. So Max was caught between his translators and Solzhenitsyn, and because of the separate contracts he had made with each under Dr Heeb's instructions, he had to abide by both.

Solzhenitsyn also demanded that Max have new translations made of both books by someone he approved. He wanted corrections made to the Glenny translation of *August 1914* before Max could reprint it. Max told his solicitors 'what is important is to soothe Mr Solzhenitsyn and prove to him that The Bodley Head certainly acted in good faith and in no small way managed to protect his interests'. To Nicholas Bethell he said 'it will take a lot of patience and paying of compensation to soothe him. Otherwise he threatens to make public disclosures of the [original] deal which he considers unethical when he goes to Sweden to [finally] receive the Nobel Prize at the beginning of December.'[16] But Bethell insisted he and Burg must be paid so long as their translation was being sold around the world, and Max was keen to sell whatever copies he still had before a new translation was printed.

On 22 November Max sent Solzhenitsyn a cheque for £3223, the difference between what he had paid Bethell and Burg according to the Licko contract and what Solzhenitsyn thought they should have been paid. But he was still in a very embarrassing position. If he stopped paying them as Solzhenitsyn demanded he would be liable for a breach of trust under the Heeb arrangement, if not of contract under the Licko agreement. Max so hated conflict that he usually turned his back on it and walked away, but there was no escaping Solzhenitsyn.

* * *

'I am arriving in New York in the afternoon of the 12th February after a short holiday in Barbados', Max wrote to Roger Straus.

> The only date I have suggested so far is the 13th February at Grosset & Dunlap, who have now definitely bought the American rights of Charles Chaplin's My Life in Pictures ... I am still puzzled as to what to do about Solzhenitsyn. There is no point in ringing Heeb up because he is in a more embarrassing situation. He has made absolutely legal a contract which Solzhenitsyn claims is illegal ... We will be accommodating but provided we get some assurance from either Solzhenitsyn, Heeb (who in future I think will be more than relieved not to be involved in strictly publishing matters) or Paul Flamand [Editions du Seuil] that we shall get the sequel to August 1914.[17]

Solzhenitsyn had given Flamand authority to act for him as of 1 January 1975 and since Straus was closer to Flamand than Max they agreed it might be more effective if Straus approached him.

'Solzhenitsyn can be very tough', Max said.

> I think we must be prepared to meet him in the same spirit. If Heeb doesn't hand our file of statements over, the office here will have to stop working for a few days to photocopy masses and masses of lengthy documents from which we will have to extract all the legal expenses we have incurred on these books and also on August 1914. The Hindi and Urdu publishers have also had letters like the one sent to you and us and they wrote to me in complete puzzlement as publishers in those two languages have never sent royalty statements to anybody. They just pay an advance and you never hear from them again and you are glad you have had the advance.[18]

Heeb had already been paid nearly £100,000 on *Cancer Ward* alone. By 29 April Max was willing to give up his foreign rights to maintain the peace but as he explained to Straus 'we cannot force the translators to surrender 12% of the author's share, unless we can come to an arrangement with them and compensate them'. If *Cancer Ward* had come to Max in the usual way, he would have commissioned a translation and paid by the word – the going rate was then about £12 for 1000 words. That way the translators would have earned about £3000 between them. But it had not and by the spring of 1975 they had been paid many times that amount. Given the situation, Max thought they ought to 'bow out gracefully and not expect further income except from the sales of the rest of the English edition in their translation'. Straus agreed. 'They have had it good and they shouldn't be greedy.'[19]

The summer of 1975 was quiet because Bethell was dealing directly with Claude Durand at Editions du Seuil and Solzhenitsyn. Max waited; he told his son-in-law Andrew Gammon just over a decade later, 'if you don't know what to do, do nothing until the way becomes clear'.[20] Bethell wanted an apology from Solzhenitsyn, and said there could be no settlement until he got one recognizing his good faith in dealing with Licko. Max confided to Straus that he doubted it would come, but he believed Bethell deserved one and he continued to work through Durand to try to secure a solution. He had offered Solzhenitsyn a £30,000 advance for *Lenin in Zurich*. Solzhenitsyn 'approves of your firm', he told Straus on 30 July, 'from which I take it that he also approves of the fact that we sold you the rights, but I agree that one doesn't necessarily follow from the other'.

On 17 September Max wrote to Straus telling him that Solzhenitsyn had agreed to give The Bodley Head his new book on 'pretty stiff terms' and in addition 'wants compensation for the excessive profits we made on <u>Cancer Ward</u>. I'd like to ask what excessive profits and how is the terrific compensation calculated? Talk about being bitten by the Capitalistic bug when you first come face to face with it. Anyway, I'll see what we can do.' By 26 September an agreement had been reached 'so you can close your files', Max told his lawyers. 'Please don't charge us too much as we have to pay all these costs ourselves and in addition have to pay a wacking big sum of compensation to AS for what he claims were our exceptional earnings on foreign rights. This is not quite correct but I am going to pay the sum to make peace and avoid a quarrel.'

Solzhenitsyn had driven a hard bargain. It included paying him another £25,000 which he deemed the translators had been overpaid for *Cancer Ward* and *The Love-Girl* because of the Licko contract. Max was able to retain the American and Canadian rights in both books but had to surrender all other foreign rights to them. Penguin and The Literary Guild were to take *August 1914* and he had an option on *October 1916* and *March 1917*.

13
Heady, Champagne Years

In most respects Max's personal and publishing lives were never separate. He became godfather to Belinda McGill's first child. He made room at The Bodley Head for the children of friends – in the sixties for Nigel Hollis and Charles Richardson, in the early seventies for Rosie Quayle – and when she finished at Chelsea College of Art, for Alexandra. He conducted business with the same kindness he showed people in private life. Contracts were agreed over drinks and written (if necessary) on the backs of envelopes. He had an almost unimaginable goodness of heart in trusting people, and was always astonished and hurt if they proved untrustworthy.

Casual meetings turned into books. His Savile friend Joe Links wrote Max a long letter about Venice when the Reinhardts were about to go there in 1965. It told them where to stay and eat and how to avoid cultural saturation by sitting in particular cafés to simply admire the view. The Chaplins also found the letter useful and amusing, so Max asked Links to expand it and published *Venice for Pleasure* in 1966, making himself and Links enough money for several more trips. Reviewers said it was not only the best guide book to that city ever written, but the best guide book to any city ever written.

The Reinhardts invited authors and sometimes members of the staff to join them on holiday at St Jean Cap Ferrat, Max putting them up at the Voile d'Or, or later at the Metropole in Beaulieu. In 1966 when Belinda McGill and Judy Taylor were there at the same time he rented a car so they could explore; on another occasion when Taylor joined Max for a rain-sodden trip in the boat with Greene, Cloetta and Chaplin, 'Charlie held his glass to catch the rain from the boat's awning to dilute his whisky'. In 1968 Max replaced his boat with a larger *Maximilian* complete with a galley, loo and ice-box. It provided swimming and water-skiing near the islands off Cannes, followed by picnics of fresh lobster and cold wine. By then the Reinhardts were renting a villa next to the Voile d'Or and when the cook brought the live lobsters back in the bus at 4 a.m. from the market she 'let them wander about on the tiled floor in the kitchen until it was time to kill them'. Greene got the idea for 'May We Borrow Your Husband?' at the Voile D'Or. He came for supper one evening and stayed for over a week watching two gay men whose eyes lit up whenever the husband of a pair of handsome honeymooners came into the restaurant. Max was fascinated how he replaced reality in the story 'so as to be unrecognizable but at the same time exact'.[1]

In 1969 Southdown Cottage became another place of entertainment. It was an old gardener's cottage in the grounds of Ione O'Brien's Park House Hotel in Bepton, West Sussex. Max got it in exchange for adding three rooms and a swimming pool to the property. On 4 March 1976 he told Alistair Cooke that 'our cottage is too small to put anybody up but next door is a hotel which belongs to friends and which has a very friendly atmosphere. I can offer tennis and a swimming pool and very lovely grass.' Greene was given a room in the hotel with a hard chair and plain table to write on. Max would leave him an agenda of points they should discuss. Could Max take an extract from Greene's introduction for a blurb? When should a new novel be published? With whom should a paperback contract be made? Max might even admit to an idea for a story, 'but know I will never be able to write it'.[2] Greene would join the family for lunch and a swim and return for supper after which he played *vingt-et-un* with Alexandra and Veronica on the floor behind the sofa. He insisted they play with real money, which the adults gave them, and used to accuse them of cheating to instigate an argument that Max said he loved and invariably lost.

Oncle Richard came regularly from Paris and stayed for weeks at a time, talking French with Max. They would play a game that required you to be a country and Max would refuse to be Turkey because he said he would destroy it. Alexandra and Veronica brought school friends for weekends and holidays. When Max thought the girls had outgrown Bepton he gave the house up and took them to America to visit friends and Joan's family. Once the Reinhardts and the Cookes swapped houses, the Reinhardts going to Cutchoque on Long Island and Max sending his blue Jaguar and driver to pick the Cookes up at Heathrow and deliver them to Pelham Crescent. One summer in California they went to Disneyland. Veronica said Max loved the pirate cave. Was he reminded of Captain Pugwash?

There were visits to Oncle Richard in France, when they were treated to fabulous restaurants and drives around Paris by Richard in his Jag, one hand on the wheel, talking all the while. There were winter holidays in the Caribbean. As the years passed, swimming vacations were added to help Max's back ailments and diet spas to remedy his expanding waistline. But Max was usually restless away from his base of influence and often obliged Joan to move on ahead of schedule. One summer a cottage was arranged for them at Manamsha on Martha's Vineyard, about an hour's ferry ride from Cape Cod. It was far too primitive for Max's liking and he refused to stay. Joan assured him there was no alternative; their reservation for the ferry to Nantucket where they had reserved rooms at a hotel for a further week was several days ahead. As usual Max got his way. Joan loaded the family back into the car and drove it to the harbour furiously repeating the impossibility of doing what he had in mind. There they joined the usual summer queue. Max got out. Half an hour later he returned and directed her to a nearby diner where they waited until an appointed time, then proceeded a different way past the other cars straight onto the ferry. Max had seen the captain and told him he was a publisher who had always been interested in ferry boats. Why did the fellow not write a book?

But behind the fun was the constant concern for Alexandra's health. Her growth had been stunted by the prednisolone she took and when she was taken off steroids and given monthly transfusions instead, the blood (then unfiltered) made her very sick. Max's letters to authors and publishers are scattered with references to her health and the dates of her transfusions, only after which he felt free to travel. In searching for a cure he had set up the Max Reinhardt Charitable Trust to fund research and pay the salary of a doctor on the unit where Alexandra was treated at Great Ormond Street Hospital. The trust also funded two projects for detecting deafness in small children, the result of which was a simple test for newborns. This was Max's way of handling a dreadful situation he could not control.

Veronica said Joan kept her concern for Alexandra to herself and did as many ordinary things as she could for both her daughters. On a nice day there was lunch in the garden. There were birthday parties. There was the great annual Boxing Day party around 5.30 to which the girls invited their friends. Max loved choosing films to show and served drinks at intervals when the reels on his 16 mm projector needed changing. One year Greene suggested *The Maltese Falcon* then decided it was a bit too violent for children, so Max showed *The Fallen Idol* instead, which may have been the more horrifying. Chaplin's films were always favourites. He was Veronica's godfather and sent splendid gifts to both girls while Max sent boxes of books for the Chaplin children. In 1968 Max wrote him that he could not 'ever remember having a better audience for anything' than the party guests who were shown *City Lights*.[3] Ralph came with special presents for Alexandra. He would spend time talking with her and acting parts to make her laugh. One of his favourites was playing the ineffectual butler who continued to bring the wrong coats to departing guests, stroking the furs all the while.

Max was a naturally affectionate father and gave both girls whatever they wanted – his unadorned Christmas cards containing £500 cash were his daughters' favourite gifts. But he maintained his privacy at home as he did at the office, especially if he thought someone might be hurt by a confession. One day when the family was together Alexandra asked him where his initialled cufflinks had come from. He refused to answer until she petted him with so many kisses that they were both overcome with laughter and he blurted out 'my first wife'. His daughters were then of an age to be enormously interested but even so his response was perfunctory. 'She was an actress, beautiful but unsuitable and we got divorced.'[4]

He was more expansive lunching with authors and colleagues at Rules, or holding forth at the many parties he and Joan gave and attended which were a necessary part of his publishing life. There Max was entirely in control of the script. Jack Ashley, who thought Max and Joan 'seemed like the figures of a lifelong friendship' said that 'Max effortlessly held centre court without pushing himself and he was such stimulating company that he provoked responses from his friends at the table. The result was some of the most hilarious and effervescent occasions I have ever attended.'[5] Euan Cameron said 'one came away feeling uplifted and reinvigorated by his affable presence and somehow flattered to be selected as one of his guests'.[6]

* * *

Jill Black called the late sixties through the seventies at The Bodley Head 'heady, champagne years'.[7] Max's lists were varied and international. There was plenty of new fiction from Greene, Heyer (until 1976), Solzhenitsyn, Paul Horgan, Paul Theroux, Jerzy Kosinski, Philip Callow, R.K. Narayan, William Trevor, Howard Fast, Eric Ambler, Rex Warner, Winston Graham and Bernard Kops. Soon Michael Mewshaw, Rachel MacKenzie, Frank Hardy, Alexander Zinoviev, Primo Levi, Robert Pirsig, Edwin O'Connor, Naomi Mitchison, Peter Dickinson, Allan Massie, Ronald Frame and Muriel Spark joined the already impressive list. On the children's side there were books, many of them prizewinners, by Pat Hutchins, Shirley Hughes, Rosemary Sutcliff, Pauline Clarke, John Prater,

Gillian Avery, Rukshana Smith, Jean Morris, Jean Ure, Susanna Gretz, Susan Cooper, Ezra Jack Keats, Betsy Byars and Maurice Sendak.

There were books of humour, popular books like Shirley MacLaine's *Don't Fall off the Mountain*, Peter Laurie's *Scotland Yard*, Maureen and Bridget Boland's big seller, *Old Wives Lore for Gardeners*, and Rixi Markus's books on bridge. *Zen and the Art of Motor-Cycle Maintenance* was a quick bestseller, as was Alvin Toffler's *Future Shock*. Mary Gilliatt's *Bathrooms, Kitchens and Dining Rooms* and *Doing up a House* took up the decorating craze. *Vogue's Book of Home and Gardens* with photos by Horst, and Horst's *Salute to the Thirties* with an introduction by Janet Flanner sat on coffee tables alongside Edgar Andrew Collard's collection of Notman photographs, Alistair Cooke and Robert Cameron's spectacular *Above London*, and Chaplin's *My Life in Pictures* with a commentary by Francis Wyndham.

There were memoirs, biographies, travel books and autobiographies, often by or about Max's friends. Jack Ashley said that when Max wanted a book

> he would introduce the subject almost casually so if one didn't pick up the signals, it could be pushed aside. Or could it? Max wasn't the kind of person whose ideas and objectives could be pushed aside and when I used general phrases like 'I'll think about it' or 'I'll see what I can do' or 'Yes, I'll do it sometime' he would gently seek specific answers, dates, chapter headings, experiences and conclusions, all done so deftly that one would agree in order to please him ... If, after that, I dallied, there would either be another phone call or another meeting to keep me up to the mark. But whatever it was, his manner was always perfect in tone.[8]

So *Journey into Silence* came into being in 1973, and later from Reinhardt Books in association with Viking, *Acts of Defiance*, which won the J.R. Ackerley Prize for autobiography in 1992, Ackerley having himself written *My Father and Myself* for Max in 1968.

Michael Millgate's *Thomas Hardy* and Samuel Hynes's *The Auden Generation* are but two examples of The Bodley Head's commitment to fine literary studies, Bernard Diederich's *Papa Doc* and *Trujillo* of its excellent historical and political commentary. Leon Edel's editions of Henry James (eleven volumes in all) were regularly added to the lengthening series of individual authors. There were important ongoing projects, like Dan Laurence's seven volumes of Shaw's plays with their prefaces (each running about 1000 pages), and his collected letters. Given the rapid rise in publishing costs and overheads, could they have been published a few years later? By 1985 when the last of the three volumes of Shaw's correspondence appeared Max told Bernard Levin, 'It's a sad state of affairs affecting not only publishing – it's been over 10 years in the making and appears at a published price of £25.00 - when volume 1 appeared in 1965 it cost 3 guineas.'[9]

In the champagne years the demand for books was large and government support for libraries and schools still high. The 1971 minutes of The Bodley Head meetings held at William Collins in Australia show that Max was pushing his foreign agents hard; his editors were doing brilliantly for him at home and he continued to think of expanding to ease the pressure on his production departments. In December 1965 G. Bell & Sons Ltd considered hooking up with his group. In 1968 he was in talks separately with Granada (who had bought 41.7 per cent of Cape in the early sixties) and with Rupert Hart-Davis about forming a company to publish educational books. In April 1969 he was talking with Cassell. Then in 1970, a few months before Allen Lane died, there was even a possible reverse takeover of Penguin.

Because of the close association of the two firms, Lane and Max had often talked about getting the companies together one day and Lane had agreed to notify Max if he ever decided to sell. When Lane became terminally ill Max was worried that McGraw Hill might take the firm over. They owned 18 per cent of Penguin's shares at the time and Max's concern was to protect his own interests and to prevent Penguin from falling into American hands. Within a few months of the collapsed Tilling's deal Heinemann had sold Rupert Hart-Davis to Harcourt Brace Jovanovitch; W.H. Allen had gone to the Americans and there was talk of Pan, the paperback house, being taken over by North American Library. In case McGraw Hill moved in on Penguin, Max tried to form a trust on lines similar to *The Economist*, the *Observer* and *The Times* trusts, and a syndicate made up of bankers, a large printer (he suggested William Clowes), Jonathan Cape, Chatto & Windus and The Bodley Head, which would acquire from the trust 51 per cent of Penguin shares. To speed his proposal Max offered to sell 49 per cent of The Bodley Head to Penguin immediately with an option for them to buy the balance as soon as the plan was finalized. It was a bold plan which came to nothing when Lane died on 7 July and the next day Penguin merged with the Pearson Longman group.

By the 1970s Max was looking even more actively for firms to buy or join so that their combined profits would be large enough to turn the entire enterprise into a public company that would eventually get a quotation on the stock exchange, making the companies more trade-able and thus more valuable. He had served with Harrap's chairman, Olaf Anderson, on the Committee of British Book Distributors Ltd, who represented their firms in the Far East; in 1970 he wrote to Anderson about a possible merger. In 1971 he tried to acquire Faber & Faber, who were then having financial difficulties. On 18 January 1972 he wrote to Paul Hodder-Williams of Hodder & Stoughton that going public would require 'a turnover of well over a million, with a profit of at least £200,000 . . . What I'm wondering is whether you and John and the rest of your Board and families might consider our joining forces to go pub-lic together. Between us we should have the necessary profit.' The same year G.V. Woodman Ltd, who were consultants to publishers and print-ers, suggested that Max might buy the Centaur Press in the north-east of England; soon after he and Macmillan were sniffing around one another and in April 1972 he was exchanging details of his group's holdings with Chatto & Jonathan Cape who had joined forces in May 1969.

At the time of their deal Cape was managed jointly by Sir Hugh Greene's son, Graham C. Greene, who appeared as an all-round busi-nessman, and Tom Maschler, who had joined Penguin in 1958, then left unexpectedly early in 1960 when Allen Lane was recovering from jaundice. In *Penguin Special* Jeremy Lewis says Maschler told Lane he had been offered something he could not refuse and something he could not disclose. This had been an offer from Michael Howard, son of Cape's co-founder Wren Howard, to become editorial assistant there. When Jonathan Cape died that year, Wren Howard and his son increased their holding in the firm according to their option, but 41.7 per cent of the firm's shares had to be sold to pay Cape's death duties. Lewis says Allen Lane agreed to buy the shares, put up £25,000, and arranged to have three disaffected Michael Joseph executives, Charles Pick, Peter Hebdon and Roland Gant, run the firm on condition that he 'would have nothing to do with Maschler'. Wren Howard agreed and Pick got Norman Collins to put up another £25,000. Collins then decided to raise his stake to £40,000 if Lane would do the same. But when Maschler heard of the deal and confronted Wren Howard about the loss of his job, Howard pulled out and the shares were picked up by Sidney Bernstein of Granada.[10]

Maschler, whose reputation was as a brilliant fiction publisher, brought Graham C. Greene to Cape two years later. According to Eric de Bellaigue in *British Book Publishing as a Business since the 1960s*, when Cape and Chatto came together, Greene was 'particularly aware of the advantages that scale allied to technology could bring',[11] and Chatto's chairman,

Ian Parsons, was beginning to feel old and not interested in the changes he saw coming. Parsons and Michael Howard became joint chairmen of that new holding company; the board was composed of three members from each side: from Chatto, Norah Smallwood, Cecil Day-Lewis and Geoffrey Trevelyan; from Cape, Graham C. Greene, Tom Maschler and Granada's representative, Robert Carr.

No one has written more knowledgeably about the post-war mergers and acquisitions in British publishing than Eric de Bellaigue. From the late sixties to the early seventies, he says they took place according to 'the theory that the combination of communication groups and publishing companies spelled prosperity'. A second phase had 'to do with US firms' initiatives in the UK, predominately those with existing media interests'. And the third, from the mid-seventies, 'saw a reversal of capital from between the USA and the UK, [and] was linked to the easing of currency controls and progressive deregulation of markets'.[12]

In his early acquisitions and his attempts to find a partner for The Bodley Head in the late sixties and early seventies Max appears to have been a bit of a loner in the process. He needed more production facilities and savings in representation, distribution and the increasingly complicated handling of rights, but he wanted at the same time to keep everything under his own control. Judy Taylor said he made the decision to join Chatto & Jonathan Cape entirely by himself. Although she was by then Max's deputy managing director, she knew nothing about the plan until she had her usual whisky with him after closing one evening in late July 1973. 'The Bodley Head was Max's company', she said. 'He owned it and he ran it. He just said he'd been in discussions with Chatto & Jonathan Cape. We needed warehousing and consolidated distribution and it made sense to join forces with them. Books were in demand. The problem was how to get them to market.'[13]

According to Graham C. Greene, Max was very keen to join his group. Max's connections with the Greene family were close and he supposed Max wanted to further tighten them through him.[14] While it is true that Max preferred to do business with people he knew, that reputation and connections meant everything to him, Max had watched the publishing takeovers by American firms and wanted to save The Bodley Head that fate. Cape and Chatto had retained their editorial independence, and both imprints shared his concern for design and typographical excellence at a time when many firms were holding back publication dates and reducing standards as cost-cutting measures. So in August 1973 joining them seemed the solution for the economies and efficiencies he wanted without sacrifice.

The new board would have three joint chairmen: Max, Ian Parsons and Graham C. Greene. The other directors would be Norah Smallwood, Hugo Brunner and Geoffrey Trevelyan from Chatto; John Hews (who became managing director of the new service company) and Judy Taylor from The Bodley Head; Michael Howard, Tom Maschler and W.R. Carr from Cape. There would be three operating companies under the holding company each with a separate board and its own managing director, Parsons continuing at Chatto (at the end of 1974 Norah Smallwood succeeded him), Max at The Bodley Head and Graham C. Greene at Cape. Eric de Bellaigue has rightly said that the union created 'the greatest concentration of literary excellence the British publishing trade had witnessed up to then'.[15] It was an admirable attempt to allow three excellent firms to compete with the giants, and for many years the arrangement was the envy of the publishing world.

The Bodley Head was valued at 35 per cent of the combined group, Chatto & Jonathan Cape at 65 per cent, which as de Bellaigue has shown corresponded closely to their turnover ratios for 1972, The Bodley Head's being £814,000 and Chatto's and Cape's a combined £1,474,000. Spicer and Pegler had suggested a closer split of 42/58 but Max told his accountants he 'was in a generous mood because it was really the quality of the partnership that was most important. As you will realize I was keen on the project and pleased that we have come to an agreement. I am quite confident in the long run it will be to the advantage of everybody.' Because Max owned almost all of The Bodley Head he ended up the largest single shareholder in the new holding company; when the shares of the firms were readjusted and added together he held 28 per cent, Greene and Maschler 7.8 per cent each, Granada 11.8 per cent, the rest of the central board of directors a combined 20.7 per cent, and other people 23.9 per cent.[16]

Max sent a letter to The Bodley Head staff on 31 July 1973, just before the merger was announced.

> What I want to emphasise is that 'joining forces' means just that. It is simply a merger – neither party is buying any part of the other. What we are doing is joining the holding company which will now be renamed Chatto, Bodley Head and Jonathan Cape Limited [the order according to the foundation date of each house], and this holding company will own all the assets of the three publishing companies.

He assured his staff that there would be 'no change whatever' at The Bodley Head.

We shall remain as we are in this building and The Bodley Head books will carry the same imprint as before. The advantage of what we are doing is only to a very small degree financial. The much larger Group, however, will enable us to undertake new ventures which we may have been too small to undertake by ourselves. I am quite confident that this new development is a good one for our firm and will benefit both ourselves and our authors.

Similar letters went to reps and right down the chain, sometimes with the rider, 'You must know by now that I have the interests of all of you at heart, and I will always see that you are well looked after.'[17]

The Bodley Head's list was added to the marketing organization Chatto and Cape had set up in 1972 and Max began to pay an overhead to the CBC group to provide him with servicing back-up. The transition seemed smooth. But a letter from Anthony Quayle on 1 December 1973 indicates that Max may have been uncomfortable with the merger almost from the first. Addressed to 'My dear old friend, up to your eyes in your own acute problems', Quayle advised him to 'keep warm, old fellow, keep afloat'.

* * *

When the merger took place Max was, by his own admission, beginning to get tired. He had finished a six-year stint on the council of the Publishers Association in 1969 and his personal letters from the next three years show his constant concern for his elder daughter's health and his occasional irritation with his own. Squash and tennis accidents had left him with intermittent back pain and by 1973 he 'thought it quite nice to have other people do some of the routine jobs I had invariably been occupied with. In fact young Graham insisted that I need no longer be involved with the small things … I welcomed his suggestion and the top-level companionship of my publishing colleagues. We were all good friends, all very proud of our lists. To begin with it was perfect, we trusted each other.'[18]

Max had always trusted his business partners, and he trusted Graham C. Greene the more because of friendships with his father and uncle. The group's financing was done with the National Westminster Bank at Lombard Street, its auditing by Spicer and Pegler; as Eric de Bellaigue has said, once things were in place, 'the publishing company executives were busy publishing, and on the holding company board there was a ready acceptance that, on financial matters, "one could leave it to Graham" '. But Graham C. Greene had many responsibilities outside the firm: he was President of the Publishers' Association from 1977 to 1979, a Trustee of the British Museum, a director of the publishers of the *New Statesman*, as well as a director of the Greene King Brewery and a board member of the merchant bankers Guinness Mahon (both family connected). De Bellaigue quotes Liz Calder, editorial director of Cape and the first woman to join its board, as saying Greene was 'a benign and somewhat remote figure, much occupied by these other responsibilities'.[19]

A year after the merger Max, always the nimble mathematician, was already 'getting worried about the financial situation of the Group'. On 31 July 1974 as he prepared for the group chairman's lunch he wrote to Ian Parsons, sending a copy to Graham C. Greene, that 'only a few months ago we had about £200,000 at our disposal which the National Westminster, Lombard Street, were investing for us and now we are overdrawn to the tune of already about £50,000'. He did not want to ask his accounting people to investigate the loss because they were overstretched in harmonizing the group's accounting procedures and reorganizing his own accounts department, but he told Parsons what he thought had happened. His itemized analysis indicates some of the rapid changes in publishing itself and the presence of a recession, the greatest impact of which was felt by CBC only the next year.

In the past Max had been used to three months' credit from many of his suppliers. They were now demanding monthly payments while his own debtors were paying more slowly, particularly those overseas who were plagued by increasing interest rates in their own countries. 'While British bills are usually paid in two months,' he wrote, 'they are taking about seven to pay and the distance makes it more difficult to put pressure on them.' As well, everyone in the new group had bought 'a considerable amount of extra paper, and quite rightly so', and Max imagined that overheads, including salaries, had increased at Chatto and Cape as they had at The Bodley Head.

Max told Parsons he could easily cope with these problems but the group was about to build a warehouse of 5000 square feet on five acres they had bought at Grantham for £35,000, and that meant investing in fixed assets as well. The building estimate was £400,000. The new DEC computer for the warehouse would add another £100,000. More financing was needed for day-to-day expenses and The Bodley Head faced a large tax bill in January 1975, which Max estimated at £50,000.

De Bellaigue says that 'management was not deflected ... from its goal of exploiting the advantages of scale to develop the central services that the three firms saw as one of the main reasons for their participation in the group'.[20] Maybe so, but Max's letter to Parsons shows that with his firm's finances out of his hands for the first time he was uneasy. 'Where will the money come from?' he asked. 'Can we do anything as a Group to make ourselves more liquid? [We need] to reduce our stock and if necessary cut our output and even delay or abandon publishing books which do not sell reasonably well and quickly.' And Grantham was not the only plan the year-old service company was about to undertake. The setting up of Triad paperbacks was also in the works. 'I'm sure there are other ways to make ourselves more liquid and that you will both have valuable suggestions to make but isn't all this making it more difficult for us to contemplate further investments in a paperback company project? Should we not give serious consideration to Penguin's offer [to paperback agreed books]?' Max had long relations with Penguin and many of his best writers continued to be successfully paperbacked there.

Grantham and Triad went ahead. The building was finished at £20,000 above cost, which was partly covered by an industrial building allowance on the construction expenditure, although that allowance came with a limitation on the amount of space allowed for dispatch operations; because the computer was bought outright they were able to write its cost off against taxes. In July 1975 Triad paperbacks was incorporated and an alliance made with Granada (headed by Cape shareholder Sidney Bernstein) to have its titles sold through them. Granada held 47.5 per cent of Triad's shares; Chatto, The Bodley Head and Jonathan Cape held 17.5 per cent each.[21]

Whatever the others thought, Max continued to worry about financing. On 14 November 1975 he wrote to Parsons again. This time his concern was the cost of the Scottish Academic Press and the University of Sussex Press which came under Chatto's umbrella. 'We have had for many years relatively easy periods when we could publish what we considered good books and be pretty sure that they would sell, and we also then had no cash problems', he said. 'I am not so sure that we can afford such luxuries any more without the possibility of doing damage to the main props of our respective businesses.'

Both presses were close to Parsons's heart, his wife Trekkie Ritchie being Scottish and their house near the University of Sussex where they had many friends. Was Max insensitive to this? Or was he simply out of step in this three-way alliance? He had come to it late, when the working relationship between Chatto and Cape was already established. And perhaps the distance between Max and his new partners was wider.

Ian Parsons had been at Chatto & Windus since his graduation from Trinity College, Cambridge, first as a typographer and from 1930 as a partner. His wife, a painter, lithographer, and illustrator of children's books, had from the war lived in an unusual, deeply loving *ménage à trois* with Parsons and Leonard Woolf. It was largely her friendship with Woolf that had brought the Hogarth Press to Chatto in 1946, and Parsons's respect for Woolf that had led him to leave Woolf with editorial control of Hogarth while relieving him of the financial and administrative responsibilities of publishing. The relationship between Hogarth and Chatto had become the blueprint for the Chatto and Cape arrangement, then for that of Chatto, The Bodley Head and Cape.

But unlike Parsons and, indeed, Graham C. Greene, whose family connections were deeply literary, it was the business end of publishing Max coveted and excelled at, which is not to say he did not value his reputation as a publisher of serious literature. He guarded it jealously. Like Parsons he also loved the feel of good paper and bindings and took pride in the elegant design of his books. But he did not share Parsons's and Greene's intellectual interests. Although he spent a great deal of time entertaining his authors, he could not recite poetry competitively from memory as Parsons and his wife did for fun, or talk about painting with the same authority. His connection with the theatre had been lifelong, his very name echoing the theatre. He had close actor friends, published theatre and movie books with them, prided himself on holding the rights to Shaw's work and, as a member of the executive council of RADA since 1965, on helping to administer one of Shaw's largest legacies. But for all that, Max was more prone to recall how he had come to publish Shaw than to quote from Shaw's plays. And while Max admired Maschler's acquisitions (Lewis reports that 'when Maschler turned up at a publishing party, the room stiffened as if a wolf had been let loose in a flock of sheep') Max and Maschler had nothing in common. Where Allen Lane may have in the beginning admired Maschler's 'irreverence and scorn for accepted wisdom'[22] Max had reached the age where he expected to be treated with the respect due his years and accomplishments.

Graham C. Greene remembered having a meal before the merger with Max and Parsons at the Garrick Club, where Max was by then more often lunching than at the Savile. Parsons kept saying, 'Graham, you must join the Garrick. I'm going to put you up.' Greene insisted he was not very clubbable because he 'felt embarrassed when Parsons treated Max as an outsider'.[23] Greene was elected on Parsons's recommendation a couple of weeks before the merger was completed, and a few days before Max was put up for election by Georgette Heyer's son, Sir Richard Rougier, on 27 July 1973; Max was elected February 1975. As the years passed Graham C. Greene hardened to Max. When Christopher Maclehose, a friend of Norah Smallwood and Carmen Callil left Chatto, Greene said Max happened to meet Ian Chapman in the street and told him offhand-edly 'that we had been hoping Maclehose would leave, which was not true'. Greene told Max that Maclehose was excellent, his leaving a loss to the firm, and he rang Chapman to say so. 'Even if what Max said had been true', Greene insisted, 'Max was hurting the fellow's chances by saying that. He just didn't get it.'[24]

Judy Taylor found the problems of the sister firms and the gossip she heard at the joint board meetings fascinating. As interesting was the 'clash of personalities' revealed as the chair rotated with each meeting. She thought Parsons 'a charismatic, attractive, very sociable man', who joined in things when the firms got together for outings. 'Parsons was a good chairman. Smallwood terrified everyone because she had a very sharp tongue and did not suffer fools well. Greene was very organized. Max was vague; meetings bored him. He was not a committee man. He didn't know what came next, didn't like that sort of thing, but he kept things going.' To Taylor's mind it did not matter because 'no one ever voted anyway. If you wanted to spend an enormous amount for an author you had to get it OKed, or if Cape wanted to sign a three book agreement it would be discussed. The board was a chance to be told what was happening. GCG, Ian and Max did the real business on the phone.'[25] Gordon Graham, head of Butterworth, to whom Max would sell HFL in 1984, 'thought the amalgamation of Chatto, Virago & Cape with the Bodley Head was ill-conceived, too much a defensive move involving incompatible personalities. Max and Tom Maschler were ... the unlikeliest bedfellows.'[26]

* * *

At the end of the 1974–75 recession the service company was in a good financial position although all three firms lost money in 1975. Max defensively told the editor of the *Bookseller* on 20 June 1978, that at The Bodley Head this was due

> to our taking a big share with our newly joined group partners in the building of a modern and efficient warehouse and a most up-to-date expensive computer (which meant running two distribution organ-isations and two computers at the same time) and also establishing a new formula for stock evaluation ... The Bodley Head has been making steady profits for the thirty years before 1975 [Max told Alan Wicks its 1974 turnover had topped £1 million for the first time[27]]

and resumed making a profit again in 1976. 1975 was the only year that we have shown a loss.

Yet even as the group's profits continued to rise, and with them its prestige (in 1980 and again in 1981 the three firms were voted Publishers of the Year by the Booksellers' Association), there were often notes of sadness and tiredness in Max's voice.

Bow Street needed repair and his team needed more room; he tried to lease 7–8 Bow Street but could not get consent from the Covent Garden Town Planning Council to use that basement for warehousing; when he later tried to rent 57–9 Long Acre/Floral Street the building went to a hotel chain. Then there was a union problem. At the beginning of February 1972 a letter had come from the Society of Graphical and Allied Trades (Sogat) asking Max to meet union representatives with the possibility of having his staff unionized. Max was intolerant of committees, bureaucracy and especially of unions. Keeping control of things was as important to him as giving his editors their head.

According to Euan Cameron even in the good years The Bodley Head paid in 'the bottom third of publishers' and the pension plan (run through Lowndes Associates in conjunction with the Scottish Widow's Fund and Life Assurance Society) was terrible. It provided people over thirty who had been with the firm for more than a year with life insurance and a pension of 40 per cent of their salary on retirement at 65. Margaret Clark said Max had promised his older staff that he would substantially raise their salaries in their last year with the firm so as to pump up their pensions.[28] What no one seems to have considered was what would happen if Max were no longer there when they came to retire. There was no profit sharing scheme for staff as there was at some publishers. Along with low salaries and pensions, this left most of the staff, especially the senior staff, financially vulnerable.

Many of the original team had lived through the war and the difficult years that followed; Margaret Clark said they were used to a different standard of living to the generation that followed. In the 1970s she still thought of Max as her protector and of her colleagues as a family working together to produce books of social and literary value. The staff may have noted that Max's stinginess with their salaries was in inverse proportion to his generosity as a host, but they were of a generation not accustomed to talk about money. Even Euan Cameron, who was younger than Clark, thought that if he and those who came in the mid-sixties had wanted to make a name for themselves (and thereby more money) they would have left after a few years.[29] But most had preferred to stay and in 1972

Max simply told A.E. Powell at Sogat that he was unable to invite him to
Bow Street because no room was large enough to hold his staff; if Powell
wanted to invite all 60 of them to his own office, Max would distribute
the invitation.[30]

With the merger many salaries were raised, including Max's – to
£10,000 supplemented by his wizardry with expense accounts. The new
service group warehouse at Grantham was unionized, and in January
1975 The Bodley Head hired a publicity designer who was, unbeknown
to Max, a member of the National Union of Journalists. By that April
it was clear that the fellow did not get along with the rest of the staff
and when he was given two weeks' notice with an additional two weeks'
wages to leave, the NUJ charged The Bodley Head with having dismissed
him for union activities. Max refused to have anything to do with the
case. He hired a QC, told Taylor 'You handle that',[31] and left with Joan
for his usual February holiday in Barbados.

In *Logos* Euan Cameron tells of going to Frankfurt with Max at about
the same time. Max walked quickly through the fair complaining 'let's
get out of here', then intimated it was unlikely they would 'be sullied' at
the restaurant he took Cameron to 'by any of the riff-raff selling or buying rights at the Fair'. For all his continued geniality to booksellers, Max
had certainly never liked Frankfurt and as Cameron says was mostly concerned with greeting his friends at publishing events. But photographs
of him in the mid-seventies show more than a disillusionment with a
publishing process of which he had become increasingly tired. There
was a little flush in his face not evident a few years earlier, and pouches
beginning under the eyes. A couple of years later he confided to Roger
Straus (who enjoyed Frankfurt) that to go to Stockholm 'I would have to
starve myself for a week in order to get into my white tie suit.'[32]

Even in the note he wrote to Straus in 1975 after stopping in New
York on his way home from Barbados he seems to lack his old enthusiasm. Harry Willetts's translation of *Lenin in Zurich* was superb and Max
thought relations with Solzhenitsyn were better, although they would
never be easy – Max's letters and memos about Solzhenitsyn over the
next decade are scattered with phrases like 'it would be nice if you were
loved by Alexander Solzhenitsyn' and 'I don't think we ought to do anything that might upset Solzhenitsyn, whether it is reasonable for him to
be upset or not.' The novel, he told Straus, 'altogether will have cost us
quite a bit of money and I don't think that we shall earn it but let us hope
that we will reap our due rewards in the future'.[33] Soon after, he asked
Anthony Quayle to resign from the board to make room for younger
working members and when he talked about Quayle's early association

with Sybil Thorndike and Lewis Casson, which had led to Shaw becoming his first signed author, he discovered that things had so changed 'very few directors knew of this past history'.[34]

The Sogat case against The Bodley Head was dismissed in June but unionization continued to be talked about and Max continued to have related problems. As Cameron predicted, the young were moving from job to job to make their names and were, as a consequence, in a position to negotiate higher salaries; in the staff files the salary differences at The Bodley Head are blatant. According to Margaret Clark, Max would say to the new staff, 'Let's keep this between ourselves.' But word got around and it created bad feelings among the loyal old guard.[35]

By March 1976 The Bodley Head had options for *October 1916* and *March 1917* and even though Collins was giving everyone the impression they were to be Solzhenitsyn's publisher, The Bodley Head had no trouble securing the English language rights to the texts of both a television and radio interview Solzhenitsyn gave the BBC. The interviews created a stir, and when the *Listener's* condensation ran out, Max quickly sold 30,000 copies of his edition, a small booklet similar in appearance to the Nobel Prize lecture.

And there was still the old pleasure of dealing with those authors who were his friends. Before he left for Crete in June 1977 for the two weeks of sea and sun which he hoped would temporarily relieve his back pain, Max wrote to Greene to say that Jill Black would be 'looking after *The Human Factor* on my behalf'. Her corrections were couched gently in the royal 'we' and included such important and charming details as: 'whooping cough is fairly rare in Britain now. Presumably Sam has had the original triple injection which every small child normally has, but also it is not necessary to stay in bed with whooping cough, though there is a six week quarantine.' At the end of four long pages, Max carefully added: 'This is the result of our combined wisdom, some of which you will see I cannot know very much about myself, but the suggestions are put forward for you to consider and decide upon as you wish.'[36]

That November Alistair Cooke came to launch *Six Men* and although Max disliked the celebrity climate that was engulfing the selling of books, he appreciated its results and his team organized the necessary parties, book-signings and television appearances that Cooke did so well. When Charlie Chaplin died on Christmas day 1977 Max had already commissioned Oona Chaplin to write her autobiography. 'Charlie was her life, and when he died she came apart', he said.[37] He wrote to Greene that 'all the children, except the youngest boy, have left home, the house runs itself with the excellent servants she has, and she has always been so busy looking after Charlie, privately and in his business affairs, that she may be feeling a little lost. Let's see what we can do. I am convinced that not only will we get a very good book once she gets going properly, but it will also be a great help to her.'[38]

The Human Factor was published on 16 March 1978 and remained at the top of the *Sunday Times* bestseller list for almost a year. But in November Avon issued their American paperback three months earlier than agreed and in order to protect themselves Penguin had to do the same in Britain, cutting into Max's hardback sales. 'There has been a palace revolution' at Penguin he told Greene, 'and the chief executive with whom we made our original agreement, Tony Mott, has now left.'[39] Even the proof copies Max had printed were being sold at high prices as first editions by second-hand dealers. Where did that leave their first edition revenues?

14
Mistakes

As de Bellaigue has shown, the group reached the 1980s in pretty good financial shape and 'when the recession of 1980 hit the publishing industry, a near-lethal combination of galloping domestic inflation and surging sterling, Chatto, Bodley Head & Jonathan Cape stayed triumphantly profitable [although] at the operating level, before contributions from Triad, all three companies were loss-making in 1980.'[1]

Max was not worried about The Bodley Head's finances, although manufacturing costs had spiralled, institutional buying was going down, interest rates were high and far too many books were being published, most of which in his opinion were of no value whatever. In America things were worse, he told Alix Meynell. 'The conglomerates intervene and are making everyone's life a misery. There are very few small independent firms left, and the conglomerates buy and sell publishing companies without any regard to the human factor.'[2] But several things occurred that year which changed everything at The Bodley Head.

On 3 September, Judy Taylor told Max she was leaving at the end of December, 'giving up my seat on the Board, the holding company Board and the Australian and Canadian company Boards'. She was moving to Gloucestershire with her new husband, Richard Hough. Although Taylor has never given any other reason for her departure, she disliked the day-to-day changes the merger had brought perhaps more than Max. 'You could sense what was happening as you went along. The three houses began to lose their individuality, then everything became impersonalized. You could see it everywhere in little things like the loss of your own trade counter. The books were at Grantham and if you wanted one you could no longer just go and get it; if you gave the copy on your shelf to an author it took weeks to replace.'[3]

Max knew some of 'the disastrous results to firms bought by conglomerates, disastrous for both parties: sacking of staff at short notice, cancelled contracts and thereby loss of authors', he told the *Bookseller* on 20 June 1978.

Estimates for budgets, turnover, expected subsidiary rights benefits, cash flow and so on can only be of use to experienced publishers whose purpose must be to find interesting books and establish close relationships with their authors, and ... this cannot be done by backroom boys far removed from the scene of operation ... The sad tales of disorganisation caused by sackings of staff with their own tragic consequences are too numerous to give any encouragement to impersonal management.

He continued to believe that publishing was best managed by publishers and as the decade changed he felt 'a warning ... due to those who may fall for the apparent attractions of joining non-publishing groups; they may get their fingers badly burned'.

The merger with Chatto and Cape had so far spared The Bodley Head such disasters but Taylor's departure left the firm vulnerable in a different way. She had been at Max's side from the first and he was unhappy in what he called 'the new world of publishing with its auctions and cost efficiency'.[4] Not having Taylor around on a daily basis was very difficult for him and far more unsettling than his gentlemanly code allowed him to say. 'I know I let Max down' Taylor admitted, 'but to give him his credit, he never said anything. He had great faith in me and it would have been an enormous compliment to [run the company] but I couldn't do that coming in three days a week so I decided to leave.'[5] It would be thirty years to the day she had been hired. From January 1981 she would come to the office one day a month and the rest of the time work from home on children's books. She would be paid £5000 as a consultant director with the promise of more money if she worked longer, and in that capacity she continued to give Max advice and to help where she could.

Ian Parsons died on 29 October 1980, leaving Norah Smallwood, who was herself seriously afflicted by arthritis (she died in 1984) in charge of Chatto & Windus. Because Chatto was financially the weakest of the group, arrangements were quickly begun to bring Carmen Callil in to co-manage that firm with Hugo Brunner. With Callil the profitable Virago came into the group although Callil, Harriet Spicer (her original secretary) and Ursula Owen (who had come to Virago later) were so concerned that their imprint not suffer in the amalgamation, it took a year before the agreement with the service company was finalized, in February 1982, and the group's name changed to Chatto, Virago, Bodley Head & Jonathan Cape. Callil became a member of the holding company board, and was named non-executive chairman in the new Virago structure. While co-managing Chatto, she continued to be responsible for the Virago Modern Classics list, leaving Spicer and Owen to jointly manage Virago.

Callil and Max had an immediate liking for one another. As Max had worked in his family's business in his youth, Callil had worked as a student in her uncles' clothing firm in Melbourne, including in its accounts department. Like Max, she had been influenced by her uncles' approach to business and she enjoyed the financial aspects of publishing. Perhaps more importantly, Max appreciated Callil's absorption in her work. Callil told Sue Bradley that Virago 'was my life, it wasn't part of it'[6] and The Bodley Head had been Max's for almost thirty years.

In the summer of 1981 Max had hired David Machin as his joint managing director. Machin had been an editor and a literary agent, moved to Jonathan Cape in 1970 for eight years, the first seven as an editorial director and the last one as deputy managing director, then headed the Society of Authors. There he and Max had exchanged letters about Michael Holroyd's biography of Shaw and Dan Laurence's editions of Shaw's work. Max had told Machin over lunch one day that James Michie was leaving and Machin had 'seized upon that and said if I ever needed anybody I was to think of him ... He had been a literary agent and he liked the new world of publishing better than I did. He followed up with a letter saying that he meant his offer quite seriously, that he wanted to leave the Society of Authors and if there was a place at The Bodley Head he would very much like to come.'[7] Machin said their discussions 'went well, as indeed did my first two or three years with Max. Then his health, which wasn't good from the start, deteriorated, and I'm afraid I found the relationship with him increasingly difficult.'[8]

Max claimed that 'a lot of people did not see eye to eye with Machin once he began to work', and gave as a ready example how soon he had to stop Machin from getting rid of John Ryder. Literary agents were another sticky point. American publishers had wooed agents for decades. James Michie had tried to get Max to do the same, but Max 'was very cagey about agents', Michie said. 'His attitude was a hangover from the old days.' Agents moved into the publishing process nonetheless, and as they did Max became even more protective of his relationships with authors. At a welcoming party for Muriel Spark at the Garrick in 1981 Max was upset when after dinner she left his side at the table to sit with

Michie, who would be her editor and was the reason she had brought *Loitering with Intent* to The Bodley Head. Michie said 'when Max left he was a little drunk and when I helped him into a taxi he said "James, you know everything about people and everything about words, and nothing about business".' At the time Michie 'could not understand why Max was so jealous. There was no other word for it.' He realized later that Max's jealousy came from the importance to his person of his close bond with his authors.[9]

André Deutsch disliked agents too, because they had access to the same pool of literary talent as publishers without having to spend capital in the hungry process of manufacturing and selling books. He was especially angry when agents moved his authors to bigger publishers who could afford to pay them more after he had nurtured them. Max appreciated his authors' loyalty as much as Deutsch but his fear was more personal, his uneasiness reflecting the very relationship between publishers and writers. As Diana Athill has said, they need each other and 'no doubt all writers know in their heads that publishers, having invested much money and work in their books, deserve to make a reasonable profit; but I'm sure that nearly all of them feel in their hearts that whatever their books earn ought to belong to them alone.'[10]

For Max the relationship was a little more complicated. He had fitted into British publishing and British society by recasting himself as an English gentleman, or perhaps more correctly, by living in the way that his old schoolmasters at the English High School in Istanbul had cast him. He knew the advantage of being among people he called 'distinguished' and given the chance would talk about himself through them. In October 1980 when he was still on the council at RADA, the queen (who with her mother was a patron) and the Duke of Edinburgh were to come to the school for an afternoon and Max had forgotten to reply that he would attend. When questioned, he said: 'I was not aware that I had to say if I wanted to be present at the Academy on the 19th of November ... In fact, I first met the Queen and the Duke at the first night of My Fair Lady, when I presented her with a specially bound copy of the book, and they kindly invited me and my wife to join them for a drink in their box in the interval. So we can pick up the link with the Academy in a personal way.'[11]

When his son-in-law Andrew Gammon was setting up a tax accountancy business later in the eighties Max told him to get 'the "best" clients even if they didn't have large accounts'. Gammon took his advice but could not understand what he called 'Max's obsession with his reputation'.[12] Michie did. 'Poor, tender Max', Michie said thinking back to the dinner for Spark. 'Max was afraid of anyone coming between him and his authors.'[13] His relationship with his authors *was* his reputation. In many respects he behaved as a good agent does today, entertaining authors, taking an interest in their private lives and performing endless favours for them, financial and otherwise. But there was one difference; by the 1980s agents were doing in Britain what had long been customary in America, auctioning books to the highest bidder after a circus of multiple submissions. The practice changed the currency between writer and publisher from patronage and artistic control to hard cash, and Max, who was the most generous of friends, could not stomach the rawness of the new environment. It was one of the reasons he hired Machin – to do it for him. Max also baulked at the large advances agents were demanding for their writers, insisting the money went mostly to the taxman and would bankrupt independent publishing houses; according to Eric de Bellaigue, in 1985 alone 'the group's increase in advances to authors amounted to £345,000'.[14] Although Max may have been in part right about the long-term effects on independent publishers, his authors clearly appreciated being better paid.

When Graham Greene's niece, Louise Dennys, became a partner in Toronto's Lester and Orpen Dennys in 1979 she wrote on the announcement of the imprint which she sent to Hugh Greene that she was hoping some day to sell a book to The Bodley Head. Soon after, on holiday with her husband and sister in the South of France, she commissioned her uncle Graham to do *Ways of Escape*. He had wanted never to write a memoir of his adult life because he thought any such endeavour would 'infringe the copyright of other people's lives'. So she editorially pulled together pieces he had written in introductions to his novels and elsewhere to form 'a kind of writer's autobiography', as she termed it.

In the tradition of publishing, if an editor commissions a book the rights are then held by that publisher, so Greene gave her world English-language rights to *Ways of Escape*, which carried a responsibility to act on his behalf (essentially as his agent) in those countries. This put her

in the position of selling the UK rights to Max – and then negotiating him up – higher, Graham told me, than he had offered before for a book of Graham's … I repeated that process in the US in a book auction involving the three publishers who had published him there, Doubleday, Viking and Simon & Schuster. Michael Korda won the book for Simon & Schuster and there too the bargaining went to a higher level than had previously been paid for any of Graham's books. As a result of our working together on *Ways of Escape*, Graham

gained a closer understanding of the traditional publishing relationships between the USA and UK and Canada ... and following that
book, he fought back Max's arguments that Canada should continue
to remain a part of his fiefdom ... Since [Graham] had been an editor
and a publisher himself, he swiftly saw a very real value of publication by a Canadian house, which ensured he received full domestic
royalties instead of 'export edition' royalties that are traditionally half
the amount.[15]

* * *

On 12 May 1981 Ralph asked Max from Toronto, 'What is on the miss in
Bow Street, what agog in Pelham?' On the surface it seemed like nothing
much. Machin was hired. Agents were dealt with. Dan Laurence's *Complete Musical Criticism* by Shaw was finished. John Dreyfus's *The History
of The Nonesuch Press* was published in a fine limited edition, appropriately launched and quickly sold out. It was followed by an exhibition
of Nonesuch books at the St Bride Printing Library. Solzhenitsyn's *The
Love-Girl and the Innocent* was retranslated by Kitty Hunter Blair and
Jeremy Brooks and would start a successful run with the Royal Shakespeare Company in September 1981. The reputation of the Georgette
Heyer Historical Novel Prize was rising on the international success of
Valerie Fitzgerald's *Zemindar*. Sales for the third of Helen Forrester's auto-
biographical sequence, *By the Waters of Liverpool*, were impressive. Things
were in place for Max to publish the official record of the Pope's visit
(scheduled for 1982), and *Loitering with Intent* was short listed for the
Booker. But was something even then amiss?

When Virago joined the group in 1982 (the year pre-tax group profits
peaked at £929,000 on a turnover of £13.3 million) Callil promised her
partners and authors that the new arrangement would bring 'full sales
and distribution service throughout the world and a distribution and
warehouse system of exceptional efficiency and other services too dreary
to list here'. She saw pretty fast that 'it cost Virago more to publish a
book through the service company than it had when we were alone'.
In fact, the overheads on CVBC books were double those of some rival
publishers.[16]

By then Max too had come to realize that the service company was
'irresponsibly run financially. Whatever we made from books was simply
put into a joint kitty at the National Westminster, which was large for
quite a while when the companies were prosperous. Everyone took out
what they needed to pay advances for the future list. The problem was

that when the kitty got smaller and each company kept taking money without telling the others, no one knew what was happening until the financial statements arrived months later.'[17] As Callil put it, 'You'd think you'd bought a book that would make money then all of a sudden some overhead came in.'[18] According to de Bellaigue the 'central overheads gave the individual companies control over less than half the overheads they bore'.[19]

The result was that between 1982 and 1986, with inflation running at 4.8 per cent, the selling and distribution costs of the service company fell a percentage point but the administrative and editorial costs rose nearly 5 per cent, raising the total operating costs of CVBC as a percentage of turnover from 36.6 per cent to 40.2 per cent.[20] In May 1984 Max bravely told an Australian reporter that the early 1980s were not 'so unhappy as some have declared' but rather 'a little pause, the result of foolish over-production in the seventies when a lot of people thought that one could publish any old thing'.[21] He was not alone in thinking a central problem in the industry was overproduction; by the mid-1980s the shelf life of an ordinary novel had shortened to four weeks or less.

But the real problem was that like Chatto and Cape, The Bodley Head relied on expensive hardbacks for its profits while the public had come to want paperbacks at a third to half the price. Triad had failed to give the group a strong paperback presence and to make matters worse, library purchases (the bread and butter of any quality publisher) had fallen sharply; Max had relied on them for years. Even Nonesuch was losing its market to trade paperback reprints. Except at Virago, where the paperback Modern Classics continued to rise in popularity, without a successful paperback arm the group was unable to increase volume sales. So as the UK book market recovered from the mid-1980s (its annual sales rising 12 per cent by 1987 and, according to Tony Willis, publishing analyst at stockbrokers, L. Messel, its profitability by eight times), CVBC seriously floundered.[22]

A small part of Max's worry is shown in a 1983 internal memo about Louise Dennys's new Canadian firm. 'If our new Agents cannot sell what is supposed to be a best seller well enough we will always have the competition of Louise Dennys who has proved that she can do better than we can. I am told she has sold 15,000 copies of Graham Greene's Ways of Escape and I wonder if you could find out how many copies she sold of Monsignor Quixote. If we don't do as well as she does (and she is distributed by Penguins as you know) we may lose some important authors like William Trevor.'

According to Guido Waldman, in the champagne years 'a literary text that breached the 3000 barrier was considered to be a success; and if a paperback house was ready to advance £1000 for paperback rights in a mid-list book, we felt amply satisfied. But this was still in the days before the literary agents had got the bit between their teeth.' Now Max and his partners needed larger volume sales and when in March 1983 Granada was sold to Collins and the group bought back its own shares at nearly £271,000 (which raised Max's holding in CVBC to 44 per cent), it was decided that Triad should be wound down and a better arrangement made for paperbacking the group's books.[23]

* * *

There was the success of Peter Dickinson's *Hindsight* that year, the prizewinning crime writer having moved to The Bodley Head from Hodder the year before with *The Last House-Party*. *The Other Man*, Greene's conversations with Marie-Françoise Allain, was doing well; *Monsignor Quixote* had continued to sell steadily and would soon be turned into a highly successful film with Alec Guinness and Leo McKern. Maurice Sendak's Glydebourne designs for Prokofiev's *The Love for Three Oranges* were published, the first of Sendak's books to originate outside the United States. Greene's *Getting to Know the General* was planned for 1984, along with Muriel Spark's *The Only Problem*, Irving Stone's *Camille Pissarro* and William Trevor's *Fools of Fortune*, which would mark his commercial breakthrough in America.

But some likely authors began to go elsewhere. Guido Waldman felt certain that had Max remained fully in charge The Bodley Head would have had Primo Levi's *The Periodic Table* and Tom Clancy's *The Hunt for Red October*, both of which he regretted losing. And the potentially best-selling autobiography that Max had been trying to get Mrs Gandhi to write since the late 1970s did not come through. In February 1983 when Judy Taylor was on a trip to India with her husband, who was writing a book about Mountbatten, Max asked her to spur Mrs Gandhi on. The Bodley Head had been Nehru's publisher for decades; Max had met him and his daughter in London in 1960, and visited Nehru at his invitation a couple of years later. He had helped Richard Attenborough secure permission to use much of Nehru's material in his Oscar winning film about Gandhi. He had then published Attenborough's *In Search of Gandhi* in December 1982, timing the book for the North American release of the film. The book and a reprint of Nehru's autobiography had sold very well on the film's massive success and Max thought its popularity and the resulting increased sales of her father's book might finally draw ink from Mrs Gandhi's pen. But she told Taylor she had never kept any notes 'and memory so often plays false'. Odd, Taylor reported to Max, considering everything they said was 'written down by Mr H.Y. Sharada Prasad who seems to organize her life and has worked for her from the beginning'.[24]

Increasing volume sales continued to be a group problem and on 23 June Max wrote to Gordon Graham at Butterworth in search of 'a suitable company to market HFL books in a better way than we do at present'. Max said he needed someone to consult on production, someone to whom he could leave the promotion and selling of the books. By October Butterworth had offered to buy HFL and by the end of the year Max had sorted out the financial flexibility he needed and his pension concerns and told Gordon Graham enigmatically 'there was a possibility'.[25]

* * *

On 10 October 1983 Ralph died. In mid-September he had gone to play tennis at Lords, dressed in his spotless whites, but not been able to move around the court much. A few days later he had the first of two strokes, concealing both from everyone until he had to be taken to King Edward VII Hospital. Veronica remembered coming home the day he died and seeing Max slumped on his desk. But only briefly. Joan quickly closed the door and told her 'your father wants to be alone for a while'.[26]

The public tributes for Ralph were understandably many, both at the memorial service held on 17 November at Westminster Abbey, and in the press. Max kept all the clippings and among them a copy of something far more touching. It was a letter he had written on 4 June 1973 to The Bodley Head's Australian agent Ken Wilder. Ralph was about to arrive in Sydney to play *Lloyd George Knew My Father* and Max said he 'would be most grateful for anything you can do for him'. As though Ralph needed introducing, Max assured Wilder

> that when you meet him you will be enchanted by him ... I want you to know that Ralph Richardson is my oldest and best friend, and in fact was the architect of my small firm joining forces with The Bodley Head many years ago. In addition, apart from his career in the theatre, he is an experienced binder, and was in fact a binder's apprentice many years ago ... His last trip to Australia many years ago was a huge success, and he was marvellous so far as his publishing activities were concerned because he kept popping into all kinds of bookshops saying: 'My name is Richardson. I am a publisher. Have

you got any of our books here?' It wasn't an act. He knows about books, cares a lot about them, and has read a great many of them. I am sure he will want to do the same again, and he will want to do it in his own, unrehearsed, but most effective way.[27]

Then in February 1984 Tom Maschler and Graham C. Greene asked Max to sell them some of his shares 'to prevent them going to Joan and the girls should something happen to me'. Since Max's daughters 'were not likely to be interested in publishing', he agreed to sell Greene and Maschler half his shares. 'I realized pretty fast that I was very foolish to agree, although at the time it seemed a reasonable request. I was 69.'[28]

This second buyback cost the group another £254,250 (339,000 shares at 75p each), a price considered fitting by Spicer and Pegler but which de Bellaigue later thought small. In return Max was confirmed as executive chair of The Bodley Head and joint chair of the group for at least another five years and the fee paid by the group for his services to HFL was increased. He was left with 25 per cent of the holding company, Greene and Maschler now having 21.2 per cent each. Greene has since said 'Max still had the controlling interest. He could still block anything. He insisted on keeping 25% for that reason but didn't seem to mind selling us the rest.'[29] Of course Max's 25 per cent was not a controlling interest if Greene and Maschler joined forces. Aside from the fact that Max was still feeling low from Ralph's death when he sold them the shares, his compliance indicates that whatever his concerns about the service company he still trusted Greene, or at least he agreed with Greene's logic that it would be better for the company to have such a large block of shares coming on the market then than in the event of his own death.

By all accounts David Machin was 'weak' in his dealings with Graham C. Greene. Margaret Clark and Jill Black both thought so. Callil liked Machin but said 'Tom and Graham did not value Max.'[30] Max said, 'Machin was very friendly with young Graham, and I guess that even though David worked for me he realized Graham was really running things.'[31] As de Bellaigue has said, pretty quickly a 'genuine feeling developed at Chatto, Bodley Head and Virago that the business was run for Cape. It was even suggested that the central sales force favoured Cape titles over others. There was firmer evidence that Cape men and women fared better when rationalization issues arose.'[32]

This soon began in earnest. Max's lease at Bow Street was due for re-examination and he had known for some time that the Covent Garden Opera House had its eye on the whole block. 'Keeping each imprint at a separate address was expensive and Graham suggested that we could economize by taking a 25-year lease on 32 Bedford Square, the premises adjoining the Cape building at Number 30. That building would be refurbished for Cape and we could move into their old building. I didn't like the idea but the debt was getting huge. I had never had a debt like that before.'[33]

In September 1984 the sale of HFL went as most of Max's business deals did – entirely without fuss and with a sense of fun. Gordon Graham recalled that after 'Max said there was a possibility' of his selling HFL, 'there was no correspondence. Then at one of the book trade's functions where Max and I generally met (we were not close friends), he touched my shoulder and said "ready when you are". I think I recall correctly that we valued the copyrights and inventory at £100,000. It was settled with one meeting in the Butterworth Boardroom, followed by champagne.'[34] To Butterworth went the publication rights in HFL books in print and under contract and Max kept the name HFL as a trading company under his own control.

Max's correspondence with the National Westminster Bank shows that by the beginning of October there were serious cash flow problems within CVBC. 'We seem to have got into a bit of a muddle', he admitted to Ken Haywood, the manager at Lombard Street, on 2 October. Shortly after this the group was given an overdraft for 1985, which had to be increased in February, by which time the group was not generating enough profit to cover the interest, let alone repay the sums it was borrowing.

Max was extremely worried. He thought it important for greater control to be exercised over the individual companies, and suggested each be allocated a specific portion of the overall facility. In the past he had rarely appeared flustered to his staff; now he was openly complaining about the expense of the refurbishments at 32 Bedford Square which, along with extending the Grantham warehouse, was adding hugely to the overheads. He was not alone in his concern. According to de Bellaigue, Liz Calder, who would soon leave Cape to set up Bloomsbury, thought the expenditure at 32 'a very bad move .... Ursula Owen says it gave the signal that overheads were out of control',[35] and the accounting system was still not working anywhere near well enough for the competitive and fluctuating publishing environment they were in.

Nonetheless, that April The Bodley Head left Covent Garden and established itself unhappily in Number 30 Bedford Square and the service company fully occupied 9 Bow Street. It was a huge upheaval and Max was very upset by it and visibly unwell. With the move the balance of power shifted tangibly. Carmen Callil said 'Graham and Tom did not treat Max well. I felt they both patronized him.'[36]

Max's major literary concern that summer was that Harry Willetts had not finished his revision of Solzhenitsyn's *August 1914* or begun to translate *October 1916* because his sister was ill. Publication had to be delayed. 'If we give him any more stress than he has already, we can only expect further delays', Max wrote to Roger Straus. 'I do not even want to ... cause him more worry and stress.' He expected both books by the end of the summer and looked forward to being able to get them into print 'but let us reach that happy stage first'.[37] Of more concern was the rising bank overdraft and the financial restructuring plan the group was awaiting from Spicer and Pegler.

* * *

On 9 September, after a meeting in the boardroom at the top of Number 32, Max suffered a massive heart attack. At the meeting everyone had been told about the winding down of Triad and a new agreement that had been made with Pan to paperback titles on a 50/50 basis. Margaret Clark was very angry because she had not been told anything about the Pan arrangement in advance, and the existing one in which her children's books were published by Puffin she thought excellent for both The Bodley Head and its authors. Max, she said, 'didn't seem to know what was going on'. As they made their way back to Number 30 he told her he had had a dreadful argument with Greene just before the meeting. He went into his room at the front of the building and she found out next day what had happened.[38]

Jill Black was told on her way up to her office that Max had collapsed, been found by a secretary, and that Greene had sent for an ambulance. He had rung Joan who remembered that when she got to Bedford Square 'Graham said the ambulance had gone. He thought to Middlesex Hospital. I waited alone at the hospital for two hours not knowing if Max would live. I was afraid to telephone Alexandra. Eventually I rang Veronica to say what had happened in case Max died.'[39]

But he did not die and everybody at Bedford Square carried on. Max had open heart surgery on 7 October to replace his aortic valve with one made from pigskin. James Michie said he 'took it with grace and stoicism when he was obviously unwell and very worried about the firm, the loans, the people'.[40] Max seemed to recover well from the surgery, which in 1985 was far longer, more complicated and dangerous than it is today, but feeling in any case not at home in Bedford Square, he worked thereafter mostly from Pelham Crescent. By November the bank overdraft had been capped at £3 million with an excess of £600,000 for six months to get the group through the peak financing period in March and April when royalty payments were due. The arrangement came with questions from the bank about whether royalty advances were recoverable should things get worse, and since Doris Lessing had not won the Booker Prize as had been expected, would there be a significant effect on trading forecasts for the year?

'We needed money', Max said. 'Our overheads were too high for the turnover we had. Even before 1985, long before my surgery, I had predicted this would happen if there was not tight financial control at the centre of the group. But they wouldn't listen to me.'[41] So Max quietly began to find a new way on his own; on 26 November 1985 he changed the name of HFL to Reinhardt Books.

The year ended with an operating loss at Chatto of £172,000, at Cape of £292,000, at The Bodley Head of £129,000, and at Virago of £5000. 'Our position was not so bad really. It was certainly much better than Cape's and Chatto's', Max said. 'Virago was in the best position because of the enormous interest in women's writing, although the Covent Garden bookshop which Carmen opened was a financial disaster.'[42] According to the *Independent*, after accounting for interest and other charges the final retained loss for 1985 was £508,000.[43]

By January 1986 the Australian property had been mortgaged and now there was an attempt to mortgage the building in Grantham for about half its £600,000 forced sale valuation. Max went to Gstaad for a short holiday and wrote to Straus on 4 February 1986 that 'it snowed most of the time and rained for a further twenty-four hours but the hotel was comfortable and I was able to start swimming again which I did with much pleasure twice a day, so I feel very much refreshed'. It was then back to business. Harry Willetts was caring for his dying sister and his Solzhenitsyn translation remained unfinished. Max assured Straus he was 'quite confident that [Willetts] is doing his utmost to let us have it as quickly as possible. When we get it, you will get it too, but as far as we are concerned, we will only make definite plans when it is in our hands.'

Soon the Putnam aeronautical list was sold to Conway Maritime and The Bodley Head's six Agatha Christie titles (*Poirot Investigates*, *The Secret Adversary*, *The Secret of Chimneys*, *Murder on the Links*, *The Man in the Brown Suit* and *The Mysterious Affair at Styles*) to Collins. 'Things haven't worked out exactly as I had planned' Max told Alix Meynell on 7 February 1986. He 'was pretty sure the situation would mean a large investor taking a stake in the company, which would dilute our control, or an out and out takeover, so I began to talk with Penguin to see what arrangement could be made'.[44] The difference in tone between Greene's correspondence with the bank at this time (which was formal and humourless) and Max's (which was friendly and rarely without mention of lunch at the Garrick) is revealing of their different ways of doing business. It also indicates, as Callil said, that Greene was making the decisions and they must have weighed heavily on him.

On 11 March 1986 the board decided that the Virago shop was to be sold, group stock to be reduced and a monitoring system developed to allow John Hews to keep closer control on revenue expenditures. By then the overdraft was close to the £3 million cap and Greene needed to ask for an increase of £855,000 for the next six months. The bank's response was that there might be a problem, so it was decided on 21 March that The Bodley Head would have to move into 32 Bedford Square and to share copyediting, production, design, publicity and rights services with Cape. The firms would remain separate, with Machin and Greene as their managing directors, but there would be redundancies.

Greene reported to the bank at the beginning of April that although what they were doing was drastic it maintained the group's basic philosophy while cutting its overheads and the pressure on its cash resources, but The Bodley Head directors said 'a move of the editorial department to 32 Bedford Square would virtually signal the end of the imprint: the practical result is that no agent or author is going to address any manuscript to any publisher other than Cape'.[45] Certainly when the newspapers got wind of the proposed move many reported that Cape was taking over. Max did his best to squash the rumours, and asked the papers to correct them so that his authors and staff would not be worried, but Euan Cameron's handwritten letter to David Machin of 28 March speaks for everyone's anger and shock. 'Did you really think I would accept what amounts to a No. 2 job … within Rupert Lancaster's department [at Cape]?' When he was unable to convince Greene that The Bodley Head's publicity department should not be joined with Cape's, he left the firm saying: 'I appreciate that cuts and drastic action are needed, even if I cannot see why The Bodley Head is being made the sacrificial Lamb, and why Cape personnel are appointed as heads of the newly merged departments in every case.'[46] Cameron had three children under fourteen at the time and was understandably alarmed. To Max he wrote sadly that after 21 years 'I shall miss you and your style of publishing more than I can say … but frankly, I am not enthusiastic about the new structure and you know yourself that life has never been quite the same since we left Bow Street.'[47]

Rather than attend his farewell party, Max took Cameron out for lunch. William Trevor had pleaded with Max not to let Cameron go and Max had replied that he wanted him to stay, giving up publicity and continuing with his editorial work. But when it came to Cameron's departure it was Hugh and Graham Greene who made sure his severance, which would otherwise have kept his family going for only six to nine months, was doubled; as a further favour Greene gave him an interview for the *Independent*, which put Cameron in line for other journalistic work. He did not resent Max; he believed it was Max's poor health that caused him to withdraw. Cameron had heard from David Machin about his redundancy late on Good Friday afternoon after he had returned from Mass. This was not Max's way of doing things. Still, over the next year Max's absence from Bedford Square and seeming indifference to the financial position of his senior staff caused many hard feelings, and brings to memory Judy Taylor's story of the day her Hoover broke in the early years. Max said simply that 'the redundancies were terrible. Nothing like that had ever happened at The Bodley Head.'[48]

* * *

When Francis Meynell had died in 1975, his widow Alix Meynell had taken over the chairmanship of Nonesuch. In May 1986 she asked Max if he would like to buy the firm; Max replied he would be 'delighted' to have Reinhardt Books take it over with 'all the rights that The Nonesuch Press have got, and the right to use the Nonesuch name' for £5000, in order to protect the press and to 'save you a certain amount of trouble' and accountant's fees. He said he had no particular plans for Nonesuch but if it proved 'more profitable than I expect, and we put the name to some good honourable use, then I would suggest that you receive, in addition, a bonus afterwards'. He later wrote to her that he had 'no intention of parting with Nonesuch which I am buying because I feel that even in a small way it is part of my publishing story'.[49] There was little discussion. On 5 November Max, Joan, Alix Meynell, John Hews (who would become a director and the Nonesuch secretary), Martin Zander and John Ryder (who would be typographic consultant) met at Pelham Crescent at 11 a.m., signed the papers, had a glass of champagne, then lunched around the corner at Max's favourite restaurant.

But this celebration was still a few months away. In June 1986, the CVBC board agreed that Robert Gavron, one of Virago's early backers and someone Alix Meynell had earlier approached about buying Nonesuch, would negotiate to buy the Virago press and shop out of the group in an arrangement whereby the press would continue to use the group services and facilities. The group was by then overdrawn £3.4 million. Clipped as the minutes are, those of 10 June also state that The Bodley Head royalties of £480,000 were being held back and some agents were pressing for payment. This was a huge embarrassment for Max who always paid his bills on time. He suggested that since The Bodley Head had been 'seriously curtailed' by the move to Number 32 it might be good to sell the children's list, which by then included Cape's. Greene replied 'No.'

Whether Max was being ironic or making an unsentimental business decision is unclear. What is clear is that Greene did not want this plum out of his hands. De Bellaigue has wondered why Greene and Maschler wanted Max's shares in 1984 when 'this same board only a year earlier had chosen to magnify the potential threat posed by Max's holding by cancelling the Granada share?'[50] Here is another question. Why did the board refuse to sell the children's list when Max was offering an entirely reasonable, and what must have been for him very sad, solution to The Bodley Head's difficulty in paying its authors? In the minutes Callil closed the issue by telling Greene he 'should withdraw from the day-to-day management of Jonathan Cape and devote time to the group and be seen as neutral'.

Proud and private, Max's anger finally erupted. Following the meeting he wrote to Greene

> it is essential (and that is being done) that we have a report on our finances with the utmost urgency. If we are advised that we are unlikely to meet our liabilities as they fall due, the Company should not continue to trade. However, I am prepared to investigate any possible solution for restructuring our financial basis which we are professionally advised will give us a reasonable chance of survival. This would probably involve either a merchant bank or a big investor taking a stake in the Company and so diluting our control, or an out and out takeover by one of the larger publishing companies in which case we can only hope it will be one compatible in character with us. I do not think a rights issue or an increase of capital raised from among the shareholders themselves will produce enough to put the Company on its feet, and I would not make any investment in the Company at its present state of affairs. If there is no probable method of meeting the need for a massive injection of new capital, we must put in train the procedures for a creditors' winding up. I sincerely hope this will not be necessary.[51]

Max subsequently refused to join Greene in giving the bank a personal guarantee before the group's facility could be raised again. And when the board decided on 24 June to raise capital through a rights issue Max told Greene that 'we could not raise enough capital from among ourselves. He and Tom Maschler said I should invest more money in the company. "Why", I said. "We're losing money. We have to sell." I refused to take my allocation because we were in so much debt that I saw no future in the service company as it was, which was why I was trying to find another solution for The Bodley Head, like Virago was, and I advised the employees who were offered shares to do the same.'[52]

Greene says he told Max 'over and over that it was in his interest to support the issue',[53] but Max refused and his holding in the firm consequently sank to 11 per cent, which soon cost him his beloved Bodley Head and a great deal of money. 'Things were being done all the time without my being consulted', he told Eric de Bellaigue. 'I had the feeling I was being pushed around.'[54]

Those left at The Bodley Head worked on. The great corrected text of *Ulysses* was published. Max told David McKetterick at Cambridge 'I am so glad that you find our new Ulysses interesting. I have got so many editions of this damned book that I can only hope that this edition will sell as it cost us a lot of money, but I do not want to have to read it again.'[55] There was talk of the next volume of Solzhenitsyn's work. 'It is quite a sobering thought', Max told Straus, 'that it will be twice the size of October 1916. However, let us take that in our stride when the time comes … There is no doubt that Willetts has had a very rough time, and has given us an equally tough time as a result.'[56] The translation arrived in September and James Michie and Jill Black had reservations about it. 'There's a lot of line-by-line editorial work to be done … It's going to be a long, hard slog editorially before there's any thought of production.'[57] It was much longer than expected. Willetts would have to be paid extra and Max was waiting for other translators to do sample chapters of work Solzhenitsyn wanted redoing. He told Durand 'that we agree to publish March 1917 on similar terms to October 1916. Roger and I are in close touch about finding a translator for this volume of La Roue Rouge, but I take it from your letter that if we are satisfied that the translator we find is a good one, we can sign him or her up immediately, and not need to refer back to Alexander Solzhenitsyn.'[58]

If nothing else the letters regarding Solzhenitsyn show Max had every intention of carrying on as usual, whatever happened at CVBC. Roger Straus dropped by on his way back from Frankfurt and on 14 October 1986 Max told Peter Carson at Penguin Books that The Bodley Head and

Farrar Straus were going to edit *August 1914* at the same time, with Jill Black finishing the job in London after discussing things with Harry Willetts. This meant the American and British texts would be the same and be published simultaneously. Since Bantam proposed to publish their mass paperback edition a year after Farrar Straus's hard cover, Max thought that if Penguin would agree to do the same it would 'give us a better chance of selling the hard cover and trade paperback edition, and we could publish it at the same time as Farrar Straus and get quite a good sale for it here and abroad which would be to the benefit of both of us as we are partners on the whole venture'. He aimed for May or June, using the same picture on the jacket as that on the earlier edition with the new lettering: 'AUGUST 1914/The final expanded text of/ALEXANDER SOLZHENITSYN'S masterpiece, newly translated.' The response from Carson was very positive, and Max proposed producing *October 1916* and *March 1917* in the same way, as joint hard and paperback ventures. John Ryder would talk directly to Penguin's production manager to ensure that the page designs would reduce satisfactorily to B format and Penguin 'would share equally the design and copy editing overhead and also the U.K. share of the translation'.[59]

* * *

In *Publisher*, Tom Maschler says that when 'Max Reinhart' (whose name he misspells) 'refused to add capital to the firm, Graham talked to various banks and managed to raise the money. All that remained was for us to come up with the collateral. Graham and I agreed to go 50/50. My "total worth" as they say, was £250,000 and so Graham gave a bank guarantee on my behalf for the balance. I was left with the interest to worry about, which came to far more than my gross salary.'[60]

The rights issue raised £923,000 but the benefit was negated by the 1985 losses and those of the current year. The issue was very divisive within The Bodley Head and caused Max 'a lot of unhappiness. Graham and Tom put up most of the money – close to a million between them. John Hews bought 1000 shares because he was told it would look bad if the accountant of the distribution company did not invest. Barney Blackley on the other hand followed my advice and he was very, very cross with me when Graham and Tom sold the company and these shares became extremely valuable.'[61]

Maschler writes of his understandable fear about his personal financial situation, and his sleepless nights during the next six months as he and Greene tried to 'form various alliances but always came up against new obstacles ... I could see no way out. Graham was constantly optimistic, with City appointments I rarely attended.'[62] During these months the board continued to find money where it could. Then on 23 September Ursula Owen told the board that 'Virago's attitude, working practices and emotional involvement were not compatible with the group's ethos ... [and that] the nature and cost of the group services provided was out of touch with their needs and had become too costly.' Virago wanted out immediately and the minutes record Max as saying the board would consider the matter without delay.

At the end of the first week of October subsidiary rights sales were already higher than those for the whole of the previous October and the arrangement with Pan was showing encouraging results. But by 10 November The Bodley Head was complaining that, as in the spring, there were again significant and embarrassing delays in royalty payments. The board decided more economy was necessary: Chatto too should move into Bedford Square and their floor in William IV Street be rented out.

On 22 December 1986 Max received a letter from Peter Mayer, who had been brought to Penguin in 1979 to sort out that group's troubles, asking if 'an injection of a large amount of cash in relation to licences might not be helpful. The Penguin Group could do it in terms of CVBC group licences, short, medium or long-term agreements. We could do that with any one company. We could do it even with a part of one company, for example, your own children's list.' The looseness of this proposal suggests that a quick solution was very possible. Mayer also said he had 'proposed to Graham some time ago an Economist type solution for your group, i.e. partial ownership but by Pearson, not Penguin. The Economist operates totally independently. I want to be as resourceful as possible and am available to you or any of your colleagues. Your group's independence is, I think, very important not just to us, but everyone in British publishing.'

Max's relationship with Penguin had always been close and friendly. Many of Penguin's first children's picture books were The Bodley Head's. Max had done some overseas selling through Penguin and The Bodley Head had sold books for Allen Lane The Penguin Press when it started up. The first paperback Max had sold was to Eunice Frost, who was then scouting for Penguin, and Penguin had continued to paperback many of Max's best authors as well as to distribute the books he published under his own imprint, one of which – Alistair Cooke's November 1986 Fulbright Commission speech 'Getting To Know You' – was in the works.

Max told Graham C. Greene of the Penguin offer and repeated his desire to take The Bodley Head out of the group. But according to Greene, after Max refused to participate in the rights issue Maschler no longer wanted to talk to him.[63] When John Hews resigned from the board on 31 December 1986 and retired from the group, Max was left even more isolated on the eve of The Bodley Head's centenary year.

* * *

After the 20 January 1987 board meeting Greene handed Max a formal letter 'on behalf of this company and each of its subsidiaries (including Max Reinhardt Limited) ("Group") with regard to the use by you of the name Max Reinhardt as an imprint on books published in the United Kingdom and distributed throughout the world'. When Max had discussed Penguin with Greene he had mentioned that he would want to continue to use the Max Reinhardt imprint from time to time for books he financed himself, books which for one reason or another The Bodley Head did not want or could not publish. A list of Max Reinhardt books had been drawn up in September 1986. It included several by Alfred Hitchcock and all thirteen volumes of The Bodley Head Shaw edited by Dan Laurence. In Greene's letter he agreed to allow Max 'in consideration of the sum of £1' to publish books 'provided the contents of such a book and its presentation should have been approved by this company and that we agree at the outset the way in which the Max Reinhardt imprint is set out'. It was further made clear that the licence that was being given to Max would continue to belong to 'the Group' who would continue 'to have full rights to the Max Reinhardt imprint' and that the licence could be 'terminated by this company on 12 months' notice'.[64]

This letter and Max's response of 30 January 1987 show how bad things between them had become. 'Your legally worded reply puzzled me because it shows that you misunderstood me completely', Max answered. 'You should at least have known that I would never agree to submit books for approval by the holding company, or to anybody else for that matter. So let us forget the whole thing. I shall in future publish any books I wish under any imprint I am legally entitled to use.' Max went on to say that he had been worried about the group's lack of central management for years, had felt that nobody was in actual charge and that this was the cause of the

financial crises which one could foresee, and which were avoided only by selling some of the company's assets, or by you and Tom putting a substantial sum of new money into the company. I do not trust the budgets, and I am concerned at the number of decisions that have been taken rather too hastily, about changes of office, changes of personnel, changes of sales organization, etc., many of which were not thoroughly thought out before hand. The most recent of which was the closing of the Trade Counter and the sub-letting of the basement and ground floor at 9 Bow Street, which I first heard of only at the last Board meeting. I feel that I do not know any more what is happening, although I can guess what is likely to happen: we shall have a crisis again in March of this year, because of everybody overspending without regard to what others in the Group may be doing. That is why I was against an increase of salaries across the board, which we cannot afford, although I am always in favour of rewarding those members of the staff who have given us good and loyal service. I do not think that I can serve any useful purpose anymore as Joint Chairman.

And so Max too 'put to the Board my resignation as such'. He was

obviously particularly worried about The Bodley Head, especially after all the references in the press about its being taken over, which has distressed many authors who, as you know, over the years have become my personal friends, or who joined The Bodley Head in the first instance because they were my friends. The only way I can see of restoring their confidence is for me to buy back The Bodley Head, provided I find a buyer who is willing to put up some of the money, but with my retaining control. If I find such a person or company I would try to arrange that the distribution and other services we get from the Group were maintained for a length of time, so as not to cause any damage.

Telling Greene that he would be in Barbados 8–22 February, he signed off 'I need not tell you that I am very sad that things have not worked out as we hoped they would.'

Greene found Max's letter 'extremely distressing' and generously accepted 'considerable responsibility' for the accounting systems that did not 'give us adequate warning of the dangers ahead'. He said he had always agreed to Max using his own name on books he published on his own account, and suggested a way to make such an arrangement legal. He asked Max to come in to the office 'at certain fixed times during the week' and 'to give everyone working for us confidence to go forward', and hoped Max would not resign as 'Joint Chairman of CVBC in which you have a not inconsiderable financial stake and with which you are so publicly associated. For all these reasons and because The Bodley Head is such a significant part of the group I frankly find the notion of it being disentangled from the rest unthinkable. The problems of doing so would be appalling and the damage done to the whole immeasurable.'[65]

Next day Max replied that he could not 'convey confidence to others if I have lost it myself'. He reckoned that

> the problems started when we were made to move from 9 Bow Street, to benefit the group. But this is all water under the bridge now. I cannot see how it would help The Bodley Head if I were more actively involved at the office than I am now. I do look after the important authors and the important projects that lie ahead, but am not involved in the choice of new books that we take. I am against the committee system, and when consulted my advice is ignored. So far as matters concerning the group go, I give my opinion when it is requested and I am obviously put off when it is completely disregarded without any explanation, as was the case with the salaries increase across the board. I know that it would be difficult to disentangle The Bodley Head from the group, but I do not think that it would be impossible to find a formula, particularly if we have to sell the whole group, which I have come to the conclusion is now practically inevitable.

He then dropped the PS: 'Graham, with whom I had dinner last night, has been aware of the situation for some time and told me that he would not entrust his new novel, which is nearly ready, to The Bodley Head if he felt that its financial problems had not been solved.'[66]

15
The Last Act

And so began the last act in what Euan Cameron later called The Bodley Head's 'ill-fated association with Jonathan Cape and Chatto & Windus', which ended in the sale of the three imprints to Random House in New York.[1] It is difficult to see how things could have been worse between the joint chairs than when Max and Joan left for Barbados. But on 19 February 1987 while they were there, Hugh Greene died; the Concorde on which Max booked a seat to return for the funeral broke down; he arrived 24 hours late and believed that his absence further estranged him from the younger Greene.

The best record of what happened thereafter is in Max's letters to Graham Greene in Antibes. Virago continued its negotiations to leave the group and Max continued to talk with Penguin to find a new arrangement for The Bodley Head. On 10 March Graham Greene sent a letter from Antibes urging Max 'again to try to buy back The Bodley Head'. If that were impossible Greene offered 'to your private company' his new novel on the promise that Max would do his 'utmost to secure the transfer of all my other books published by The Bodley Head to your own company. This would mean buying them back from The Bodley Head, and I hope you will succeed in doing so.'

On 19 March, as she often did, Joan cooked English sausages for Greene and Max at Pelham Crescent – Greene's fried, Max's roasted. They ate them by the fire and shared a bottle of claret. Next day Max sent a copy of Greene's 10 March letter by hand to the younger Greene and proposed that 'we should transfer to Reinhardt Books Graham's backlist titles published by The Bodley Head, when we have agreed on a price', which he told him how to calculate. The younger Greene replied on 23 March with great concern that his uncle would move to Reinhardt Books: 'I know that you have an unusually intimate publisher/author relationship with

Graham and I hope that this will enable you to devise a way of publishing Graham's new novel under The Bodley Head imprint which would make him happy, which would protect him from any fears he may have and which would also protect our publishing relationship.' He closed by suggesting that 'to pursue the course you are proposing would seem to me an act of very considerable aggression'.[2] Given the situation, these seem rather strong words unless he was intending to deny The Bodley Head the same possibility of leaving the group the board had given Virago. Greene made a point of saying he was not sending a copy of the letter to his uncle, with whom he admitted he was on very bad terms, but that Max should send it on if he wished.

Max read the letter to Greene over the telephone the next day along with the 24 March piece from *The Times*'s 'Londoner's Diary' in which the younger Greene was quoted as saying that rumours Carmen Callil was 'deep in negotiations over [Virago's] future' and that Virago was set to leave Chatto, Bodley Head and Cape were 'pure fantasy'.[3] Why did he say this? Graham Greene immediately sent *The Times* a letter (dated 24 March and published on the 28th) saying that his nephew's statement 'that rumours of changes are "pure fantasy" seems to indicate that he is living himself in a fantasy world. Publishers depend on authors, and I am sure that I am not the only author who will consider leaving the group should there be none of the necessary changes in the administration.' Two days later Max told the *Independent* that 'he would like to buy back The Bodley Head and run it more independently and in a more personal way, so that it is smaller and more intimate – instead of being run by committee'. He confirmed that Virago had been negotiating to leave the group for some time and told 'Londoner's Diary' that 'the negotiations were concluded'.[4] A CVBC press release of the same date confirmed the Virago negotiations but contradicted Max's desire to buy The Bodley Head back.

On Monday 30th a meeting was held at Max's house with 'three other key directors' followed by a full board meeting on Tuesday 31st of nine directors at which Max formally resigned as joint chairman of CVBC because, as he told Barry O'Brien at the *Daily Telegraph*, 'I am not very much involved in the day-to-day running of the company. I am much more involved in the editorial affairs of The Bodley Head.'[5] He would remain a director of the holding company and executive chairman of The Bodley Head. The next day he told O'Brien that 'I have all the assurances I want and so has Graham Greene. I spoke to him on the telephone yesterday at his home in the south of France. We are perfectly happy at the moment', and confirmed that discussions about the Virago buyout 'had reached an advanced stage'.[6] Another press release dated 2 April said an agreement in principle had been reached for the sale of Virago to its management, with a sales and distribution agreement with the group for five years.

What had happened? On 1 April Max told Graham Greene 'the press have been truly persecuting me'. They wanted to know

> the arrangement that the other directors had agreed which made me say that I would not withdraw The Bodley Head from the group and, of course, I wouldn't tell them, although Carmen Callil, Graham and Tom Maschler know and have agreed to it, that is that we sell the group and that you and I favour selling to Penguins. I haven't of course told the press that but I have told Peter Mayer. If the others favour Pan I will only agree provided we can then take The Bodley Head out of the deal and sell The Bodley Head to Penguins. I made that very clear and I hope that, prodded by Carmen who is entirely on my side and Peter Mayer who is willing to come back from New York the moment I ask him to, we will solve our problem.

In a statement to the *Sunday Telegraph* on 5 April Max corrected various errors of fact that had seen print and when 'The Times Diary' wondered if 'a predatory Penguin [would] soon be stalking the corridors of Chatto, Bodley Head and Jonathan Cape . . . in the hope of pecking off The Bodley Head' he said he was 'sure they are interested in buying us – but for the moment it won't happen'.[7]

As though to lighten this gathering nightmare with farce, a letter arrived almost immediately from Alexander Flegon offering Max a 50/50 partnership in a firm he was setting up to publish Russian books. All Max had to do was invest £10,000 for a desk-top publishing system and he would make a fortune. Max wrote back reminding Flegon, 'you know very well that we are Alexander Solzhenitsyn's publishers and have many books of his still to publish. You will also remember the famous case we fought against you when you tried to publish an English edition of August 1914 before us. We are therefore the last publishers to consider your proposition.'[8]

Eric de Bellaigue quotes Tom Maschler as saying that Graham Greene's blistering letter to *The Times* on 28 March 'sold us down the river'. Or did it speed, at least from Greene and Maschler's point of view, a highly successful financial solution to their problem? Maschler says that 'one day in March 1987, I received a phone call from my friend Bob Gottlieb.

He asked whether, if Si Newhouse were to fly over, we would be willing to talk to him.'[9]

Without telling Max about the call or the meeting set up for two weeks later, Graham C. Greene received Max's formal resignation as joint chairman of the board on Monday 31 March, and he watched Max make the statements he did to the press in the following few days, statements which indicated that both Max and Greene's Uncle Graham would not leave the group. Maschler told de Bellaigue 'we were scared [Max] would muck things up in any negotiations'.[10] What he would have done was negotiate to take The Bodley Head out of the group, which he was trying to achieve through Penguin even over the next weeks before they signed the deal with Random House.

According to *Publishing News* 'Greene was careful to keep news of the meeting [on 10 April] secret. Deliberately he made no entry in his diary and no one else in the group was aware of what was happening when he and Maschler slipped quietly into The Connaught that morning' to meet Newhouse for breakfast in his suite.[11] They were surprised that Newhouse – who, as Maschler tells us in his book, was 'the sixth richest man in America',[12] the owner of Condé Nast, *Vanity Fair*, the *New Yorker*, the Random House publishing group (which included Knopf, many newspapers and television companies) – did not want to put money into CVBC but rather to buy it outright. The price was tempting. According to Maschler, as the day passed Newhouse said he would double their current salaries of £40,000 and give them both ten-year contracts. Then he said, ' "The price I offer you is twenty million pounds, to include the company's debts" (they came to four million). It happened so suddenly.'[13] After a walk around Hyde Park Greene and Maschler 'agreed to the deal and that it should be concluded as quickly as possible (within three weeks)'. They felt that Random House was a good match because they already shared some authors – Doris Lessing, William Faulkner, VS Pritchett – and because Sonny Metha, who had left Pan to take over Knopf when Bob Gottlieb went to the *New Yorker*, was an old friend. Maschler readily admitted they knew Max 'would be furious' but 'we were not obliged to consult him. The fact that he had declined to put up the money we desperately needed had resulted in Graham and I holding over 50 per cent of the company between us, i.e. we were in control.'[14]

On Tuesday 21 April Max went to Paris to see Oncle Richard who was seriously ill and on Thursday 23rd, while he was away, an emergency board meeting was held. Present were Greene, Maschler, Machin, Callil, J.F. Charlton, R.H. Kirkpatrick, C.A. Ryder Runton, M.R.M. Lancaster and

J.E. Peck. Greene said his secretary had been unable to contact Max, that he was understood to be abroad. The minutes say that because of 'talks currently being held with other parties' to whom Greene needed to give confidential information, he needed 'formal Board approval' which he was given and for all the subsidiaries.

Thursday 7 May, with Max's 'apologies received', Greene reported to the same directors plus G.A. Rutherford that at 1.15 a.m. that morning he and Maschler had sold their shares in the group to Random House in New York, and that Random House would offer the remaining share-holders the same price they had received. He hoped the legalities would be completed in a month. He understood that the group would continue 'in substantially the same structure'. The staff of The Bodley Head and its fellow companies was gathered and told by Greene of the sale. The next day the papers reported the takeover as having brought the group's shareholders £18 million.

Max behaved elegantly – on another occasion Alistair Cooke had told him: 'You hide your disappointments with great grace.'[15] He told the press mutedly that he welcomed the sale although it had 'been done in the darkest secrecy'. He had found out about it only the night before when Greene, Maschler and Callil arrived at Pelham Crescent to tell him. Callil remembered being taken by Greene and Maschler so she could convince Max to sign the papers. Because of the firm's articles, unless 90 per cent of all shareholders agreed to the sale the shares had to be offered to all the other shareholders. Max's letters show him vague on this point until the middle of May, when even then he might possibly have held things up but clearly did not wish to; in any case he would presumably have had to top the Random House offer to succeed. 'Max liked me', Callil has said, 'and Graham and Tom thought I would be able to calm him down because they knew he would be astonished and deeply offended.'[16] Max said Greene rang him and insisted ' "Look, Tom and I and Carmen want to come and see you." When they arrived at Pelham Crescent Carmen said "Max, you must be thrilled. You are a millionaire." I asked "What do you mean?" and she replied, "Well, we have sold the company to Random House and you will get more than a million pounds".'[17] In fact, his share came to almost double that – £1,947,956.76.[18]

Max was very fond of Callil and thought her a brilliant publisher. 'She made a great success of Virago, but she was really an innocent in this. I think they had just told her in the taxi what we would get for the shares. She didn't seem to know much about what was going on. I told them, "No. I don't want to sell to Random House. We will have trouble if we do.

Why don't you talk to Penguin?" But Greene told me "it's too late. We have arranged for you to have lunch tomorrow with Si Newhouse and Bob Bernstein, just you alone with them at the Connaught. They will convince you of what a good idea it is".'[19] Max wondered why Random House had paid them far more than any one else was willing to; the *Bookseller* called 'it rich reward for poor management'.[20]

> I went to the Connaught and Si Newhouse asked, 'Would you like a drink?' I said 'Yes, thank you, what are you having?' He said he would have a Perrier. 'I cannot have an alcoholic drink if you are having Perrier' I said, and I made him drink wine. The lunch lasted three hours. He told me the story of his life, and Robert Bernstein had brought me a little book to which I had contributed something about one of the directors of Random House. My own firm had old connections with Random House which had begun when someone at The Bodley Head had asked them if they would publish a book in America and they replied they weren't a publisher, so they were asked if they would do it at random. The lunch was pleasant enough and a few hours later Graham told me 'Tom and I are becoming directors of Random House America.'[21]

Max sent a packet of newspaper clippings to Graham Greene in Antibes on 11 May and his accompanying letter shows how bruised he was. He wrote to Greene again on 15 May to say he had lunched with Sandy MacGregor, a vice-president of Random House who, along with vice-president, Howard Kaminsky, chairman Bob Bernstein and their team had come to London to close the deal. MacGregor and Bernstein were to join the British board; Greene and Maschler the American one. MacGregor, Max reported, 'was quite appalled at the fact that I wasn't told of the arrangements that Random House had made with Graham and Tom'. Max agreed to help 'reorganise The Bodley Head ... provided it was made clear that I wasn't taking any instructions from Graham and MacGregor accepted that and that when the time came, which would be when your next book came to be published, I would resign as Chairman of The Bodley Head, publish your book at Reinhardt Books and distribute it whatever way we want'.

Five days later Max told Greene he no longer minded what inaccuracies the papers continued to print. 'I mean that.' He repeated what he had said in his 15 May letter, that he had given Random House 'a copy of the letter you sent me about giving me your next book and my trying to buy from the group your back list. They know exactly where we stand.

Penguins are just waiting for the word to take over the distribution of Reinhardt Books but I don't want to make any announcement until the deal with Random House is settled to our satisfaction. I have a lot of very friendly notes from other publishers who all want to help but as we've arranged we'll stick with Penguins.'[22]

* * *

In return for the little book Newhouse and Bernstein had given Max when they met him at the Connaught, Max sent Newhouse a copy of Mary Connell's *Help is on the Way*, which Max Reinhardt Ltd had published in 1986; with it he wished the new venture success and said he would help however he could through the delicate proceedings he knew would follow. That he sent this book shows his canniness and sense of fun for it at once confirmed his right to publish under his own name, his and Graham Greene's continuing loyalty to one another and, almost incidentally, that as a publisher he too crossed the Atlantic.

This young Texan writer and artist had first written to Greene in 1978. Her voluminous letters had amused him and his sister Elisabeth Dennys, who was then his secretary. As a favour to Connell, Greene had sent her novel to Max in 1983. It had been rejected by Knopf. The Bodley Head reader had judged it 'fairly pedestrian [although] ... an honest attempt'. Connell had taken Max's rejection with equanimity and continued to send him letters addressed to 'Dear Max of the House of Reinhardt' or 'Max Reinhardt, an Angel ... [which] is higher than a prince; and even higher than a sheriff'. Graham too had been persistent. A year and a half later he suggested Max publish a small selection of Connell's poetry, which was original, witty and wise in a style that owed something to Stevie Smith.

At that point Max had turned Connell over to Joan. 'One would deduce you enjoy the good fortune of being somehow related to Mr. Max', Connell wrote her. 'I applaud you if you chose it, and congratulate you if it was hereditarily bestowed. He seems a precious man; so sweet and wise, and the relationship must give you great pleasure.' Picking up the fun Joan had replied, 'Yes I do enjoy good fortune as I am Mrs. Max!' They would print a small book of Connell's poetry under the Max Reinhardt imprint.[23] Max knew he was bound to lose money on it but he was carried along by Greene's enthusiasm. What he did not know was that when the book was published CVBC had decided no longer to distribute Max Reinhardt books in the usual way, and no UK rep or American agent had a sample copy to sell. Greene saved the day when he discovered that

Connell's brother was Jim Wright, the majority leader in the House of Representatives. So Max sold the book to an American distributor and had it passed around Washington cocktail parties – along with Greene's endorsement on the cover, and his favourite Mary Connell lines: 'Am I kissing wrong frogs?/ Or am I kissing frogs wrong?'

Nonetheless, Max had taken a terrible blow. In his *Memories* he said simply 'the circumstances of the takeover ... were not normal ... I cannot deny that what had happened was deeply upsetting.' Privately he allowed that

> if I had been asked earlier I might well have said Hurray! Someone had to buy CVBC because we didn't have any capital ... But the deal was made without my knowing anything about it and I thought that the way it was done was more than a little discourteous. I didn't like someone else selling off part of my inheritance. Although I knew things were in very bad shape, and Random House saw immediately that what I had been complaining about for some time was true, that things had not been well managed. I had continued to trust the people I worked with as I had all my life. No one had ever done anything like that to me before so it was an enormous shock.[24]

To his solicitor he said he liked the Random House people. What disappointed him was 'the behaviour of my colleagues who made the deal without consulting me'.[25]

Greene senior was furious about the way his old friend had been dealt with and, probably responding to a 22 May note from his nephew telling Max to stop talking to the press about the takeover, sent a letter dated the same day to the *Independent*. It was published on 3 June: 'The American takeover of the CVBC group will obviously aid the unsatisfactory financial situation of the majority of shareholders, but if the new American owners allow the administration of the group to remain in the same hands as in the past, I think that many authors besides myself will prefer to take their books elsewhere. An author is not a chattel. My loyalty is to my publisher, Max Reinhardt, and not to a group.' He had used similar words in his July 1961 letter to the *Observer* after the failed Heinemann merger, and to his friend A.S. Frere whom he nonetheless soon after thanked for his years of kindness in a prefatory letter to *The Comedians*, his first Bodley Head novel. Graham C. Greene could not have failed to hear the echo.

The same day, what Max had warned the younger Greene would happen filled the business pages of the papers. Simon Master, managing

director of Pan Books, was to leave Pan at the end of the week to become
chief executive of the group. He had been appointed international vice-
president of Random House and made responsible for non-American
operations. Greene would remain chairman but he, Maschler, Callil
and Max would report to Master. According to Patrick Hosking in the
Independent, when the announcement was made in New York on 1 June
Robert Bernstein had left no one in any doubt, 'Simon Master will have
ultimate authority at CVBC.' The *Evening Standard* put it more coarsely:
Simon Master would now 'rule the roost over the likes of Tom Maschler,
Max Reinhardt and Graham C. Greene'.[26]

Greene and Maschler were said to welcome the appointment because
they had had close business relations with Pan over the years. With dry
irony Max told the *Bookseller*: 'What we have needed is stronger central
management. That is what we are now getting.'[27] Of course by the time
Simon Master set up office in the board room at 32 Bedford Square at the
end of June, Max had already arranged to leave The Bodley Head, taking
Graham Greene's new book with him.

* * *

That summer London's trade journals, literary columns and party conversations were rife with comment. Gossip had it that Random House
was about to buy Pan itself making 'a massive foothold in the British
book world, linking one of our most aggressive paperback publishers
to the older and grander traditions of the Chatto group'.[28] Quoting
Oscar Wilde, 'We have everything in common with America except
language', Giles Gordon wrote in the *Bookseller* on 12 June that 'the
casualty of international publishing must be the diminution of the
idiosyncrasies of local language, of individual identities ... The publisher's balance sheet may well be healthier. The craft of publishing is
likely to become more brutalising, and the writing more bland.' Several
newspapers predicted that erstwhile Cape authors would go over to Liz
Calder at Bloomsbury. It was said in the *Sunday Telegraph* that agents
were refusing to send material to Cape. By mid-June there was specula-
tion that Graham Greene would give his new novel to Reinhardt Books.
If he did it would be a humiliating blow for CVBC. But that 'foxy old
general of British publishing', as the *London Daily News* dubbed Max,
said 'nothing has been decided yet. If he gives his new book to me, of
course I will publish it ... we are very old friends ... Why not wait until
July when there will be something really interesting to say', and left for
France.[29]

Max saw Oncle Richard for the last time in early June. He died on 13 August, well into his nineties, and was buried in Montparnasse leaving Max to deal with his personal affairs. In his early Paris years Richard 'had bought space for three tombstones at Montparnasse. The first was for Anya [who had died in 1958], the second for my mother [who had died in 1960] and in the middle was going to be his tombstone.' Max had been given Richard's power of attorney in the mid-1960s and had been handling his money for him since then. Now he had to carry out the instructions that Richard had left about his housekeeper and various girlfriends.[30] So Max was back and forth between London and Paris, in London lining up his first Reinhardt and Nonesuch publications, in Paris and the south of France meeting Greene, by late September together with the Random House people to discuss buying Greene's backlist.

On 6 October Max and Anthony Rota gave a small party at the Garrick for John Ryder's seventieth birthday and on 9 October Max resigned as chairman of The Bodley Head and as director of the CVBC board. In his letter to Simon Master he said he could not 'but have strong, affectionate feelings for The Bodley Head, its authors and remaining staff after running it for nearly thirty years, mostly happy ones', and that he would continue to give Random House any help he was asked for. He would also continue to publish under his own imprint, Reinhardt Books, and that of The Nonesuch Press 'since publishing is my life's work and the area in which I have made most of my friends'.

Greene and Max had another of their sausage suppers on 8 October. Then, on 13 October *The Times* literary editor, Philip Howard, reported that Max, 'Graham Greene, Alistair Cooke, Maurice Sendak, and other valuable and distinguished authors are striking a blow for the old-fashioned small publisher against the big new conglomerates'. The Reinhardt Books list, Howard said, was not going to be a big list but it would be a classy one, starting with Greene's novel *The Captain and the Enemy*, his play *The House of Reputation*, and *Reflections*, a newly collected edition of his political essays. An agreement with Penguin to handle the marketing, distribution and representation of Reinhardt Books had been arranged.

* * *

Max had lost The Bodley Head but won 'a notable victory for the pub-lisher as civilized literary friend and mentor as opposed to publisher as Big-Bang, whizz-kid accountant', Philip Howard said. 'Max Reinhardt and The Bodley Head have always made a big thing, as a small, exclusive publishing house can afford to, of the need for tender, loving care of ... their authors. It was the loss of this personal touch in the new world of publishing as an anonymous assembly line that Graham Greene complained about.'[31]

Max had become a kind of hero. 'Moreover', Robert Winder wrote in the *Independent*, he had become 'a peculiarly British kind of hero', standing up for books having a value different from other commodities. Winder said there was a shudder of glee in London publishing circles at Max's decision, 'as though a national treasure (Graham Greene) had somehow been airlifted out of New York, spirited away and brought home safe and sound'.[32]

Letters of congratulation came from colleagues and friends. Simon Hornby, Chairman of W.H. Smith offered his full support. Sir Robert Lusty, who had retired as managing director of Hutchinson in 1973, was delighted by the splintering of the conglomerates and wished Hugh Greene were still around to see it. He hope there was time for a postscript to Jack Lambert's *The History of The Bodley Head* which he looked forward to reading.[33]

Max replied to most letters with his customary humour and apparent humility. 'I don't know why the papers are making such a meal of what is only a minor extension of my publishing activities', he told Brooke Crutchley. 'I suppose that with the news that large publishing firms are gobbling up other large publishing firms it's a change to go back to cottage industry life. The irony is, of course, that all the technical side of my publishing will be the responsibility of one of the biggest conglomerates: Pearson!'[34]

Bit by bit the story of what had happened came out, Max all the while telling the press his move to Reinhardt Books had nothing to do with the takeover, and never allowing more about it than that his former partners had been 'a little bit discourteous'. But Max was angry, Graham C. Greene believed because he knew he had made a business mistake.[35] Certainly Max knew he had made a mistake in selling Greene and Maschler his shares in 1984. He readily acknowledged it. But the larger error, and the one that stuck with him he told Roger Straus, 'was to merge the firm with partners who thought differently'.[36] Greene and Maschler's refusal to allow Max to take The Bodley Head out of the group symbolized to him the greedy process of buying, selling and swallowing that he had tried to avoid when he joined with Chatto and Cape.

Max and Straus, who had survived an overture from Random House in 1986, were the end of the line of post-World War II publishers. As Straus told the *New York Times*, they had come to publishing because 'it was a literary kind of life ... Making money was not the greatest impulse'.[37] The Bodley Head's advances and salaries might have been small, but the prestige of the firm was large. The changes in publishing had come fast. Callil saw them as soon as she took over Chatto; at Virago she had been able to buy old books for a few hundred pounds; at Chatto she had to advance tens of thousands to acquire new novels.[38] The only way you could get the money back was to sell mass printings. In 1987, 5000 copies made an author about £5000, which was nowhere close to the large advances being paid out. So if the film and paperback rights or a prize were not achieved, the bank manager wanted an explanation.

Under CVBC's umbrella, Max had been able to continue publishing elegant books of literary quality for many years, and he had kept his list of prominent authors, headed by Graham Greene. But even this small conglomerate had failed; Eric de Bellaigue gives as reasons the group's 'separate editorial fiefdoms [which] shielded for a long time a large slice of costs from critical scrutiny', the lack of a paperback arm, the 'management of the share registry ... [which] inhibited the group's development' by narrowing its equity base and finally, the management structure which was too dependent on Graham C. Greene.[39] In the end, Max was unwilling to be told what to do, certainly not by Greene and Maschler, brassy agents and large conglomerates.

Publishers have a foot in both the worlds of commerce and of letters. Max's weight was usually in the world of commerce. But in leaving The Bodley Head he made a protest against the commercial pressures on editors and authors and returned to the ideal literary relationship he had had with his writers and staff, a relationship he thought essential to publishing books of quality. It was based on the principle that the author should call the tune. Graham Greene wanted that too and their success in getting Reinhardt Books off the ground when they were both old men shows their loyalty to that principle as much as to each other.

* * *

If Max had 'cock[ed] a snook at the world of multinational conglomerates', as Anthea Hall wrote in the *Sunday Telegraph*,[40] a heavy price had been paid by his old Bodley Head people. Simon Master told the *Bookseller* that for at least the past year the 'working environment for the other Bodley Head staff has been difficult – they have had to put up with a lot of uncertainty and damage to their own relationships with authors while Max has been so unhappy'.[41] For the past eighteen months Max had hardly been in Bedford Square and Margaret Clark, who worked through the transition, said this was the most difficult thing. 'I don't understand why he didn't take care of the staff. Max just left and we didn't know what was happening. It made things very hard.'[42] The fact was, as Max told Greene on 19 October 1987, he would have made his intentions clear sooner but unofficial negotiations at the time 'with Penguin over a much bigger deal' had caused his partners to 'beg ... me not to take any action until they had time to reconsider the whole situation'. And then, as it turned out, Max himself did not know what his partners were doing while he was trying to find a solution for The Bodley Head.

Guido Waldman knew Max was 'absolutely mortified that he could not better protect his staff at the close'.[43] The patriarchal loyalty on which Max had based his life had proved useless in the face of conglomerate publishing and in the end, for all his graciousness, Max too had to fight to save himself. Margaret Clark said that when the sell-out took place she was preparing Sendak's *Caldecott & Co.* for publication. It had been costed and was ready to go when Max rang and said 'you're not doing the book. I am.' She thought this 'very mean'. Although she acknowledged how kind Max had previously been to her, she never forgave him.[44]

The most poignant description of those months was written by Barney Blackley to Max on 7 September 1987.

The whole business of the group's decline into near bankruptcy and eventual sale to Random House has left me with a very nasty taste in my mouth. When we were independent you often used to discuss with me the state of the company's affairs and your plans for its future. I knew what was going on and had some say in it. So did others. One felt valued. Almost from the moment we joined Chatto & Cape this feeling ceased. Things began to happen without one being consulted or even forewarned. It was degrading, and I suppose I shouldn't have stayed. But I loved The Bodley Head, it had been a central part of my life, my nature includes a strong streak of loyalty, and I thought that I could help to preserve something of the firm's character, which many of us valued. It didn't take me long to realise that no one in the rest of the group gave a damn about The Bodley Head's character. I also had a growing sense of things getting out of control. You were often clearly worried and unhappy, and this was infectious. I felt increasingly irrelevant and excluded from any policy-making discussions. It was a wretched time. Things went from bad to worse and eventually we had the rationalisation of last summer when The Bodley Head was shoehorned into No. 32. When David suggested that it would help with the space problem if I agreed to work mainly at home for my last year, I welcomed the chance of getting away from that atmosphere. At the same time he asked me to resign as a director. I found this a bit hurtful, but it seemed important to him, for some reason which he did not explain, so I agreed.

Blackley killed himself six months later. Although his widow assured Max that the reasons had nothing to do with what happened at The Bodley Head, as Max said, 'it was a very, very sad ending'.[45]

Max did not attend the party to celebrate The Bodley Head's centenary at the Garrick on 22 September 1987, or the party at Hatchards on 11 November to celebrate *The History of The Bodley Head*. Jack Lambert, with whom Max had sat on the RADA council and whom he had commissioned to write the book, was dead; under pressure of the deadline and the sale to Random House Guido Waldman and many others in the office, including Max himself, added bits to it as Michael Ratcliffe finished the book. It was dedicated to Max and was without the postscript Robert Lusty had hoped for. Instead it cut off with a funereal 'Envoi' that buried the details of the firm's demise. A few days later, on 19 November, Max gave a lecture to the Wynkyn de Worde Society about The Nonesuch Press; he remembered what fun it had all been working with Francis Meynell.

16
Reinhardt Books

Max began to rebuild his small empire when he changed the name of HFL to Reinhardt Books in 1985. Adding Nonesuch the following year was important to him; it provided the continuity and personal prestige that was threatened within the group. 'Reinhardt Books Limited is [a] family-owned business' his announcement read. 'It is particularly appropriate that the association between the Meynell and the Reinhardt families will be maintained as Max Reinhardt has been a director of The Nonesuch Press since 1953, with Sir Francis' widow, Dame Alix Meynell, as Chairman, and they are now reversing their roles, with Dame Alix remaining as a director.' As the CVBC fiasco played itself out, Max's larger concern had been keeping The Bodley Head. When it was sold he moved quickly into what he called 'our small operation' with Penguin. Reinhardt Books was neither part of the Penguin group nor entirely separate from it but operated as something of a cottage industry under the Penguin umbrella in a quiet arrangement between Max and Peter Mayer. Max had wanted to call the imprint Max Reinhardt Books. But the sale of The Bodley Head made that legally impossible.

As chairman and managing director of the new firm Max made the editorial decisions with the help of Joan, who was named co-editor, and from March 1988 with Judy Taylor as his consulting editor. Headquarters were at Pelham Crescent. Everyone came and went to check in with Max and lunch with authors at nearby restaurants. Penguin provided office accommodation at 27 Wright's Lane along with distribution, sales, marketing, production and some editorial services, sharing the costs and profits of Max's books. Initially there were about six titles a year, books Max wanted to publish and Penguin agreed to. They were designed by John Ryder with the help of Michael Harvey. John Hews took charge of accounts. Annabel Huxley kept things going until the move into the

Penguin building on 18 January 1988 when Elizabeth Bowes-Lyon was brought in as assistant publisher. When she married in the summer of 1990 Amanda Hargreaves replaced her – among the instructions Bowes-Lyon left Hargreaves was this note: 'we receive letters and typescripts from unknown authors all the time. Try to turn around the obviously hopeless ones straight away. Others – log in the book, then tick off when you've returned them. If you discover a gem, get an opinion from Judy or Max!'

To some at The Bodley Head it looked like a confused weakness when Max walked away as things fell apart. But his old friend Joe Links commended him.

> I have always admired your character but never more than as shown over this takeover caper. With anyone else there would have been little left but rancour: you take the only correct view – that you have achieved what you wanted and, if others have ended with a good deal of what you should have had, so much the better: you have enough. You are of course absolutely right but few would have seen as clear-headedly.[1]

Links understood that Max's instinct to leave what he could not control was also one of his great strengths. It was what he had done in his youth as Istanbul became hostile to foreigners, and as a young man leaving Paris in the face of war, abandoning his family for the kind of British life he had learned from his gentle headmaster. He had been lucky. Oncle Richard had financed his move, Harold Laski guided him into British life, Ralph Richardson taught him the role of British gentleman, Graham Greene helped make him a British publishing giant. He seemed to have needed the approval of these men, and in starting Reinhardt Books again Graham Greene guided him. If his letters to Graham Greene during the CVBC troubles had been sometimes filled with nothing but apology for what had happened and the accusation of behaviour he could neither stomach nor understand the reason for, he was quick to transform what may have looked to some like diffidence into his more customary step forward.

When Greene delivered the manuscript of *The Captain and the Enemy* to the new firm in mid-December 1987 Max wrote to Peter Mayer about 'the new arrangement – it's starting well'. Mayer agreed, 'It's ... a fine book for us to begin this new association.'[2] By then two new books of Greene's writing had been picked up, Christopher Hawtree's *Yours Etc.*, a collection of Greene's letters to editors, and Judith Adamson's *Reflections*, a selection of his journalism which she had gathered as she wrote about his politics in *The Dangerous Edge*. There was a contract for the auto-biography of Kenneth Lo, the famous tennis player and founder of the Memories of China restaurants in London and the first school of Chinese cookery in Europe. And by March 1987 Max had bought at Greene's insis-tence *The Broken Commandment*, a first novel by an entirely unknown Irish writer named Vincent McDonnell. His wife had sent Greene the manuscript after the book was rejected by seven publishers (including The Bodley Head) and Max had sent McDonnell £1000 advance. Under-standably, McDonnell was very grateful. 'You are responsible for ending the most terrible writer's block I have ever endured' he wrote to Greene, 'and which I felt certain would be for the rest of my life ... In six months my life, our life, has been transformed. You have been responsible for it all.'[3]

So the new Reinhardt list began and with the move to the Penguin building Max's back stock was transferred to Harmondsworth. There was Mary Connell's *Help is on The Way* (which Viking continued to sell in New York), Douglas Day's *Journey of the Wolf* (which had been chosen by the literary editor of *The Times* as one of the best novels of 1987), Paul Reilly's *An Eye on Design* (a book by a friend who, as director of the Council of Industrial Design, had been at the centre of the design world for thirty years), Jerome Weidman's *Praying for Rain* (which had been transferred from Heinemann when Greene and Heyer had come to The Bodley Head), and Helen Bannerman's by then controversial *Little Black Sambo*.

Bannerman had written this book in India in 1898 for her young daughters. Unfortunately when Grant Richards published it in London the following year he failed to protect the American copyright and debased versions of the original soon appeared, partly because new reproduction techniques rendered Sambo blacker and blacker. The more serious political problem arose when some American editions changed the setting to the deep south and by 1963 when the copyright reverted to Bannerman's heirs and Ian Parsons secured it for Chatto & Windus (along with those for the other Sambo books) *Sambo* had been tagged racist. Ten years later Teachers Against Racism demanded that Chatto & Windus withdraw the books but Parsons said the teachers were implant-ing in innocent minds the idea that there was something derogatory in having coloured skin and continued to sell about 10,000 copies a year.

Then in 1981 Bannerman's daughter, Elizabeth Hay, published *Sambo Sahib*, a biography of her mother, and the National Library of Scotland put up an exhibition of Bannerman's work. The accusations eased off until Chatto transferred its children's list to The Bodley Head at the beginning of 1983 and a year later *Little Black Sambo* appeared in the new children's catalogue, sent to 40,000 schools throughout Great Britain and Ireland. This time complaints came from the Inner London Educational Authority and soon British newspapers filled with letters either calling the book racist or its discontinuation censorship.

The children's list was then under Margaret Clark who decided to stop publishing all the Sambo books because she thought The Bodley Head's reputation as a publisher aware of the multicultural needs of its market was being damaged. The imprint's main customers were teachers and librarians who did not consider when and why the book was written but the social context of the children for whom they ordered it. Clark realized that by dropping the books she was exercising a form of censorship of which she did not approve but she believed that adults who had not known the book in childhood might find it stereotyped and was certain that most would not recognize it had been written nearly a hundred years ago. As evidence she told Max about a young black journalist who had asked her for Bannerman's telephone number.[4]

Max did not want to surrender the copyrights to the owners who, he predicted, would quickly sell them to another publisher for a large sum of money. So when the licence renewals came up again in April 1986 he had Sambo moved to Reinhardt Books, and once settled in the Penguin building, he ordered a reprint of 10,000 copies that 'We should be able to get rid of in a year or so', he told Penguin. But Penguin would not distribute them. Max had 'masses' of letters from the public 'begging me not to suppress the book and telling me that they would be distressed if they couldn't have their children read it after their grandparents and parents themselves had been brought up on it. I personally feel that it's perfectly innocuous and Sambo ends up being a little hero' he told Peter Carson.[5] But too many librarians and other interested groups disagreed. In January 1988 the NUJ decided that a book 'notorious for its racism' should not be connected with Penguin and froze the stock.

Judy Taylor had loved *Sambo* as a child, and the book had been a best-seller for 50 years so Max asked John Hews to ask Margaret Clark for the file copies of the other Sambo books – he thought it better coming from Hews because he had not spoken to Clark since his resignation – and transferred the distribution rights of the books to Ragged Bears Limited in Andover, Hampshire, a company run by Charles Shirley, a former director of Methuen Children's Books. Max told him to expect 'absurd publicity'; he himself had 'recommended to the reporters ... that they take a minute to read the book themselves and see whether it is objectionable and whether Little Black Sambo isn't a successful little hero'.[6] 'The main thing', Judy Taylor told Shirley, 'is to avoid causing distress in Wright's Lane.'[7]

Things went smoothly until 1 August 1989 when Shirley reported that a new buyer at Selfridges had removed *Sambo* from the shelves, although the new bookshop at the Louvre had 50 copies. Taylor replied that Harrods was keeping its stock in a locked cabinet and even then salesmen were derided for carrying it. By February 1991 Shirley had removed the book from his catalogue but ordered another 7500 copies he knew he could sell without the listing; at a recent London book fair people had been delighted to see it on his shelf.

By the end of 1992 *Sambo* was in the press again. A shop in Edinburgh had withdrawn the book because anti-racist campaigners had said it was offensive. It had been on display for three months without objection but the *Edinburgh Evening News* found it shocking to see the book at Christmas 'when parents were buying gifts for their children'. Waterstone's said they would only refuse to carry copies (of which they had none at the moment) if the book were declared illegal.[8] But *Sambo* continued to sell and the next February when PEN disclosed that 60 per cent of children's authors claimed to have been censored by politically correct publishers, Max and Judy Taylor felt proud not to be among them. Max published *Sambo* until 1995 when he passed the publication rights over to Ragged Bears.

* * *

In early July 1988 Greene turned up at Wright's Lane to sign pre-publication copies of *The Captain and the Enemy*, be interviewed for the radio, eat sandwiches of smoked salmon and drink champagne. Judy Taylor told Max that the inscription in her copy would 'set the tongues wagging in twenty years' time – "For Judy, with many years of love, from Graham"!'[9] When the novel was released in September some critics grumbled about continuity but most accepted that the novel's disjuncture was caused by the book having been started in 1974, picked up again in 1978, then in 1981, 1984 and finally in 1987. Some wondered if the great novelist was just getting old. Salman Rushdie wrote in the *Observer* that in the first 79 pages 'Greene writes like a dream' and if technical problems hurt the rest, 'half a novel's worth of vintage Greene is not to be sneezed at. We should be grateful for that initial champagne.'[10]

Peter Mayer told Greene that he was 'very glad to see what you, Max and I organised a year ago – which had its risks – has turned out so well.

There are very few new publishing associations that have given me as much pleasure.'[11] Greene told the *Sunday Express* 'I feel a loyalty to my publisher not to criticise it too severely, but it's been a difficult book.'[12]

What interested him more was Vincent McDonnell's *The Broken Commandment*. He had nominated it for the *Sunday Express* book of the year award and was pushing it hard, telling the papers how the book had come into his hands. The twist came a year later when he was asked to judge the 1989 Irish Guinness Peat Aviation Award, which was worth £50,000 for the best book written by an Irish writer in the past three years. Philip French, Fay Weldon, Hugo Kenner and Gerry Dukes were to read the 30 to 40 entries and draw up a shortlist of five, from which Greene agreed to pick the winner. Everyone knew he favoured McDonnell's novel; he was quoted on the book's jacket saying it was 'sad, merciless, unforgettable'.

As it turned out *The Broken Commandment* was not on the Guinness Peat short list, which included Seamus Heaney's *The Haw Lantern*, and John Banville's *The Book of Evidence*, a novel similar thematically to McDonnell's. Banville's was the book the assessors thought should win. But Greene was relentless in a cause; he got the sponsors to provide a second prize of £20,000 for best first novel (awarded to McDonnell) before he would name Banville as winner of the £50,000.

When McDonnell got wind of what was going on he told Greene he would refuse the prize. Max sent him a telegram saying if he did he 'would be most unfair to [Greene] and his publisher who hoped to sell more copies of the book as a result'.[13] So McDonnell changed his mind and the Irish papers carried a photo of a somewhat amazed looking young writer, and at his side as they celebrated in Dublin's old House of Lords, a distant, very determined looking Graham Greene.

This is a small story beside the success of *The Captain and the Enemy*, which *Publishing News* listed among the bestsellers in October 1987 and of which Max had sold 60,020 copies at home and 26,328 abroad by the time McDonnell received his prize. But it is a story of Greene's compassion and tough mindedness and of his influence on Max's publishing life. *The Broken Commandment* was a promising first novel, and McDonnell continued to write. 'Graham and I both thought that you had it in you to be a writer', Max told him on 23 December 1994 when McDonnell wrote to thank him for his help and to announce the publication of his fourth book. By then Greene was dead and Michael Sheldon's biography of him had been published, as had the second volume of Norman Sherry's. 'I think that we need laws to protect people who can no longer speak for themselves', McDonnell wrote Max. 'I like to remember Graham as I knew him and he was never anything but kind and considerate.'[14] In publishing *The Broken Commandment* Max and Greene did what they had always done as a publisher-writer team, what Charles Evans had done for Greene when he bought *The Man Within* in 1928, what the conglomerates who were gobbling up smaller firms like The Bodley Head were doing less and less. Without the huge advance and publicity budgets of the conglomerates, they gave a chance to a new writer.

* * *

Even before these two books were published Reinhardt Books had begun to make a profit and Max had begun the difficult and sometimes delicate task of trying to get the rights to Greene's books from Simon & Schuster, Heinemann and The Bodley Head. 'According to Graham's agent here', Max told Peter Mayer, 'all the contracts that he signed ... with Heinemann and The Bodley Head stated that the paperback rights of his books could not be licensed or the licence extended without his permission.'[15]

The scheming started on 11 March 1988 when Max sent Greene the draft for a letter Greene was to send to him. With the draft came Max's explanation of 'the intricacies and relationships between the various firms so you can see why I have written it as I have'. The intricacies were held in lively snapshots of various publishers who disliked various other publishers 'which is why I haven't mentioned' their names, and what of this publishing soap opera should be told to whom, when, and in what context.

Greene's response was identical to Max's draft, beginning: 'As you know I have been thinking for some time about the state of my collected edition, both in America and in the UK.' He said he would write to Michael Korda himself to say that Max would offer 'a sum which would compensate them for any loss of future earnings'. He would also write to Simon Master to ask 'if he would consider a fair offer to transfer The Bodley Head rights'. Would Max negotiate with Paul Hamlyn, who was then head of Heinemann, 'an old friend of yours and I also remember him from our boating days at Cap Ferrat'. The Heinemann hardbacks were probably not making much money but he thought the paperback editions still did. If Max could make a deal for the lot, Greene would have a complete collected edition in the UK and that edition could then be transferred to the USA. He was prepared 'to write new introductions where necessary'.[16]

So Greene told Korda that he 'would very much like in these last years of my life to see a complete collected edition of my books available in the USA as well as the UK' and wanted it to be Max's.[17] And Max wrote to Paul Hamlyn that Greene would be 'very grateful if all his books could be under the control of one publisher, both in the States and in the UK. As he and I, as you know, have been friends for a very long time he would like it to be me.'[18] But he would not approach The Bodley Head directly. He told Maître Paschoud 'the new people are not particularly interested in the backlist of authors which I particularly care for ... They will guess that I may be the instigator in all these requests for reversion of rights, but I don't want this to be admitted officially. However, I do very much care for the important books that I had published, particularly those of my friends, and would want to see that their interests are properly safeguarded.' Max also wanted Greene's children's books and Chaplin's autobiography, all out of print with The Bodley Head. Would Paschoud see what he could do?[19]

* * *

Alexandra had married in 1988 and 'rented a flat with her husband in the cheapest district in London, South Audley Street, around the corner from the Connaught!' Max told Oona Chaplin.[20] Her husband Andrew Gammon said that before the wedding Max had shown him how to double the money his family would otherwise have received for their shares in his father's Indian construction company. Max's rules were that Andrew was to visit him every Saturday morning, that there was to be no debate about what Max told him to do, and that he had to do *exactly* what Max said. 'If you do, it will work out all right.' It did. 'Max was brilliant', he said, 'and he never liked to talk about his achievements. When I asked how I could thank him he replied: "Love your wife. That's your payment to me. And be good to her".'[21]

Veronica too had left home, first for St Andrew's University. When she graduated she had been awarded a place as a trainee at the BBC in London. She would go on to direct and produce several documentary series for them, and later for Channel 4, work which would take her all over the world. Since Max was having difficulty with the stairs at Pelham Crescent, Joan began looking for a large flat on one floor.

Although Max told Roger Straus on 25 January 1989 that 'publishing life couldn't be more horrendous on both sides of the Atlantic', Reinhardt Books had had a satisfactory start. To have this small personal set-up within the resources of Penguin was unique and certainly seemed to many a wonderful position in publishing. Judy Taylor had begun to accumulate a strong children's list with *Tom's Pocket* by Sarah

Garland, Maurice Sendak's *Caldecott & Co.*, and Mitsumasa Anno's *Anno's Faces*.

So while Joan looked for another place to live, Max began to expand in a small way. Proposals came from agents – a biography of Conor Cruise O'Brien, a collection of John Buchan's *Spectator* pieces. Max had heard on 'Desert Island Discs' that Dame Josephine Barnes wanted to write a book and asked Elizabeth Bowes-Lyon to talk to her. George Millar had a novel for Max to look at, and wondered if Max might republish his personal experiences of the war. By February 1989 Max was planning The Nonesuch Storytellers, a series he wanted to start with Greene. The books would be 'looked after as we used to in the grand Bodley Head days' he told William Trevor, who wanted to add a volume but could not extract his new collection from Random House. The Maugham estate gave its approval for an edition, and Max was trying to line up ones by Scott Fitzgerald and Victor Pritchett.

But even as Max expanded, the problems with his Penguin set-up began. In May Alistair Cooke's *America Observed* had been published to good American reviews. The first printing (by Knopf) of 15,000 copies had sold out within a couple of months. But in Britain 'the book did not receive the reviews it deserved, largely because of the bitchiness of the media' Max told Ronald Wells, who had compiled and edited the collection.[22] Almost all the articles had first appeared in the *Guardian* and Cooke had given the paper an exclusive interview in return for free republication. Max was only able to sell about 5000 copies in Britain and a year later Cooke complained that 'Ron Wells has not yet had a penny from Penguin !!!!!!!!!!!!!! After almost 20 months! What goes on?'[23] 'Unfortunately', Max answered, 'Penguins are no longer the friendly intimate firm it used to be and a lot of the individuals I knew have left.'[24]

* * *

The Nonesuch Press was revived with a small luncheon party at the Garrick on 23 August 1989. The press's previous publication had been *The History of The Nonesuch Press*, so in a sense Max was beginning with a clean slate. On 28 September he published Greene's *Why the Epigraph?* and a definitive edition of Robert Louis Stevenson's *The Wrong Box*, a book Graham and Hugh Greene had both wanted to publish for many years. The Stevenson edition secured Max a new copyright and kept 'the imprint "The Nonesuch Press London with Viking, New York" against all the other earlier Nonesuch books which were with Random House', he emphasized to Christine Pevitt, editor in chief at Viking Penguin.[25]

Why the Epigraph? was bound in fine olive cloth with gold lettering and printed on thick paper the colour of clotted cream. It contained all Greene's epigraphs in chronological order with a short comment about each and an author's note explaining that 'a plot is not what a book is about ... The epigraph is what the novel is about.' The 950 signed copies were sold at £30 before notice of the book's publication was even circulated. As Peter Quennell said in the *Spectator*, Max was once again 'in a flourishing condition'.[26] Greene, he might have added, was elusive as ever; more than one reviewer noted his comments about the Thomas Traherne epigraph for *Rumour at Nightfall*: 'I am sure that this epigraph described my intention, but I have suppressed the novel. I have never reread it and I have quite forgotten what my intention was.'

The Wrong Box was an equally elegant edition, of 1850 copies. This rather absurd black comedy of the railway age had a complicated plot involving a corpse found in a water-butt, a grand piano, and a funny bore named Joseph Finsbury. Ernest Mehew added an introduction explaining that the story had been written by Stevenson and his American stepson, Lloyd Osborne, but since the corrections Stevenson had made to the proofs never reached his American publisher, what Max was publishing had never seen print. With the Reinhardt-Greene stamp on it, even at £36 the book sold out almost as fast as *Why the Epigraph?*

There were also trade editions of Lewis Carroll's complete works, and Geoffrey Keynes's edition of Blake's prose and poetry. In January 1990 John Hayward's Donne and Swift were reissued in equally splendid volumes. If they were not quite up to their original standard because photo printing lacked the crispness of the hot metal process, reviewers were delighted to see Max's well edited and beautifully produced books in shops again.

But critical success did not necessarily lead to financial gain. When *Caldecott & Co.* was published in June 1989 it also got wonderful reviews. Sendak's honest description of his New York boyhood filled with images of Mickey Mouse and Shirley Temple, Brooklyn and Manhattan, gave reviewers as much pleasure as his comments on Beatrix Potter, Edward Ardizzone, Kate Greenaway and especially Randolph Caldecott, the god of American children's books, whose impact on *Where the Wild Things Are* is obvious. Sendak's voice was like 'some old mariner talking of reefs and icebergs' said Edward Blishen in the *TLS* on 13 July 1989. 'Fascinating, very funny, and compulsive reading' said Sebastian Walker in the *Telegraph*, 'overflow[ing] with Sendak's love of children: it is a love that has a classical discipline and above all dignifies children and childhood'.[27]

But Penguin decided not to paperback the book and Max was unable to sell it on.

His team were finding other difficulties working at Wright's Lane. Mistakes were being made in print runs and things done to some of the books without Max's authorization. Penguin needed an eighteen-month lead time and Max was in a hurry. At the same time, he had agreed to Penguin's need to paperback his books after twelve months but found he needed longer to sell his hard copies.

Greene's copyright problems were a further irritant. 'There is so much confusion at The Bodley Head since they have been declared "dormant"' he told Greene on 7 August 1989. 'The whole Group with Hutchinson is moving again to another office in Vauxhall Bridge Road in November. Nobody there seems to know what the others are doing.' And 'Heinemann (now owned by Octopus, and themselves owned by Reed International), are trying to get the rights for Mandarin, a very recently created paperback firm, which would mean taking them away from Penguins.' Further, 'The Bodley Head, now owned by Random Century, would like the paperback rights for their own Arrow (so far, very insignificant) ... The difficulty will be that Heinemann (who are only a small part of rich Reed International) may stubbornly sit back and refuse to sell.'[28]

'Graham's policy', Max told Penguin on 4 January 1989 'is that if Heinemann and The Bodley Head could not sell the paperback rights in his books, they may be more amenable to make a deal for him to buy back the rights.' This reasoning worked with The Bodley Head, who accepted Penguin's offer and renewed Greene's paperback licences with Penguin, which was what Greene and Max wanted. But the offer to Heinemann was turned down.

What had become clear, Max told Greene on 23 July 1990 was that 'the publishing climate has completely changed and one is no longer dealing with publishers who wish to co-operate with their authors, but with toughies who only care for their short-term selfish interests, irrespective of whatever compliments they pay'. By then Greene was pretty ill and wanted something done fast. He drafted a letter to *The Times* to try to stop Octopus from paperbacking his books with Mandarin against his wishes should Penguin not succeed in reopening negotiations with Heinemann.

By the end of 1989 *Yours Etc.* had been published. Hawtree's editing was found very useful by reviewers who said Greene emerged from the letters as a formidable conversationalist, marshalling with integrity a wide range of public interests. His sincerity and his loyalty impressed them, and 'his ability to pounce on unsuspected lapses and to produce startling gobs of intelligence'.[29] *Reflections* had been delivered and Max was 'very enthusiastic about the collection. 'Each time I go back to it I find more that is rich and fascinating' he told Louise Dennys,[30] who had the Canadian rights.

Joan had found a flat around the corner from Pelham Crescent in Onslow Square, which was accessible by elevator, spacious, and with enough room for all Max's books and papers. She moved them over a week in March 1990 while Max retreated to a suite at the Berkeley Hotel where she joined him after each day's work. By then Veronica had a flat of her own in Battersea where Max once pushed the cart around Sainsbury's for her happily filling it with wine for them both. He had recently learned that Joe Links regularly did all the household shopping at Marks & Spencer.

The Last Word and Other Stories was published in July 1990. It was Greene's first collection in over twenty years and only four of the stories had appeared before in book form; 'A Branch of the Service' was previously unpublished. Reviews were mixed, and again Max felt that Penguin's sales people should be doing a better job for him. *Reflections* brought excellent reviews and was mentioned on several 1990 Christmas lists. To avoid the hardback returns he had had with *The Last Word* Max got Penguin to agree not to publish their paperback edition for 15 months. But in Canada, Lester and Orpen Dennys had gone into receivership and try as he did, Max could not get the rights reverted to Reinhardt Books and transferred to Penguin UK. So the book was never paperbacked there and the hard covers were kept in print but out of bookshops by the firm that took them over. And the Nonesuch Maugham had not been a financial success; although everyone admired its looks and production Maugham's stories sold better in Heinemann's cheaper edition.

There was no way around the fact that things were not working well. Max's breathing had become laboured and for all their loyalty to one another, Max was too ill to keep his finger on things and Greene was so unwell that he was spending five or six hours every two weeks in hospital having blood transfusions. 'It's a very tiring business getting old',[31] he told Max, who could only agree.

Max's decline was all too evident on 7 September 1990 when he was called to testify in a suit between Macmillan and William Collins over C.S. Lewis's Narnia copyrights – the first five Narnia books had gone to Collins and Geoffrey Bles, the other two (chronologically in the story the first and last) to The Bodley Head. The American solicitors were relentless. At first it seemed Max could not remember much of what they wanted to know and he tried to sidetrack them with the highlights of his career – his relations with Shaw, the Coronation Shakespeare, the publishing of Chaplin's autobiography, his friendship with Greene. But as they led him deeper and deeper into the trail of documents he had signed, it became clear, as he readily admitted, that contracts had been handled by various editors 'or somebody of equal authority. I wouldn't sign anything unless I trusted the people completely.'

There had been no in-house counsel or legal staff at The Bodley Head. Lawyers had not been consulted when these kinds of increasingly complicated licensing arrangements were drawn up. Unless the author

> happened to be a friend of mine. In, the case of Graham Greene, for instance, I mean the children's department prepared the contract with Graham Greene for his four children's books that we published, and I looked at it very carefully because he was a great personal – he is a great personal friend of mine ... At the time we didn't have the kind of integrated publishing, where one publisher did hard covers and paperbacks as well – I mean <u>we</u> didn't have it ... I published for fun ... I'm fond of finely produced books.

Max seemed very old, operating on trust and charm in the fast world of conglomerate publishing, and the record shows the terrifying effect on him of his growing sense of his own diminishing talents. Publishing could no longer be done just for fun. Soon afterwards he told Joan 'I've lost my touch.'[32]

On 3 April 1991 when Graham Greene's daughter, Caroline, telephoned to say her father was dying Joan answered the phone. Max was just leaving to see his cardiologist. His breathing was very bad by then and not wanting him to miss the appointment, Joan said nothing until they returned to Onslow Square. By then Greene was dead. Again Max's deep loss was hidden, the statement he issued diminutive: 'Graham was a marvellous friend and those to whom he gave his friendship benefited from his wisdom and kindness. I was fortunate to have been a friend and to have had the privilege of working with him as a colleague in publishing when I was in charge at The Bodley Head and also to have been his publisher there and under my own imprint. His death will leave a great void.' Max did not attend the funeral in Vevey. He had always hated funerals and he was too ill himself. But when a Requiem Mass was held for Greene in Westminster Cathedral on 6 June, he and Joan took the protective care of Yvonne Cloetta that Greene would have expected. She might otherwise have been forgotten except by journalists eager for her photograph.

* * *

When a copy of Penguin's complete Lewis Carroll had arrived in May 1991 Max wrote to Peter Carson that the book was 'very interesting as the copyright is vested in The Nonesuch Press ... Why on the title page doesn't it mention that it is published by Penguin in association with The Nonesuch Press?' A month later Amanda Hargreaves had to point out that 500 copies of Sarah Garland's *Oh, No!* had disappeared. 'Is this what happened to Nonesuch Blake and Nonesuch Carroll between November and December 1990 too? If so, why does this keep happening?' She was glad to hear that Penguin were reprinting 500 copies of *Anno's Aesop* but wanted to know 'why do we find out by accident'? A few months later Taylor complained that 'we are all embarrassed by not yet having a signed contract to send to Kingsley [Amis]'s agent more than a year after terms were agreed between us', and 'once again we are awaiting a contract' for Sarah Garland's *Billy and Belle*.[33]

Irina Hale's *The Big Small Bad Boy* was published that June. Hale had studied with Kokoschka, sculpted with Manzù, won the city of Salzburg prize, published with Macmillan and André Deutsch, and had a book on the National Curriculum list. Max and Taylor thought this book would be a success; as Hale's paintings and sculptures were being exhibited in London slides were made of her work for publicity purposes and an arrangement made to have the book displayed in the gallery. But review copies never got through the Penguin system; the book sold badly and by the end of December Penguin had decided not to paperback it in the usual way.

The next two years were personally tough for Max too. Alexandra had become severely depressed. She later said it 'took hold of me like bindweed'. At first she was agoraphobic, then she became aggressive and began to make huge sculptural collages of tubes, needles and other medical equipment she had endured living on blood transfusions. According to Veronica things became very tense at Onslow Square and where Max was usually reasonable and calming when crises arose, she thought he felt impotent in the face of what was happening to her sister. He did not know what to do. His money had paid for the research that had helped keep her alive, but money was useless here.[34]

And Max was increasingly breathless. In July 1992 he needed open heart surgery again, to replace the aortic valve with a mechanical one. Alistair Cooke was about to have an arthritic knee replaced. 'You think of me and I'll think of you', Max wrote him.[35] To cheer one another on they agreed that the next time the Reinhardts were in New York the two couples would go dancing at the Rainbow Room.

The operation was lengthy and Max remained exhausted and anxious afterward. Joan thought 'he was never quite the same again ... But he continued to make valiant attempts to keep going.'[36] By September when Jack Ashley's *Acts of Defiance* was published he had lined up book signings, a wide range of newspaper, radio and television interviews (many associated with the Labour Party Conference which was to begin on 26 September), and an impressive book launch for noon, 22 September. Politicians, friends, reporters and publishers nibbled rounds of cocktail sandwiches and assorted canapés on the Pavilion Terrace at the House of Commons. *The House Magazine* said 'the surgeon who took away [Ashley's] hearing ... took away the best prime minister the Labour Party never had ... This is a hugely entertaining story of an outstanding member of Parliament.'[37] In a short speech at a subsequent party at the House of Lords on 8 October Max said 'to publish a book that one likes by an author who one admires and who is also a friend, is one of the most satisfying elements for the publisher involved'. *Acts of Defiance* had by then been nominated for the Ackerley Award but despite Max having assured Penguin the book would sell well through the Hearing Research Trust, with which he and Joan had been associated since its origin in 1985, and the Royal National Institute for the Deaf, the book got few reviews and when paperbacked 'once again under the Penguin imprint Reinhardt Books had not been mentioned'. Max asked that 'the complaint [be passed] on to the proper department so if there is a reprint the correction is made'.[38]

Judy Taylor was not having much luck either. When Penguin decided not to paperback *Big Small Bad Boy* she asked about the four other children's books she had in the system. Penguin's response was that they could not guarantee that books signed up for Puffin would actually be paperbacked. By 1992 most paperback picture book lists were suffering and a run as small as 7000 or 8000 was considered uneconomic. So in December Taylor and Max decided to see these four books through and to close down their Reinhardt children's list.

Maureen Roffey's *Ten Little Teddy Bears* and Gerald Rose's *Polly's Jungle* were entered for the W.H. Smith Illustration Award. Kingsley Amis's *We Are All Guilty*, which he had written between the publication of his *Memoirs* and his seventieth birthday, brought back to life a seventeen-year-old Cockney youth he had created for a TV play fifteen years earlier; it posed a social question Taylor thought perfect for young people – is society responsible for an individual's actions, or is he? The copyrights to Greene's four children's books had still not been sorted out and Max decided it would be simpler for Ardizzone's estate and Bruce Hunter, the new agent Greene's son had appointed to take care of his father's work, to deal directly with Penguin/Viking. The plates for the books could not be found by The Bodley Head and that meant securing and insuring the original drawings. As Taylor saw Sarah Garland's *Who Can I Be?* and *What Am I Doing?*, the last two of Reinhardt's fifteen children's books, through the Penguin system, she wrote to Mitsumasa Anno that 'The British publishing scene is in a very bad way. I think you would be wise to allow Philomel to have the British rights [to *Anno's Grimm*]. If they are unable to find a publisher at least they would be able to sell their edition direct, not only in Britain, but in Australia, New Zealand and South Africa, all small but valuable markets.'[39]

Max wrote to Alistair Cooke that 'although I feel recovered from what the operation was supposed to have done, I still find that I'm forgetting intimate friends' names. I've therefore listed the few friends I have left in my diary, and before I go to lunch at the Garrick I look at it very carefully.' Cooke was on his way to California and Max added wistfully, 'If you happen to get to San Francisco do be sure to give my love to the Huntingdon … The club with its swimming pool across the way, and the pleasant light lunches with a lot of continental waiters, who always treated me as if I were the other Max Reinhardt, gave me an extra pleasure.'[40] He continued to encourage Cooke to prepare another volume for publication but their letters were more often filled with aches and pains, borne on both sides with wry humour.

There was sadness even in publishing *A World of My Own* where there should have been nothing but joy for Max in this final Greene book. Max's handwritten additions to the contract show his concern that Louise Dennys's Knopf Canada edition not be published before his, and that his name and Yvonne Cloetta's be prominent on it. Greene had selected the dreams he wanted included and at Dennys's suggestion Cloetta had added a foreword and then, after talking with Max, 'a dedication' that they wanted to appear before it: 'According to the expressed wish of the author this book is published in Britain by his great friend and publisher for many years Max Reinhardt, and in Canada by his niece and publisher Louise Dennys.' Since Greene had left specific directions about the book's publication, including that he wanted it dedicated to Cloetta, Dennys told Amanda Hargreaves that 'technically it shouldn't be called that [a dedication]. He [Greene] in fact dedicated the book to Yvonne, but she chose not to include any such reference feeling that her involvement with the Foreword was sufficient. She suggested this wording to reinforce Graham's wishes with regard to publication.' The placement Dennys thought 'very conspicuous but Yvonne, to whom I was speaking again yesterday, confirmed that this was Max's desire. If so, we will of course leave it there.'[41]

In this Max was beginning to sound like Francis Meynell, who on 5 November 1960 after reading 'Whitefriar Talking' had sent him a swift note about the prominence of the Reinhardt name. 'Other people than "Whitefriar" tell me that they have the impression that Nonesuch is part of your "set-up". I think this may be due to your letter-paper, or notice-board at Earlham Street or Catalogue. You will agree that it is important that Nonesuch should publicly be associated with Bodley Head etc. only in the sense that its <u>distribution</u> is the same. Will you give this a minute's thought?' In publishing, perhaps more than anywhere, prominence of name and timing are important and experience had made Max guard both jealously. This would be Greene's final book and he understandably wanted his own name associated with his old friend in this final way. After the book was published he encouraged Cloetta to write (with Marie Françoise Allain) her invaluable *In Search of a Beginning, My Life With Graham Greene*, which he arranged for Euan Cameron to translate but did not live to see published by Bloomsbury in 2004.

* * *

In the early 1990s there were serious overstocks of the Reinhardt Books hard-cover edition of *The Captain and the Enemy* in New York. Although the paperback was selling, Viking had sold only two hard copies in 1993 and none at all in 1991 and 1992. Penguin had 4827 in the warehouse and wanted to pulp all but 500 of them. Pulping cost money, offended even dead authors, and reflected on a publisher's business acumen, except that Max was not the cause of the problem. In the old days he would have been able to control print runs more accurately; now he apologized for reprinting so many and instructed Viking to try a book club first. If that did not work they should send 100 copies to his office, keep 500 and pulp the rest. There was also an overstock of *Yours Etc.* which puzzled Max. These were the first edition and they should have been sold. 'Publishing seems a shadow of itself these days', he told William Trevor. 'Quality slips away, as it does from so much of the contemporary world.'[42]

When Greene's friend and travelling companion Bernard Diederich sent Max his manuscript *Graham Greene and The Comedians* the following year, Max was no longer publishing new books. He had closed the office in the Penguin building and retreated to his study overlooking Onslow Square. There he could rise slowly from his desk to take a book he had published from the shelf for a visitor to appreciate, or to read a dedication a satisfied author had inscribed to him. At The Bodley Head Max would have published Diederich's book as he had so many other excellent critical works. 'It's a sad state of affairs', he wrote Diederich 'but most publishers are cutting their lists as there are far too many books being published at present'.[43] In September he pulped 2500 sheets of the Nonesuch Maugham and told Alix Meynell that 'when Francis asked me to join him in becoming Mr Nonesuch again, it was one of the happiest events of my publishing career. The discussion at all our meetings always ended effortlessly by our agreeing on all matters.'[44]

Penguin's evaluation of the future success of its joint titles with Reinhardt Books over the next 15 years was disappointing. Max pointed out that many of the children's books had not yet been reprinted as paperbacks, that Sarah Garland's *What Am I Doing?* was tipped for the prestigious Kate Greenaway Award, and that there would most probably be another book coming from Alistair Cooke. He was sure that when these and his remaining stock were sold the income would be higher than Penguin estimated. There was also a little stock of the Nonesuch Blake, Donne, Swift and Lewis Carroll, all in hardback. They were selling slowly, as was a paperback edition of the Carroll. But Max did realize the end was close.

That Christmas he wrote to Alix Meynell that 'the publishing world is turning upside down and many of the smaller firms have been gobbled up, and so I have decided to stop publishing any new books with a Reinhardt book imprint and continue to sell whatever stock we have through Penguin, who have also had a tough time'. He

wanted to save the Nonesuch Press in case anything happens to Reinhardt Books, and have decided to buy the company personally at the price at which Reinhardt Books bought it from you. This also means that Reinhardt Books will no longer be considered a group owning other companies and will not need to have any annual audit and neither will the Nonesuch Press ... This will also save the Nonesuch Press as an entity of its own and the only directors will be you, Joan and myself ... and we will see that it is well protected.[45]

In May 1996 as he was slowly trying to wind up his co-publishing with Penguin he told Judy Taylor

they have suggested remaindering all our stock, but I don't want to remainder the Nonesuch titles or the Graham Greenes, with the possibility of one or two exceptions. As for the children's books, I would like to have your advice ... I am enclosing a list of stock they are holding and the value they expect to get for remaindering them. We mustn't forget that they own a remainder company! I don't want to make things difficult but I think we ought to consult the authors, don't you? ... I see they have listed <u>Little Black Sambo</u> which they refused to take on, but you will be amused to know that somebody rang me from the Children's department saying that they would like to take it on now, but it is a bit late, and I want the Ragged Bears to continue selling it. They also want to remainder a number which they are willing to reprint.

Taylor thought 'it a great pity to have to remainder everything but I can see no alternative ... What a sad ending.'[46]

'The greatest analgesic in history', Cooke wrote to Max, 'is barleyensis vulgaris ... but it may be purchased over the counter under several trade names: eg. Johnny Walker's, Dewars White Label, J & B etc.'[47] Max replied 'I note your cure ... but I (alas or no) am still advised to stick to reasonably good white wines.'[48] It was bridge at the Garrick that kept him going. He played on Tuesdays and Thursdays with Richard Rougier, Wyndham Lloyd-Davies (Jill Black's surgeon husband) and until his death in 1997, the theatre director Harold French with whom he had been playing since the Margaret Leighton days. Max had always loved games, club gossip and intrigue. According to Rougier he was among the top four or five players at the Garrick, 'a sound good club player' who was accommodating to his partner, read the cards well and counted them reliably. 'If you're a good club player, you never lose it', Rougier said. 'Max's bridge did not fall off.'[49]

His back worsened though and other things had to be given up. In 1996 after thirty years he resigned from the council of RADA. He had a deep affection and admiration for the academy, which he had seen successfully through years of cuts in public funding, the alterations to the GBS Theatre in 1983, the purchase of 18 Chenies Street in 1990, and the Centenary Project in 2004. Richard Attenborough was sad to see him go. 'I shall long be personally in your debt during the difficult times we have been through and I know everyone ... is deeply grateful for your exacting period as Chairman of Finance and General Purposes.'[50] Through his charitable trust Max set up a scholarship in his name to be awarded annually to a RADA student; he was very pleased in June 1997 to get to the Vanbrugh Theatre to see its first recipient, Philippa Waller, appear in *The Jealous Wife*. In 2008 Attenborough opened a new rehearsal room dedicated to Max.

Nonesuch remained active enough for Max to pretend he was still publishing. But in the spring of 1997 he wrote to Roger Straus: 'Do you realize, Roger, that I started publishing a couple of years after you? And although our main distinction at The Bodley Head was to be the founders of Penguins, we also had one or two good authors who remained faithful to us.'[51] There was a finality in his voice and a sad confusion of subjects, with Max at first part of The Bodley Head he was so proud of, then as 'one or two authors who remained faithful to us' tumbled out, almost as an afterthought in the humble, yet royal, 'we'.

17
Last Words

On 18 March 1997 Alistair Cooke wrote that he had hired 'a dreamboat . . . she's caught on in two weeks to the variety of little things that attach to my free-lance life'. Max was 'so glad that you have found a dreamboat to work for you. So have I, in the form of Belinda who used to be my secretary at The Bodley Head thirty years ago and whom you met at Bow Street when The Bodley Head was a proud independent company.'[1]

Belinda McGill remained Max's handmaid for the rest of his life. She had been with him when he built The Bodley Head and she would help him through the bewildering end of his decline. When she came Max was still getting out to restaurants despite his back problems, which were sometimes relieved with epidurals, and the Warfarin he took because of his metal heart valve. 'It limits drinking, diet and other activities', he told Cooke. But McGill said 'he had lost confidence in himself when I went back and I had to keep saying "Yes Max, you can do it" to cover his anxiety as best I could'.[2]

Max had always been a great raconteur and a home-grown project had begun to get him to record his past. The tapes eventually became *Memories*, and while the paper and typeface for this small book were being chosen, Onslow Square was like a real publisher's office. Max kept the book light and full of the stories about his famous friends he had told when he was centre stage. He was too expedient to expose his angst about the demise of The Bodley Head, which had come to obsess him like Kim Philby's loyalties had Greene at the end. He left it to Eric de Bellaigue to sort out the sadder details in the *Bookseller* the following year. And when soon after *Memories* was published privately for friends at Christmas 1998, and the skilled Sue Bradley came with her tape recorder to interview Max for *National Life Stories*, he was pretty forgetful about things he did not want to remember. Or perhaps he was just too polite to reveal what he did remember; Jill Black was not the only person to say she never saw him be rude to anyone.

For all his graciousness as a host Max was an exceedingly private man, even at home. It was helping with the tapes that Veronica began to understand something of his past. 'He never told us anything', she said. She had never heard from her father the disturbing story he told Euan Cameron about the impaled heads on the Galata Bridge, or what it was like to be a Jew in Paris in 1938, or what had happened to his relatives during the war. 'He just wanted everyone to be happy.'[3] Max had wanted the same thing at The Bodley Head; by reassuring his talented editors about money, he had created conditions in which they produced some of the finest books in the world and had built a children's list second to none. As his extended family, his staff had worked happily for him for decades.

But while he was for the most part a gentle patriarch with the appearance of an immensely confident man, McGill thought that being cut off from his family so early because of the war had left him more vulnerable than he looked. Perhaps that is why he was as shrewdly reticent about himself as he was about financial matters, his conversation, as Euan Cameron has said, being generally anecdotal. Certainly 'membership of such institutions as the Savile or the Garrick ... mattered to [Max] and he loved the company of those he considered "distinguished"'.[4] He was proud to be of service to them, and he appreciated the praise and friendship they returned.

Many of them were older men who trusted him as a father might a son. Francis Meynell inscribed Max's copy of the autobiography Max published for him, 'To Max who made it and much of me.' Even though Max knew that what happened at The Bodley Head was caused in the first instance by changes in publishing that were beyond his control, he continued to believe that if his partners had done what he had advised the group could have been saved, and if when its sale became inevitable they had allowed him to buy back The Bodley Head, he could have kept it going. In his failure on both counts he felt he had let his staff down, and perhaps that was why he so resented what his partners did. They diminished his sense of his own genteel responsibility.

* * *

In September 2000 Max's first grandchild was born. Honouring Max's initials, Veronica named her Marina Reinhardt and she gave her grandfather enormous pleasure in his final years. When Max could no longer get to the Garrick on Tuesdays and Thursdays, and finally could no longer walk, he had to be taken to a nursing home. It was appropriately called Galsworthy House and it backed onto Richmond Park in Kingston. Shortly before the end, which came on Tuesday 19 November 2002, Belinda McGill took him out into the garden in his electric wheelchair. 'What's wrong with me?' he asked her. 'Why can't I go home?' She thought long and carefully before answering. 'Well Max – let's just say you have a very serious case of old age.' Her response sent him into such a fit of laughter she thought he would topple his chair.[5]

There was no funeral. At the crematorium his family and extended family read poems they liked and bits from *Memories* and *The History of The Bodley Head*. They listened to Kiri Te Kanawa singing Gershwin's 'Love is Here to Stay' and Scott Joplin's 'Elite Syncopations'. Max had so loved to dance. At the celebration of his life held at the Garrick on 4 February 2003 the habitués of the Card Room were particularly pleased because Max had left them £10,000; they had decided to use it to host an annual dinner in his memory for themselves as near as possible to his birthday. He had always been such a gracious host and happiest when giving pleasure to his friends. Judy Taylor talked about her publishing work with him, Richard Attenborough about what his old friend had done for the Royal Academy of Dramatic Art. The broadcaster Michael Charlton read Ian Chapman's message as Chapman had been taken ill. Euan Cameron stood on a chair to read Jack Ashley's eulogy. Joan recalled fond memories of 46 years of marriage and ended with Max's favourite recommendation, 'Let's have a drink.' So everyone drank magnums of champagne and in remembering Max talked about 'the happy times of publishing, when one's word was worth more than a written commitment'.[6]

Notes

Prologue

1. The Max Reinhardt interviews were recorded by Sue Bradley for *Book Trade Lives*, and are housed in the the British Library Sound Archive. Bradley also recorded interviews with Judy Taylor and Belinda McGill from The Bodley Head, and with Carmen Callil. Further quotes from these tapes will be noted as BTL, prefaced with the initials of the person interviewed. The British Library reference numbers are: for Max Reinhardt – C872/07, Judy Taylor – C872/55, Belinda McGill – C872/28, and Carmen Callil – C872/116. Callil's tapes are closed until 30 May 2026; it is with her permission that I listened to them and she maintains copyright of what I have quoted.

1. From Istanbul to London on the Orient Express

1. Euan Cameron, 'Max Reinhardt', *Logos*, 2005, 178.
2. Max Reinhardt (hereafter MR), interview with author, 1996. I taped several interviews with Max Reinhardt from 1994 to 1998 and met with him frequently thereafter. Some of the material from these tapes is in his *Memories*, published privately in 1998; a copy is in the British Library. If information quoted here from my interviews is not in *Memories*, it will be noted simply as MR, followed by the year.
3. *Memories*, 2; emails from Gavin Wraith, 21/12/04, 23/12/04, 22/3/06; Istanbul Jewish Genealogical Project.
4. Interview with Andrew Gammon (hereafter AG), 13/1/06.
5. Telford Waugh, *Turkey Yesterday, Today and Tomorrow*, Chapman & Hall, 1930, 267; *Memories*, 10.
6. Letter from MR to Graham Greene (hereafter GG), 2/1/68. Unless otherwise indicated, all the letters quoted are in MR's personal archive which is privately housed.
7. MR, 1996.
8. Letter from MR to G. Waterfield, 20/6/78.
9. Philip Mansel, *Constantinople*, St Martin's Griffin, 1995, 400.
10. MR, 1996.
11. Ibid.
12. Ibid.
13. MR, BTL.
14. Letter from Stathy Eugenidi (hereafter SE) to MR, 23/8/43.
15. MR, BTL.
16. Ibid.
17. MR, 1996.
18. MR, BTL.
19. Letter from C.H.R. Peach to Mr Jordan, 12/09/38.

2. Enemy Alien, Student, Spy

1. MR, 1995.
2. Ibid.
3. James Agate, *Ego*, Harrap, 1940, 117.
4. MR, 1995.
5. *Memories*, 15–17 and MR, 1995.
6. MR, 1995.
7. Gary O'Connor, *Ralph Richardson: An Actor's Life*, Methuen, 1999, 124–5.
8. Letter from MR to SE, 20/7/43, *Memories*, 20.
9. *Memories*, 20.
10. Letter from MR to SE, 20/7/43.
11. Letter from MR to SE, 13/1/44.
12. LSE Records.
13. MR, BTL.
14. LSE records, letter from MR to SE, 19/12/44.
15. *Memories*, 22–3 and MR, 1995.
16. MR, BTL.
17. Ibid.
18. MR, 1997 and MR, BTL.
19. LSE records.
20. MR, BTL.
21. Letter from Ralph Richardson (hereafter RR) to MR, 6/7/46.
22. LSE records, MR, 1997.

3. The Accountants and George Bernard Shaw

1. *Memories*, 25.
2. Email from Gavin Wraith, 21/12/04.
3. Letter from George Bernard Shaw (hereafter GBS) to Lewis Casson, 23/7/47.
4. *Memories*, 28.
5. MR, 1997 and MR, BTL.
6. Telephone interview with James Michie, 7/3/06.
7. Letter from MR to Anthony Quayle (hereafter AQ), 26/8/47.
8. Letter from GBS to AQ, 5/9/47.
9. Letter from GBS to MR, 17/10/47. This and MR's other letters from GBS are in the Max Reinhardt Papers, Special Collections Research Centre, Georgetown University. Copies are in Reinhardt's personal archive.
10. Letter from GBS to MR, 8/1/48.
11. Letter from GBS to MR, 25/4/48.
12. Letters from MR to GBS, 2/9/48, GBS to MR, 16/9/48.
13. Letters from GBS to MR, 10/12/48, 17/4/49.
14. Letters from GBS to MR, 8/6/49, 29/6/49.
15. Letter from AQ to MR, 21/6/49.
16. Telegram from AQ and MR to RR, undated.
17. *Ralph Richardson: An Actor's Life*, 202.
18. Letter from MR to AQ, 5/1/50.
19. Letter from MR to AQ, 2/4/48.

20. MR, BTL.
21. Letter from T.E. Hanley to J. Schwartz, in the Hanley Collection, Harry Ransom Centre, University of Texas, Austin.
22. Letter from T.E. Hanley to MR, 15/9/53.
23. Ibid., ?/12/54.
24. *Ralph Richardson: An Actor's Life,* 214; John Miller, *Ralph Richardson: The Authorized Biography*, Pan, 1995, 156.
25. Telephone interview with Diana Fowles, 14/3/05.
26. MR, 1995.
27. Telephone interview with Diana Fowles, 14/3/05.
28. Letter from MR to Rex Warner, 5/2/64, Reading University.

4.   Nonesuch

1. Francis Meynell, *My Lives*, The Bodley Head, 1971, 307.
2. Letters from MR to Francis Meynell (hereafter FM), 14/8/52, FM to MR, 21/10/52.
3. Letters from FM to MR, 21/11/52, 1/12/52, MR to FM 21/1/53.
4. *Memories*, 32; MR 'Lecture to The Wynkyn de Worde Society', 19/11/87.
5. Letter from FM to MR, 12/2/53.
6. Letter from MR to FM, 26/5/53.
7. Letter from MR to AQ, 4/9/53.
8. Letter from MR to George Macy, 10/4/54.

5.   The Bodley Head

1. MR, BTL; MR, 1997.
2. Letter from RR to MR, 17/4/56; MR, 1995.
3. Letter from Derek Verschoyle to L.A. Hart (hereafter LAH), 10/11/56.
4. Letter from MR to LAH, 18/9/56.
5. Letter from MR to Henry Ansbacher & Co, 8/11/56.
6. Letter MR to LAH, 12/11/56.
7. Ibid.
8. Letter from MR to LAH, 17/11/56.
9. Quoted in J.W. Lambert and Michael Ratcliffe, *The Bodley Head 1887–1987*, The Bodley Head, 1987, 298–9.
10. Letter from MR to LAH, 29/11/56.
11. *The Bodley Head 1887–1987*, 301.
12. Letter from MR to R. Pegler, 8/10/56.
13. Letter from LAH to R. Pegler, 21/12/56; *Memories*, 44.
14. Letter from Joan Reinhardt (hereafter JR), 5/12/07; interview with JR, 3/10/04.
15. Letter from RR to MR, 1/2/57.
16. *The Bodley Head 1887–1987*, 302.
17. Ibid., 318.
18. Interview with JR, 1/10/06.
19. Ibid., 26/2/06.
20. Judy Taylor (hereafter JT), BTL.
21. Letter from John Goodwin, 25/1/06.

22. Letter from Guido Waldman, 25/1/06.
23. *Logos*, 2005, 180.
24. JT, BTL.
25. Belinda McGill (hereafter BM), BTL.
26. Eric de Bellaigue, *British Book Publishing as a Business since the 1960s*, The British Library, 2004, 138 and *The Bodley Head 1887–1987*, 306.

6.   Enter Director Graham Greene

1. Letter from GG to MR, 18/6/57.
2. Letter from GG to MR, 17/10/57.
3. Letter from MR to GG, 18/12/57.
4. Letters from GG to MR, 16/1/58, 17/10/57; 17/10/57; MR to GG, 22/10/57.
5. Letter from GG to MR, 23/9/57.
6. *Memories*, 47.
7. Letter from J.B. Priestley (hereafter JBP) to MR, 13/10/58.
8. Letter from MR to GG, 3/11/58.
9. Letter from JBP to MR, 9/1/59.
10. MR, 1996.
11. Letter from JBP to MR, 27/5/59.

7.   Charlie Chaplin: The Great Coup

1. Telegrams from GG to Charles Chaplin (hereafter CC), undated; 18/12/58.
2. MR, 1997.
3. Letter from MR to CC, 11/6/59.
4. Letter from MR to Amanda Saunders, 26/10/92.
5. Letter from MR to CC, 11/6/59.
6. Letter from MR to GG, 11/2/60.
7. MR, 1996.
8. Telegram from MR to GG, 21/11/60, quoted in letter from MR to Josephine Reid, 21/11/60.
9. Letters from GG to MR, 5/12/60, MR to GG, 29/12/60.
10. Letter from MR to GG, 21/6/61.
11. *Memories*, 59.
12. Letters from GG to MR, 23/5/62, 10/8/62.
13. James Michie, 'Charlie Chaplin', *The Oldie*, 18–19.
14. Letter from JT, 5/12/07.
15. Telegram from Eileen Burnier to MR, 31/8/62.
16. MR, 1997, and letter from JR, 5/12/07.
17. Letters from MR to GG, 1/4/64; quoted in ibid., 1/6/64.
18. Letters from MR to GG, 24/2/64, MR to RR 14/4/64, MR to GG, 24/2/64.
19. Letters from MR to Georgette Heyer (hereafter GH), 17/5/64, MR to GG, 12/5/64.
20. Letter from JR, 5/12/07; MR, 1997.
21. Letters from MR to CC, 22/9/64, Oona Chaplin to MR, 31/9/64 in *Memories* 60.

8. The Reinhardt-Greene Team

1. Letter from George Ansley to Lionel Fraser, 5/6/61.
2. Letter GG to A.S. Frere, 16/10/62, quoted in Richard Greene, *Graham Greene: A Life in Letters*, Little, Brown, 2007, 262–3.
3. *The Bodley Head 1897–1997*, 327; letter from MR to Dwye Evans, 10/2/61.
4. Letter from GG to MR, 2/12/60.
5. Letter GG to A.S. Frere, 16/10/62.
6. Letters from GG to MR, 1/4/62, to Muriel Spark, 10/9/62, to David Cornwall, 17/7/64.
7. Letter from MR to Marlene Dietrich, 1/15/65, Reading University.
8. Letter from GG to various London reviewers, 1/3/65.
9. Letters from GG to MR, 25/6/62, 24/6/63, 18/2/65, 18/5/65, 20/10/67.
10. Letters from MR to GG, 2/8/67, GG to MR, 1/12/68.
11. Letters from GG to MR, 22/1/68, MR to GG, 22/1/68, Josephine Reid to MR, 2/6/69.
12. Letters from JBP to MR, 4/12/62, 1/5/64.
13. *Memories*, 71.
14. Letters from GG to Geoffrey Eley, 30/4/65, undated draft letter.
15. Letter from MR to Charles Pick, 10/8/66.

9. Georgette Heyer

1. *Memories*, 65.
2. Letters from GH to MR, 20/7/63, MR to GH, 24/7/63, GH to MR, 22/11/63, ibid., 22/3/64.
3. Letters from GH to MR, 24/10/63, 19/12/66.
4. Letters from GH to MR, 23/10/65, 7/4/66.
5. Letter from GH to MR, 7/4/66.
6. Letter from MR to GH, 7/12/65; MR, 1997.
7. Letters from MR to GH, 5/4/66, 14/12/65.
8. Letters from GH to MR, 18/9/66, MR to GH, 19/9/66, GH to MR, 11/10/66.
9. Letter from GH to MR, 19/6/72.
10. MR, 1996.
11. Letter from MR to K. Falk 13/6/78, Reading University.
12. Letters from MR to GH, 22/11/67, GH to MR, 23/11/67, MR to GH, 25/5/72.

10. The Bodley Head Books for Children

1. JT, BTL.
2. Ibid.
3. Ibid.
4. Ibid.
5. Interview with JT, 23/3/07.
6. Letter from MR to LAH, 17/10/74.
7. JT, BTL.

11.   From Bow Street to the World's Bookshops

1. Letters from MR to JBP, 21/9/65, JBP to MR, 25/9/65.
2. Letters from MR to RR 9/12/66, to GG, 7/1/66.
3. *Logos*, 2005,181.
4. Letter from GG to Viking Press, 1/2/66.
5. Norman Sherry, *The Life of Graham Greene*, Vol. 3, Viking, 2004, 410; Richard Greene gives a fuller account in *Graham Greene: A Life in Letters*, 256.
6. JT, BTL.
7. Letter from James Michie, 7/3/06.
8. Letter from Guido Waldman, 25/1/06.
9. Letter from MR to FM, 20/6/66.
10. Interview JT, 10/1/06.
11. BM, BTL.
12. *Logos* (16/4), 180.
13. Letter from MR to unidentified bookseller, ?/1/71, Reading University; interview with BM, 16/3/05.
14. Letter from MR to Ken Wilder, 15 January 1965, MR's letters to Wilder are at Reading University.
15. Letter from MR to Ken Wilder, 3/1/67.
16. Letter from MR to Ken Wilder, 10/8/66.
17. Letters from MR to GG, 5/4/68, 23/8/68.
18. Letter from MR to RR, 10/10/68.

12.   Alexander Solzhenitsyn and Copyright

1. Victor Erlich, *NYT*, 6/11/68; Vladimir Petrov, *NYT*, 22/6/68. The best account of Solzhenitsyn's publishing affairs is in Michael Scammell's *Solzhenitsyn*, Norton (1984).
2. BM, BTL.
3. Letter from MR to Roger Straus (hereafter RS), 4/11/70.
4. MR, *NYT*, 6/10/68. According to Scammell, The Bodley Head translation was 'less than distinguished', 733.
5. MR, *The Times*, 14/12/70.
6. Letter from MR to George Kennan, 28/3/69.
7. Letter from MR to Dr J.F. Heeb (hereafter JFH), 16/3/70.
8. Letter from MR to JFH, 23/4/70.
9. Letter from MR to RS, 7/10/70.
10. Ibid.
11. Letter from MR to RS, 4/11/70.
12. Letter from MR to JFH, 13/10/70.
13. 'Law Report', *Sunday Times*, 26/11/71.
14. Ibid.
15. Letter from MR to RS, 21/11/74; *Memories*, 74.
16. Letters from MR to Peter F. Carter-Ruck, 22/11/74, to Nicholas Bethell, 22/11/74.
17. Letter from MR to RS, 15/1/75.

18. Letter from MR to RS, 27/1/75.
19. Letters from MR to RS, 14/5/75, RS to MR, 29/5/75.
20. Interview with AG, 13/1/06.

13. Heady, Champagne Years

1. Letters from JT, 5/12/07, JR, 5/12/07, MR, 4/4/92.
2. Letter from MR to GG, 6/12/79.
3. Letter from MR to CC, 12/1/68.
4. Interview with AG, 13/1/06.
5. Letter from Jack Ashley, 30/1/06.
6. *Logos*, 2005, 181.
7. *The Bodley Head, 1887–1987*, 332.
8. Letter from Jack Ashley, 30/1/06.
9. Letter from MR to Bernard Levin, 23/4/85.
10. Jeremy Lewis, *Penguin Special: The Life and Times of Allen Lane*, Viking, 2005, 309, 339, 338–40.
11. *British Book Publishing as a Business since the 1960s*, 136.
12. Ibid., 3–4.
13. Interview with JT, 10/1/06.
14. Interview with Graham C. Greene (hereafter GCG), 12/1/06.
15. *British Book Publishing as a Business since the 1960s*, 132.
16. Ibid., 139–40.
17. Letter from MR to F.J. Gibb 9/1/74, Reading University.
18. MR, 1996.
19. *British Book Publishing as a Business since the 1960s*, 148, 142, 141.
20. Ibid., 140.
21. Ibid., 141.
22. *Penguin Special: The Life and Times of Allen Lane*, 309.
23. Interview with GCG, 12/1/06.
24. Ibid.
25. JT, BTL.
26. Email from Gordon Graham, 28/2/06.
27. Letter from MR to Alan Wicks, 23/12/74.
28. Interviews with Euan Cameron (hereafter EC), 21/3/05, with Margaret Clark (hereafter MC), 12/1/06.
29. Interviews with MC, 12/1/06, with EC, 21/3/05.
30. Letter from MR to A.E. Powell, 14/2/72.
31. JT, BTL.
32. *Logos*, 2005, 182; letter from MR to RS, 17/11/78.
33. Letter from MR to RS, 18/1/75.
34. Letter from MR to AQ, 20/3/75.
35. Interview with MC, 12/1/06.
36. Letter from MR to GG, 20/6/77.
37. MR, 1997.
38. Letter from MR to GG, 12/09/78.
39. Letter from MR to GG, 15/12/78.

14. Mistakes

1. *British Book Publishing as a Business since the 1960s*, 142.
2. Letter from MR to Alix Meynell (hereafter AM), 1/11/79.
3. Interview with JT, 10/1/06.
4. MR, BTL.
5. JT, BTL.
6. Carmen Callil, BTL.
7. MR, 1997.
8. Letter from David Machin, 12/3/05.
9. Telephone interview with James Michie, 7/3/06.
10. Diana Athill, *Stet: A Memoir*, Grove Press, 2001, 132.
11. Letter from MR to R. O'Donoghue, 16/10/80.
12. Interview with AG, 13/1/06.
13. Telephone interview with James Michie, 7/3/06.
14. *British Book Publishing as a Business since the 1960s*, 147.
15. Email from Louise Dennys, 18/11/07.
16. *British Book Publishing as a Business since the 1960s*, 144; telephone interview with Carmen Callil, 31/1/06.
17. MR, 1998.
18. Carmen Callil, BTL.
19. *British Book Publishing as a Business since the 1960s*, 153.
20. Ibid., 146.
21. MR, *The Age* (Melbourne), 9/5/84.
22. Jane Rippeteau, 'Thriller With a Chapter or Two to Come', *Financial Times*, 20/5/87.
23. Email from GW, 25/1/06; *British Book Publishing as a Business since the 1960s*, 151–2.
24. Letter from JT to MR, 15/3/83.
25. Letter from MR to Gordon Graham, 2/2/06.
26. *Ralph Richardson: An Actor's Life*, 306–7; Veronica Reinhardt (hereafter VR), telephone interview, 6/7/07.
27. This letter is at Reading University.
28. *British Book Publishing as a Business since the 1960s*, 152; MR, 2000.
29. Interview with GCG, 12/1/06.
30. Interviews with MC, 12/1/06, Jill Black, 11/1/06, telephone interview with Carmen Callil, 31/1/06.
31. MR, 1999.
32. *British Book Publishing as a Business since the 1960s*, 153.
33. MR, 1999.
34. Letter from Gordon Graham, 2/2/06.
35. *British Book Publishing as a Business since the 1960s*, 147.
36. Telephone interview with Carmen Callil, 21/3/07.
37. Letter from MR to RS, 18/7/85.
38. Interview with Margaret Clark, 12/1/06.
39. Interview with JR, 22/3/05.
40. Telephone interview with James Michie, 7/3/06.
41. MR, BTL.
42. MR, 1999.

43. Patrick Hosking, *Independent*, 10/4/87.
44. MR, 1998.
45. *British Book Publishing as a Business since the 1960s*, 146.
46. Letter from EC to David Machin, 10/4/86.
47. Letter from EC to MR, 22/4/86.
48. MR, 1997.
49. Letter from MR to AM, 19/8/86.
50. *British Book Publishing as a Business since the 1960s*, 152.
51. Letter from MR to GCG, 10/6/86.
52. MR, 1998.
53. Interview with GCG, 12/1/06.
54. *British Book Publishing as a Business since the 1960s*, 154.
55. Letter from MR to David McKetterick, 17/6/86.
56. Letter from MR to RS, 28/8/86.
57. Letter from Jill Black to MR, 15/9/86.
58. Letter from MR to Claude Durand, 22/9/86.
59. Letter from Peter Carson to MR, 24/10/86.
60. Tom Maschler, *Publisher*, Picador, 2005, 231.
61. MR, 1998.
62. Tom Maschler, *Publisher*, 232.
63. Interview with GCG, 12/1/06.
64. This letter is at Reading University.
65. Letter from GCG to MR, 5/2/87.
66. Letter from MR to GCG, 6/2/87.

15. The Last Act

1. *Logos*, 2005, 182.
2. Letter from GCG to MR, 23/3/87, Reading University.
3. *The Times*, 24/3/87.
4. The *Independent*, 30/3/87: *The Times*, 30/3/87.
5. *Daily Telegraph*, 31/3/87.
6. Ibid., 1/4/87.
7. *The Times*, 6/4/87.
8. Letter from MR to Alexander Flegon, 15/4/87.
9. *British Book Publishing as a Business since the 1960s*, 156; Tom Maschler, *Publisher*, 232.
10. Ibid., 156.
11. *Publishing News*, 15/5/87.
12. Tom Maschler, *Publisher*, 232.
13. Ibid., 234.
14. Ibid., 234.
15. Letter from Alistair Cooke (hereafter AC) to MR, 1/31/85.
16. Telephone interview with Carmen Callil, 31/1/06.
17. MR, 1996.
18. Letter from MR to Barry Francis at Beachcrofts, 27/5/87.
19. MR, 1996.
20. The *Bookseller*, 1/1/88.

21. MR, 1996.
22. Letter from MR to GG, 20/5/87.
23. Letters from Mary Connell to JR, 27/6/85, JR to Mary Connell, 27/6/85, 22/10/85.
24. *Memories*, 82; MR, 1996.
25. Letter from MR to Riou Benson, 18/5/87.
26. *Evening Standard*, 3/6/87.
27. The *Bookseller*, 5/6/87.
28. *Evening Standard*, 3/6/87.
29. *Sunday Telegraph*, 17/6/87.
30. MR, 1997.
31. *The Times*, 13/10/87.
32. The *Independent*, 28/10/87.
33. Letters from Simon Hornby to MR, 16/11/87, from Robert Lusty to MR, 13/10/87.
34. Letter from MR to Brooke Crutchley, 2/11/87.
35. Interview with Graham C. Greene, 12/1/06.
36. Letter from MR to RS, 14/4/97.
37. *New York Times*, 9/23/96.
38. Carmen Callil, BTL.
39. *British Book Publishing as a Business since the 1960s*, 156–7.
40. *Sunday Telegraph*, 18/10/87.
41. The *Bookseller*, 16/10/87.
42. Interview with Margaret Clark, 12/1/06.
43. Letter from GW, 25/1/06.
44. Interview with Margaret Clark, 12/1/06.
45. MR, 1997.

16.   Reinhardt Books

1. Letter from Joe Links to MR, 9/8/87.
2. Letters from MR to Peter Mayer, 16/12/87, Peter Mayer to MR, 16/2/88.
3. Letter from Vincent McDonnell to GG, 16/3/87.
4. Letter from Margaret Clark to MR, 1/10/85.
5. Letters from MR to Peter Carson, 16/1/88, 29/1/88.
6. Letter from MR to Charles Shirley, 14/3/88.
7. Letter from JT to Charles Shirley, 11/5/88.
8. *Edinburgh Evening News*, 26/12/92.
9. Letter from JT to MR, 23/8/88.
10. *Observer*, 11/09/88.
11. Letter from Peter Mayer to MR, 12/9/88.
12. *Sunday Express*, 4/9/88.
13. Telegram from MR to Vincent McDonnell, 28/10/89.
14. Letter from Vincent McDonnell to MR, 5/12/94.
15. Letter from MR to Peter Mayer, 23/5/88.
16. Letter from GG to MR, 16/2/88.
17. Letter from GG to Michael Korda, 1/4/88.
18. Letter from MR to Paul Hamlyn, 27/3/88.

19. Letter from MR to J.F. Paschoud, 27/5/88.
20. Letter from MR to Oona Chaplin, 1/11/89.
21. Interview with AG, 13/1/06.
22. Letter from MR to Ronald Wells, 3/5/89.
23. Letter from Alistair Cooke (hereafter AC) to MR, 27/6/90.
24. Letter from MR to AC, 5/6/90.
25. Letter from MR to Christine Pevitt, 31/8/88.
26. The *Spectator*, 30/9/89.
27. The *Telegraph*, 6/5/89.
28. Letter from MR to GG, 2/2/90.
29. C.J. Fox, *Sunday Times*, 3/12/89.
30. Letter from MR to Louise Dennys, 2/11/89.
31. Letter from GG to MR, 4/12/90.
32. Interview with JR, 20/3/07.
33. Letters from MR to Peter Carson, 16/5/91, Amanda Hargreaves to Peter Carson, 10/6/91, JT to Peter Carson, 1/10/91.
34. Telephone interview with VR, 6/7/07.
35. Letter from MR to AC, 15/7/92.
36. Letter from JR, 5/12/07.
37. *The House Magazine*, 85.
38. Letter from MR to Peter Carson, 25/7/94.
39. Letter from JT to Mitsumasa Anno, 30/8/92.
40. Letter from MR to AC, 23/10/92.
41. Letter from Louise Dennys to Amanda Hargreaves, 26/5/92.
42. Letter from MR to Trevor Cox (William Trevor), 3/5/93.
43. Letter from MR to Bernard Diederich, 19/6/94.
44. Letter from MR to AM, 20/9/94.
45. Ibid., 5/12/94.
46. Letters from MR to JT, 8/5/96, JT to MR, 13/5/96.
47. Letter from AC to MR, 12/2/95.
48. Letter from MR to AC, 22/2/95.
49. Telephone interview with Richard Rougier, 9/2/06.
50. Letter from Richard Attenborough to MR, 6/1/97.
51. Letter from MR to RS, 14/4/97.

17. Last Words

1. Letter from MR to AC, 24/3/97.
2. Ibid.; interview with BM, 16/3/05.
3. Telephone interview with Veronica Reinhardt, 6/17/07.
4. Interview with BM, 16/3/05; *Logos*, 2005, 181.
5. Interview with BM, 16/3/05.
6. Letter from MR to AM, 5/11/90.

Index

Shaw, George Bernard, 2, 32, 39, 104
and MR publishes Shaw-Terry
correspondence, 32, 33–6, 40
and Shaw-Achurch correspondence,
39–40
Sheldon, Michael, 181
Sherek, Henry, 37, 38
Sherry, Norman, 102–3, 181
Shirley, Charles, 179, 180
Sholokhov, Mikhail, 117
Simon & Schuster, 34, 35, 69, 73, 74,
144
Simon, Richard, 34–5
Sinyavski, Andrei, 111
Smallwood, Norah, 58, 129, 130, 135,
141
Smith, Lillian, 93
Smith, Rukshana, 126
Soldati, Mario, 81
Solzhenitsyn, Alexander, 1, 110–21,
125, 137, 138, 145, 151, 156
Southern, Terry, 83
Spanish Civil War, 14, 16
Spark, Muriel, 81, 125, 142–3, 147
Spencer, Roy, 97
Spicer, Ernest Evan, 15, 17, 30, 31
Spicer, Harriet, 141, 142
Spock, Dr Benjamin, 81
Stark, Leslie, 47
Stellar Press, 31, 40, 47, 85
Stevenson, Robert Louis, 184, 185
Stokes, Walter, 36–7
Stone, Irving, 147
Stone, Reynolds, 44
Stonier, Brian, 106–7
Straus, Roger, 64–5, 112, 113, 115,
116, 117, 120, 121, 137, 151, 152,
156, 172–3, 183, 195
Sutcliff, Rosemary, 93, 97, 125
Sutro, Gillian, 102
Sutro, John, 65, 102

T. Werner Laurie Ltd, 55, 56, 100
Taylor, Iris, 58, 103
Taylor, Judy, 2, 56–7, 57–8, 61, 92–9,
103, 104–5, 106, 122, 129, 130,
135, 140, 141, 147, 148, 176, 179,
180, 183–4, 189, 190, 193, 194,
198

Taylor, W.G., 49, 54
Terry, Ellen, 2, 32
Theroux, Paul, 125
Thomas Tilling (company), 77, 78, 85,
127
Thompson, Kay, 94
Thorndike, Sybil, 32, 138
Titus, Eve, 94
Toffler, Alvin, 126
Trevelyan, Geoffrey, 129, 130
Trevor, William, 1, 104, 125, 147, 154,
184, 192
Triad paperbacks, 133, 146, 147, 151
Tube Investments, 23, 26
Turkey, and modernization of, 7–8

University of Sussex Press, 133
Unwin, Fisher, 55
Unwin, Rayner, 54, 98
Unwin, Sir Stanley, 2, 56–7
and sale of The Bodley Head, 49–51,
53, 54
Ure, Jean, 126
Usherwood, Molly, 24, 28
Ustinov, Peter, 55

Verschoyle, Derek, 48, 49
Vevers, Gwynne, 97
Virago, 141, 145, 153, 154–5, 158,
162, 163–4
see also Chatto, Virago, Bodley Head
& Jonathan Cape

Waldman, Guido, 60, 104, 147, 174,
175
Walker, Sebastian, 185
Waller, Philippa, 194–5
Warburg, Frederic, 78, 79
Warner, Rex, 41, 67, 125
Waugh, Sir Telford, 8, 9, 19, 20, 21
Webb, Kay, 97
Weidman, Jerome, 178
Weldon, Fay, 181
Wells, Ronald, 184
Whistler, Rex, 92
Whitbread, Stanley, 17, 31
Wilder, Ken, 107, 148